Hypothesis Testing and Model Selection
in the Social Sciences

Methodology in the Social Sciences

David A. Kenny, Founding Editor
Todd D. Little, Series Editor
www.guilford.com/MSS

This series provides applied researchers and students with analysis and research design books that emphasize the use of methods to answer research questions. Rather than emphasizing statistical theory, each volume in the series illustrates when a technique should (and should not) be used and how the output from available software programs should (and should not) be interpreted. Common pitfalls as well as areas of further development are clearly articulated.

RECENT VOLUMES

DATA ANALYSIS WITH Mplus
  Christian Geiser

INTENSIVE LONGITUDINAL METHODS: AN INTRODUCTION
TO DIARY AND EXPERIENCE SAMPLING RESEARCH
  Niall Bolger and Jean-Philippe Laurenceau

DOING STATISTICAL MEDIATION AND MODERATION
  Paul E. Jose

LONGITUDINAL STRUCTURAL EQUATION MODELING
  Todd D. Little

INTRODUCTION TO MEDIATION, MODERATION, AND CONDITIONAL
PROCESS ANALYSIS: A REGRESSION-BASED APPROACH
  Andrew F. Hayes

BAYESIAN STATISTICS FOR THE SOCIAL SCIENCES
  David Kaplan

CONFIRMATORY FACTOR ANALYSIS FOR APPLIED RESEARCH,
SECOND EDITION
  Timothy A. Brown

PRINCIPLES AND PRACTICE OF STRUCTURAL EQUATION MODELING,
FOURTH EDITION
  Rex B. Kline

HYPOTHESIS TESTING AND MODEL SELECTION IN THE SOCIAL SCIENCES
  David L. Weakliem

Hypothesis Testing and Model Selection in the Social Sciences

David L. Weakliem

Series Editor's Note by Todd D. Little

THE GUILFORD PRESS
New York   London

Library of Congress Cataloging-in-Publication Data

Names: Weakliem, David L., author.
Title: Hypothesis testing and model selection in the social sciences / David
  L. Weakliem.
Description: New York : Guilford Press, [2016] | Series: Methodology in the
  social sciences | Includes bibliographical references and index.
Identifiers: LCCN 2015043221 | ISBN 9781462525652 (hardcover)
Subjects: LCSH: Social sciences—Statistical methods. | Statistical
  hypothesis testing. | Social sciences—Methodology.
Classification: LCC HA29 .W395 2016 | DDC 300.72/7—dc23
LC record available at *http://lccn.loc.gov/2015043221*

In memory of
Herbert A. Weakliem (1926–2015)

Series Editor's Note

Why do so many false dichotomies exist, I wonder? Frequentist versus Bayesian seems to be one. Granted, the two camps have very different historical roots and some purveyors of either camp have strong agendas. David L. Weakliem provides us with an amazing interplay of depth and balanced comparison between these two major traditions. His vast experience is clearly evident as he walks us through meaningful examples without creating a sense of right versus wrong; rather he instills the simple yet important value that the approach to be used is that which serves the analytical goals at hand. By grounding the statistical theory in its philosophical origins, Weakliem teaches us one of the most important things we all should learn about statistics: *how* to think, instead of *what* to think. Weakliem carefully provides arguments that highlight the utility of both frequentist traditions and Bayesian practices, and without advocating for either the status quo or radical revolution, crafts a guide to how traditional practices can be wedded to Bayesian ideas to improve scientific discovery.

Weakliem also underscores another important feature of being a thoughtful researcher, namely, model selection. In the world of confirmatory modeling, there appears to be a lack of appreciation for the importance of testing competing models and determining which to select from a set of possible models. Selecting the appropriate model is a critical issue of social justice, since the model selected is the one that will inform both policy and

practice. Weakliem is a strong advocate of principled and thoughtful application of all our modeling techniques.

Wealkiem is like a master chef who explains the relations among all the elements of cooking without providing you with a single recipe. You are given all the ingredients and the principles of combination that allow you to create your own recipe—one that is the perfect combination for the research meal you desire to create. He shows us how to create such masterful works by walking us through real research questions with real data.

One final feature of this book that I love is the wonderful set of bibliographies that Weakliem has assembled at the end of each chapter. This book is bound to be a mainstay reference guide to model selection, specification, estimation, and evaluation, and the bibliographies are rich fodder to feed the intellectual hunger that he elicits in each chapter. They are a qualifying-exam's worth of influential readings that graduate students should take full advantage of. And, of course, put Weakliem's book on your exam's reading list, because it really will be your roadmap going forward.

As always, "enjoy!" Oh, and "make good choices."

TODD D. LITTLE
Snowbound in Boise City, Oklahoma

Preface and Acknowledgments

This book has a long history. My interest in hypothesis testing began in graduate school when I worked with my advisor, Chuck Halaby, on some research that used non-nested hypothesis tests. A few years later, I was studying the relationship between social class and voting choices. A model that seemed reasonable in principle fit pretty well but could still be rejected using standard hypothesis tests. A colleague, Ron Breiger, told me about a new (to sociologists) statistic for model selection called the BIC (Bayesian information criterion). I tried it, and it gave the answer that I was hoping for.

However, I wanted to understand why it gave that answer, and my efforts eventually led to a paper on the BIC (Weakliem, 1999). A few years later, Chris Winship invited me to edit a special issue of *Sociological Methods and Research* on model selection. In the introduction to that issue (Weakliem, 2004), I explored some of the questions that are considered at greater length in this book. A few years after that, after an email exchange, Andrew Gelman invited me to be a coauthor for a paper on the problems of statistical inference involving small effects (Gelman and Weakliem, 2009). Work on that paper also influenced my thinking. A number of participants at meetings of the Methodology Section of the American Sociological Association have given helpful comments. I also thank Cornell University, Indiana University, the Center for Advanced Study in the Behavioral Sciences at Stanford University, and the University of Connecticut for their support.

C. Deborah Laughton of The Guilford Press, and Series Editor Todd D.

Little deserve special thanks for their patience and support during the long process of writing. Several anonymous readers made helpful comments on an early draft of the book, and Chris Winship and Andrew Gelman gave valuable comments on a later draft. Finally, I thank my wife, Judith Milardo, who helped in many ways.

Contents

3 • The Classical Approach   43

4 • Bayesian Hypothesis Tests   75

8 • Hypothesis Tests 158

The companion website
www.guilford.com/weakliem-materials provides
data and syntax files for the book's examples.

1

Hypothesis Testing and Model Selection

This chapter outlines the purpose and scope of the book. It begins by summarizing the conventional procedure of hypothesis testing and some alternatives to the usual standards of "statistical significance." It then describes the problem of model selection.

1.1 INTRODUCTION

Hypothesis tests are central to quantitative research in the social sciences. The standard format for research papers is to draw on theory to make a case for a positive or negative association between the values of two variables, report a measure of association between those variables after controlling for other potentially relevant factors, and present a test of the "null hypothesis" that the association is zero. If the estimate for the parameter representing the association has the expected sign and is more than about twice its standard error, the researcher can claim support for the theory that underlies the prediction. In textbooks and media reports, the research will be described as having found a "statistically significant" relationship. If the parameter estimate has the expected sign but is less than twice as large as its standard error, the research will be regarded as inconclusive, at best. Many studies

1

have found that papers that do not obtain statistically significant results are less likely to be published: an early example is Sterling (1959/1970), and a recent one is Gerber and Malhotra (2008). Although the great majority of the space in a research paper may be devoted to reviewing the literature, developing the theory, describing the sample and data, and discussing the potential implications of the findings, the paper's "life" hinges on the single figure representing the test of the null hypothesis.

The conventional standard of statistical significance is defined in terms of the probability of *the data, given the null hypothesis.* The logic of the test is that if the observed data would be unlikely to occur if the null hypothesis were true, we should "reject" that hypothesis and turn to an alternative. However, ultimately researchers almost always want to make judgments about the credibility of *a hypothesis, given the data.* Standard practice does not offer explicit rules for doing this, but it is safe to say that a "statistically significant" estimate is regarded as substantially enhancing the credibility of the hypothesis of an association between the variables. However, some statisticians argue that standard levels of statistical significance actually provide little evidence against the null hypothesis and may even provide evidence in favor of it. Savage et al. (1962, p. 181) put it this way: "No one is too ignorant of statistics to know that a $|t|$ of 3 . . . strongly disproves the null hypothesis. I wish we didn't all know that, because it is false. Actually, in circumstances not very unusual, a $|t|$ of 3 is mild evidence in favor of the null hypothesis."

Savage did not offer a definite alternative to conventional standards of significance, but Schwartz (1978) proposed an easily calculated statistic that has come to be known as the "Bayesian information criterion" (BIC, or sometimes SBIC), and has been widely adopted. The BIC implies that a t-ratio must be at least $\sqrt{\log(n)}$ in order to provide *any* evidence against the null hypothesis. This standard is considerably more conservative—that is, favorable to the null hypothesis—than the conventional .05 and .01 levels of statistical significance. The minimum t-ratio needed to produce evidence against the null hypothesis is 2.14 in a sample of 100, 2.63 in a sample of 1,000, and 3.03 in a sample of 10,000. At about the same time, Akaike (1974/1998) proposed another easily calculated alternative to standard hypothesis tests based on the principle of minimizing prediction error. In the "Akaike information criterion" (AIC), the minimum t-ratio needed to favor including an additional

parameter is $\sqrt{2}$ regardless of the sample size—considerably *less* stringent than the conventional standard for statistical significance.[1] Because of the widely differing standards implied by the different criteria, the debates over hypothesis testing are not only an issue of statistical theory but also crucial for almost anyone who does quantitative research.

Model selection is an extension of hypothesis testing. A conventional hypothesis test can be used as a way to choose between two models, one in which a parameter is free to take any value and another in which it is fixed at a specified value. However, research is rarely limited to two models: in most cases, a large number of potential models are estimated. For example, a researcher who is interested in the association between x and y after controlling for "relevant" variables may try many combinations before deciding on the model to be presented to readers. Even if no control variables are considered, a researcher may explore different functional forms or specifications of the error term. This process of model selection raises additional questions. One is: Which model selection strategy will have the best chance of selecting the correct model? A second is: How should hypothesis tests be interpreted when the model is chosen from a number of possibilities rather than specified in advance? For example, suppose we are interested in the proposition that "the greater the value of x, the greater the value of y." An investigator begins by estimating the regression

$$y = \alpha + \beta x + e; \, e \sim N(0, \sigma^2) \tag{1.1}$$

and finds that $\hat{\beta}$ is positive but not statistically significant at conventional levels; he/she then follows by estimating:

$$y = \alpha + \beta x^\gamma + e; \, e \sim N(0, \sigma^2) \tag{1.2}$$

in which $\hat{\beta}$ is positive and statistically significant. Should conclusions about the proposition be based on the test statistic from Equation 1.1, the test statistic from Equation 1.2, or some combination of the two?

----

[1]Akaike (1974/1998) proposed AIC as an acronym for "an information criterion," but it is now universally taken to stand for "Akaike information criterion."

1.2 STANDARD PROCEDURE OF HYPOTHESIS TESTING

This section gives a summary of the standard procedure for hypothesis test-ing, which is based on the "classical" theory of hypothesis testing developed by R. A. Fisher, Jerzy Neyman, and Egon Pearson. This is often called the "frequentist" theory because it can be based on a definition of probabilities as relative frequencies, but it is also compatible with a definition of probabili-ties as "propensities" (Giere, 1975, pp. 218–219). The frequency interpreta-tion is more familiar because of Neyman's advocacy and the historical links between hypothesis tests and sample surveys, but the propensity interpreta-tion is more appropriate for most data in the social and natural sciences. The summary is purely descriptive: the extent to which the procedure can be jus-tified by logic or statistical theory will be discussed in Chapter 3. The discus-sion assumes that we have a statistical model that has been estimated by the method of maximum likelihood and that interest centers on one parameter θ or a number of parameters $\theta_1 \ldots \theta_m$, although the model may contain other parameters.

1.2.1 One Parameter

1. State a "null hypothesis" of the form $\theta = k$: that is, that the parameter has some specific value. Usually k is zero; if k is some other value, it is pos-sible to define a new parameter $\theta' = \theta - k$ and test the hypothesis $\theta' = 0$. Therefore, subsequent discussion will assume that $k = 0$.

2. Compute the "t-ratio" of the parameter estimate to its standard error: $t = \hat{\theta}/s(\hat{\theta})$.

3. Choose a "critical value" obtained from a standard normal distribution. The critical value, c, is chosen so that it would be "unusual" for a random variable from the appropriate distribution to fall outside the range $(-c, c)$. The conventional standard for what should count as "unusual" is a prob-ability of .05, in which case, $c = 1.96$, but sometimes .10 or .01 are used. The symbol α is sometimes used to represent the chosen standard.

4. If the absolute value of the ratio from Step 2 is greater than c, "reject" the null hypothesis at the standard used to calculate c. If the null hypothesis

is rejected, the parameter estimate is often described as "statistically significant at the α level." Sometimes α is given in percentage terms—for example, "at the 5% level." An alternative way to reach the same conclusion is to calculate the probability that a random variable from a standard normal distribution would fall outside $(-t, t)$. This probability is known as the p-value; if it is less than α, then the null hypothesis is rejected at the α level. Sometimes the exact p-value is reported in addition to the result of the hypothesis test.

5. If the hypothesis is rejected, conclude that the parameter is approximately equal to $\hat{\theta}$ and ask if that value is "substantively significant"—that is, large enough to be of interest from a theoretical or practical point of view. The assessment of "substantive significance" is often neglected—see McCloskey (1985) and Ziliak and McCloskey (2008)—but all textbook accounts agree that it is important.

6. If the hypothesis is not rejected, "accept" the null hypothesis. Accepting the null hypothesis does not mean claiming positive evidence in its favor but simply saying that there is no compelling evidence that it is false. Some observers avoid the term "accept" on the grounds that it suggests positive support. For example, the American Psychological Association's Task Force on Statistical Inference states, "Never use the unfortunate expression 'accept the null hypothesis' " (Wilkinson, 1999, p. 602). However, this prohibition has no historical basis: according to Neyman (1952, p. 55), "A test is nothing but a rule by which we sometimes reject the hypothesis tested and sometimes accept it."

1.2.2 Multiple Parameters

1. State the "null hypothesis" of $\theta_1 = \theta_2 \ldots = \theta_m = k$: that is, that several parameters all have a specific value, usually zero. For example, $\theta_1 \ldots \theta_m$ might be the regression coefficients for dummy variables representing a categorical variable such as ethnicity or region. In this case, the null hypothesis means that the categorical variable does not affect the outcome.

2. Fit a model imposing the restriction in question and the "full" or unrestricted model by maximum likelihood, and record the value of the log-

likelihood for each. Compute -2 times the log-likelihoods of the restricted and full models. Because -2 times the log-likelihood will appear frequently in the subsequent discussion, I will refer to it as the "deviance," following McCullagh and Nelder (1989), and represent it by D.

3. Compare the difference in deviance to a critical value obtained from a chi-square distribution with m degrees of freedom. As with tests for a single parameter, it is also possible to compute the p-value: the probability that a random variable with two degrees of freedom would be smaller than the difference in log-likelihoods.

4. If the difference in deviance exceeds the critical value, reject the null hypothesis. Rejecting the hypothesis $\theta_1 = \theta_2 \ldots = \theta_m = k$ does not mean concluding that all of the parameters are different from k, only that at least one of them is.

5. If the difference in deviance does not exceed the critical value, accept the null hypothesis. As in the one-parameter case, this should not be regarded as positive evidence for the null hypothesis, just as a lack of clear evidence against it.

6. If the null hypothesis is rejected, the estimate of each θ might be reported and discussed. Alternatively, intermediate models that place some structure on the values of the parameters might be considered—for example, models that specify that certain groups of parameters are equal to one another while others are distinctive.

1.2.3 Likelihood Ratio and Wald Tests

The test involving the difference in deviance is known as a "likelihood ratio test," while the t-test is an example of a "Wald test." In a model with normally distributed errors, likelihood ratio and Wald tests produce exactly the same results, but in general they are only asymptotically equal. Most of the discussion in this book will assume that we are using likelihood ratio tests, but Wald tests have the practical advantage of requiring estimation of only the full model. If only the results from the full model are given, it is possible to calculate the difference in deviance between the full model and the restricted model produced by setting a single parameter equal to zero: it is approximately equal to the square of the t-ratio for that parameter.

1.2.4 Types of Hypotheses

This book will consider hypothesis tests in the context of statistical models.[2] In general, a model is a probability function $f(Y; \theta)$—that is, the model expresses the likelihood of the observed data as the function of the values of a number of parameters. A hypothesis is a statement about the value of one or more of the parameters. The models considered in this book will all involve a "response" or "dependent" variable whose distribution is predicted from a number of "independent" variables. More precisely, the model includes an equation in which some function of the expected value of y is predicted from the x variables:

$$g(\hat{y}) = h(x) \tag{1.3}$$

and a probability function connecting y to $\hat{y}$. This class includes a wide range of models, including generalized linear models, nonlinear regression, and duration (event-history) models (Lindsey, 1997; McCullagh and Nelder, 1989).

A hypothesis is a statement that the value of a parameter falls in a predetermined range (θ_a, θ_b); a hypothesis involving multiple parameters is a combination of statements about individual parameters. If the upper and lower ends of the range are the same, it is known as a "point hypothesis." The great majority of hypotheses tested in research are point hypotheses, and the procedures described above assume a point hypothesis. The most common use of a point hypothesis is to represent the claim that a variable has no effect on y.[3] Another common use is to represent the claim that two variables have the same effect—this includes the hypothesis that a variable has the same effect in two different groups. A third use is to represent the claim that the ratio of parameter values is the same in different groups. For example, the hypothesis that the ratio of two parameters β_1 and β_2 is the same in two groups can be tested by comparing the full model:

---

[2]Thus, it will not consider pure nonparametric tests.

[3]In itself, a regression coefficient merely shows that there is an association between two variables after controlling for other variables. I use the term "effect" for brevity and because researchers often interpret regression coefficients in causal terms. See Morgan and Winship (2015) for a discussion of causality and statistical models.

$$y = \alpha + \beta_{1j}x + \beta_{2j}z + \text{controls} + e \tag{1.4}$$

to the restricted model:

$$y = \alpha + \gamma_j\,(\beta_1 x + \beta_2 z) + \text{controls} + e \tag{1.5}$$

where j represents the groups.

If θ_a and θ_b are not the same, we have an "interval hypothesis." The most common use of interval hypotheses is to test claims about the sign of a parameter: $\theta \geq 0$ or $\theta \leq 0$. In the conventional approach, such hypotheses lead to "one-tailed" tests, which are exactly the same as ordinary tests except that the α critical value is equal to the 2α critical value in a two-tailed test. For example, the .05 critical value in a one-tailed test of the null hypothesis that $\theta \leq 0$ is 1.65, which is the .10 critical value in a test of the hypothesis that $\theta = 0$. The interval hypothesis $-\delta \leq \theta \leq \delta$ can be used to represent the proposition that θ is approximately equal to zero. Although a test of this hypothesis may be attractive in principle, there is no generally accepted standard for what should count as "approximately equal," so it is rarely used in practice. Apart from a discussion of one-tailed tests in Section 3.4, this book will focus on point hypotheses.

1.2.5   Non-Nested Hypotheses

In both of the examples described above, the model representing the null hypotheses is a special case of the full model. In this situation, the models are said to be "nested." Standard hypothesis tests apply only to nested models, but there are some situations in which one might want to choose between models that are not nested, for example, probit and logit models for a binary outcome. It is possible to develop tests for non-nested hypotheses. These involve two parts, one in which the first model is taken as the null hypothesis, the other in which the second hypothesis is taken as the null hypothesis. As a result, there are four possible outcomes: the first model is accepted while the second is rejected, the second is accepted while the first is rejected, both are accepted, and both are rejected. That is, a non-nested hypothesis test does not necessarily produce a decision in favor of either model: the conclusion might be that both are acceptable or that neither is acceptable (see Weakliem, 1992, for more discussion and references).

1.3 MODEL SELECTION

A hypothesis test can be regarded as a way to choose between two models. The problem of model selection arises when there are more than two possible models. An example is choosing among the regressions

$$y = \alpha + \beta_1 x_1 + \beta_2 x_2 + e;\ e \sim N(0, \sigma^2) \tag{1.6}$$

$$y = \alpha + \beta_1 x_1 + e;\ e \sim N(0, \sigma^2) \tag{1.7}$$

$$y = \alpha + \beta_2 x_2 + e;\ e \sim N(0, \sigma^2) \tag{1.8}$$

and

$$y = \alpha + e;\ e \sim N(0, \sigma^2) \tag{1.9}$$

Despite its simplicity, the example illustrates the central issues involved in the process of model selection. First, the use of hypothesis tests does not necessarily result in the choice of a single model: it might result in accepting both Equations 1.7 and 1.8. Second, different sequences of tests could lead to different destinations. For example, one possible strategy is to begin with the null model, add variables one at a time, and retain them only if they are statistically significant. Another is to begin by including all potential variables, remove them one at a time, and restore them only if they are statistically significant. Suppose that β_1 was not statistically significant in Equation 1.7 and β_2 was not statistically significant in Equation 1.8, but that both parameter estimates were statistically significant in Equation 1.6. In this case, the first strategy would lead to the null model: neither Equation 1.7 nor Equation 1.8 would be chosen over it, so Equation 1.6 would not be attempted. The second strategy, however, would lead to model Equation 1.6, which would be chosen over both Equations 1.7 and 1.8. With only two potential variables, an investigator would almost certainly estimate all of the models, but the number of potential models becomes very large as the number of variables increases: with p potential independent variables, there are 2^p possible subsets. Usually only a small fraction of the possible models are considered, making the potential difference between different paths of model selection an important concern.

Practices of model selection developed from experience, and there is no single procedure that is universally accepted; in fact, many textbooks do not discuss the issue. However, it is possible to identify some common features in standard practice. First, the usual goal is to select a single "final" model. Sometimes it is not possible to make a clear choice and a few models are treated as more or less equally good, but in either case most of the models that are estimated are simply set aside. Second, decisions are made by fitting a sequence of nested models, using hypothesis tests with standard levels of significance (usually .05) to decide whether to add or remove parameters from the current model. The exact sequence of models cannot be specified in advance since it depends on the outcome of previous tests, but the direction is usually from simpler to more complex; for example, an investigator might begin by including a small number of core control variables and then experiment with adding others. Third, automatic methods like stepwise regression are not normally used and are generally regarded as undesirable. Decisions about the models to be considered and the order in which they should be estimated are supposed to be guided by theory or substantive knowledge.

1.4   PURPOSE AND PLAN OF THE BOOK

This book is intended as a guide to the major approaches to hypothesis testing and model selection. It will examine the logic of the different approaches to hypothesis testing and model selection using simple examples, and illustrate their application to real examples from research. Two related questions might be asked about this approach. First, why is there continued disagreement among statisticians who have thought deeply about these issues? Second, given that there is disagreement, why not take an empirical approach and use simulations to assess the performance of various criteria? The answer to both questions is that all of the methods considered are mathematically correct, but they answer somewhat different questions. In order to decide which one to use, social scientists must first decide on the question we want to answer. Simulations are useful for exploring secondary issues, such as small-sample adjustments to test statistics, but are not necessary for understanding the fundamental differences among the criteria.

Chapter 2 summarizes the major criticisms of conventional hypothesis

testing and illustrates model selection by classical hypothesis tests, the AIC, and the BIC, using four examples. Chapter 3 examines the theory of classical hypothesis tests in more detail and then discusses the validity of the criticisms outlined in Chapter 2. Chapter 4 examines the Bayesian approach to hypothesis testing. The chapter is not limited to the BIC, which represents only one of the possible Bayesian hypothesis tests. Chapter 5 discusses the AIC, covering both its rationale in terms of prediction and a Bayesian rationale. Chapter 6 considers a Bayesian perspective on an alternative to the standard test of $\theta = 0$ versus $\theta \neq 0$: a three-way test of $\theta < 0$, $\theta = 0$, and $\theta > 0$. Finally, Chapter 7 discusses issues of model selection, and Chapter 8 offers conclusions about the use of hypothesis tests in social science research.

2

Hypothesis Testing: Criticisms and Alternatives

This chapter begins by distinguishing among different uses of hypothesis tests. It then summarizes the major criticisms that have been offered. Two alternatives to standard tests, the AIC and the BIC, are described, and the different criteria are applied to four examples. The examples show that model selection by the AIC, BIC, and classical hypothesis tests can lead to dramatically different conclusions.

2.1 HYPOTHESIS TESTING AND ITS DISCONTENTS

Classical hypothesis tests became the subject of severe criticism almost as soon as they began to be widely used: Berkson's (1938, 1942/1970) critiques are well known and are still cited today. The criticism has continued and even intensified since that time. Cohen (1994, p. 997), a psychologist, charges that hypothesis testing "has not only failed to support the advance of psychology as a science but also has seriously impeded it." Mason (1991, p. 343), a sociologist, holds that "much, perhaps most, use of statistical inference in the social sciences is ritualistic and even irrelevant. . . . Those asterisks that adorn the tables of our manuscripts are the product of ritual and little, if anything, more than that." McCloskey (1998, p. 111), an economist, proclaims that "statistical significance is bankrupt; all the 'findings' of the Age

of Statistical Significance are erroneous and need to be redone." Gill (1999, p. 647), a political scientist, speaks of "the insignificance of null hypothesis significance testing." The philosophers Howson and Urbach (1994, p. 50) assert that "the principles of significance testing . . . are simply wrong, and clearly beyond repair." Lindley (comment on Johnstone, 1986, p. 582), a statistician, maintains that "significance tests . . . are widely used, yet are logically indefensible."[1] Further examples of such views could easily be found.

Although their critics have been more vocal, hypothesis tests have some defenders. The basic argument in their favor was made by Mosteller and Bush (1954, pp. 331–332; see also Davis, 1958/1970, and Wallis and Roberts, 1956) 60 years ago: "The main purpose of a significance test is to inhibit the natural enthusiasm of the investigator." Without some accepted standard, researchers would be able to claim any parameter estimate with the expected sign as favorable evidence or, alternatively, dismiss any deviations from a preferred model as "trivial." Hypothesis tests have survived and spread in the face of criticism because they fill an important need. However, even if some standard is necessary, it is reasonable to ask whether conventional hypothesis tests provide the *best* standard, and this question will be explored in the following chapters.

2.2   USES OF HYPOTHESIS TESTS

Before considering the criticisms of hypothesis tests, it is necessary to distinguish the different purposes for which they are used. This section discusses the major ones, drawing particularly on Cox (1977; see also Anscombe, 1961, and Krantz, 1999).

2.2.1   Conclusions about Parameters of Interest

An important use of hypothesis tests, and the one that has received the most attention in statistical theory, is to evaluate theoretically based propositions

---

[1]Articles in statistics journals are often followed by short comments and replies. Comments will be included as separate entries in the bibliography if they have distinct titles, and otherwise indicated as in this reference.

about the value of a parameter. In most cases, the proposition is that the value of an independent variable x will have a particular association—positive or negative—with the outcome variable y after controlling for other variables. Sometimes the proposition of theoretical interest involves other aspects of the model such as functional form. The usual procedure is to fit an equation of the form $\hat{y} = \alpha + \beta x + \gamma_1 z_1 \ldots + \gamma_k z_k + e$, where x is the variable of interest and $z_1 \ldots z_k$ are other variables that might influence y.[2] The claim that x is associated with y implies that the null hypothesis $\beta = 0$ is false. Therefore, if the null hypothesis is rejected and the parameter estimate has the expected sign, that counts as support for the prediction derived from theory.

If a theory predicts an exact value for a parameter, it is possible to test the null hypothesis that it has that value. Accepting the null hypothesis then is a success for the theory in the sense that it is not refuted, although it does not provide positive evidence in favor of it. In the social sciences, it is rare for a theory to predict a specific nonzero parameter value, but sometimes a theory implies that there will be *no* association between two variables after appropriate controls are included.

2.2.2 Choice of Control Variables

In most research, there are many variables that might affect the outcome but that are not of theoretical interest. Omitting variables that affect the dependent variable will usually produce biased estimates of the parameters of interest, so the best strategy for minimizing bias would be to include every potential control variable. However, the inclusion of controls reduces the precision of the estimates of the parameters of interest, especially in small samples. As a result, it is necessary to have some procedure to decide which potential control variables should be included and which should be omitted. Hypothesis tests are often used to make these decisions: accepting the hypothesis that the coefficient for some variable equals zero means that it can be omitted. In contrast to conclusions about parameters of interest, the sign of the parameter estimate is not of interest for control variables: the only question is whether it is different from zero.

---

[2] I assume a linear model for simplicity of exposition.

2.2.3 Primary Structure

"Primary structure" (Cox, 1977, p. 52) involves parts of the model specification that define the parameters of theoretical interest. For example, many theories in the social sciences propose a relationship of the form "the larger the x, the larger the y." Hypotheses of this kind can be represented by:

$$y = \alpha + \beta f(x) + e \qquad (2.1)$$

where $f(x)$ is any monotonically increasing function of x. The parameter of theoretical interest is β, and the nature of $f(x)$ is an issue of primary structure.

Simplicity of interpretation or ease of estimation are often important considerations in the choice of $f(x)$. In this example, one might begin with a linear model and test it against a quadratic model

$$y = \alpha + \beta_1 x + \beta_2 x^2 + e \qquad (2.2)$$

Even if the hypothesis that $\beta_2 = 0$ could be rejected, a researcher might still prefer to use a linear regression as long as it provided a good approximation.

However, the precise specification of primary structure is sometimes important. For example, Myrskylä, Kohler, and Billari (2009) analyze the relationship between socioeconomic development and fertility in nations of the contemporary world (see Section 2.6.2 for a more detailed discussion). There is a strong negative association over most of the values of development, but they propose that at higher levels of development the relationship is reversed: that is, $\partial y/\partial x$ is positive when x is near the highest levels observed in the data. Conclusions on this point are sensitive to the exact specification of the relationship between x and y, so the issue is more important than it would be if the research question simply involved the general direction of association.

2.2.4 Secondary Structure

Secondary structure involves aspects of the model that are relevant to the estimation of parameters of interest but not to their definition. In the case of linear regression, the assumptions that the errors are independent, follow a normal distribution, and have constant variance are aspects of secondary structure. If these assumptions are incorrect, the parameter estimates will

still have the same interpretation, but ordinary least squares will be an inefficient method of estimation. As in questions of primary structure, the null hypothesis is often regarded as a convenient approximation rather than as a proposition that might be exactly true.

2.2.5 Goodness of Fit

The idea of a goodness-of-fit test is to assess the fit of a model to the data without specifying an alternative model (Anscombe, 1963). However, many goodness-of-fit tests can be understood as tests against a very general alternative. For example, the chi-square test for independence in a contingency table implicitly compares the model of independence to a "saturated" model in which each cell has its own parameter μ_{ij}. The defining feature of a goodness-of-fit test is that the alternative model is not adopted if the null hypothesis is rejected—rather, the result is taken to mean that it is necessary to continue searching for a satisfactory model.

Tests against a saturated model are not always possible—for example, in a standard regression model, the estimate of the variance is undefined if we fit a separate parameter for each observation. However, some specification tests are designed to detect a wide range of potential flaws in a model without specifying a serious alternative. For example, Davidson, Godfrey, and MacKinnon (1985) propose testing the hypothesis $\gamma = 0$ in the time series regression:

$$y_t = \alpha + \beta x_t + \gamma(x_{t+1} + x_{t-1}) + e \tag{2.3}$$

Because it is logically impossible for future values of x to influence y, Equation 2.3 would not be adopted if the hypothesis were rejected. Rather, the result would be taken to mean that the independent variable and the error term are correlated in the regression

$$y_t = \alpha + \beta x_t + e \tag{2.4}$$

Such correlation could result from a variety of causes, including omitted variables or errors in the measurement of x, so if the null hypothesis were rejected it would be necessary to carry out tests for the particular possibilities and modify Equation 2.4 in an appropriate fashion.

As this example illustrates, the distinction between a goodness-of-fit test and a test of a specific hypothesis is a matter of degree: a test may indicate a number of possible problems in the model without being completely general. Whether a given test should be regarded as a goodness-of-fit test thus depends to some extent on the purposes of the researcher. For example, serial correlation in the residuals of a time series regression may result from the omission of a relevant variable or misspecification of the functional form. If the hypothesis of no serial correlation is rejected, a researcher might estimate the model using a "correction" for serial correlation, or might conduct a wider search for different kinds of misspecification.

2.3 CRITICISMS OF CONVENTIONAL HYPOTHESIS TESTING

This section describes some of the most important criticisms of the conventional practices described in Section 1.3. The validity of the criticisms will not be considered here but rather left until after the discussion of the classical theory of hypothesis testing in Chapter 3. The first three criticisms involve the scope of hypothesis tests: they hold that there are situations in which conventional hypothesis tests cannot be applied or that there are important questions they cannot answer. The fourth and fifth involve ambiguity or paradoxes. The sixth, seventh, and eighth criticisms are more fundamental and raise questions about the logic of conventional hypothesis testing.

2.3.1 Sampling

Almost all textbook presentations of hypothesis testing involve random sampling from a population, or a process that can be repeated under identical conditions such as plays in a game of chance. In that case, p-values represent the proportion of random samples for which the test statistic would be greater than or equal to the observed value. However, hypothesis tests are often applied to data that do not represent random samples. For example, many statistical analyses involve the span of time for which data on the variables of interest are available. Such data could be regarded as a sample from the history of the unit (past and future) but cannot plausibly be regarded as a

random sample. Other research involves complete populations, for example, all nations in the contemporary world.

Some observers maintain that conventional hypothesis tests, even if they are valid in principle, can properly be applied only to data that represents a random sample from some population. Moreover, they hold that tests should be interpreted only in terms of sampling error, not in terms of general uncertainty about the parameter values. According to Morrison and Henkel (1969/1970, p. 186), "Significance tests . . . are not legitimately used for any purpose other than that of assessing the sampling error of a statistic designed to describe a particular population based on a probability sample." McCloskey (1996, p. 40) quotes this remark and adds that "no one disputed their declaration because it is indisputable. That is what 'statistical significance' means, mathematically speaking." Similarly, Schrodt (2014, p. 293) says that the use of significance tests on data that are not from probability samples requires "six-impossible-things-before-breakfast gyrations." As Schrodt's comment implies, there is disagreement on this point: some observers argue that conventional hypothesis tests can legitimately be applied to populations and nonrandom samples. This issue will be discussed in more detail in Section 3.1.

2.3.2 Credibility of Point Null Hypotheses

Many null hypotheses are not credible in principle. For example, standard variables such as gender, education, marital status, income, or ethnicity can be expected to have at least some slight association with almost any individual-level outcome that is of interest to social scientists. Turning to another unit of analysis, Mulligan, Sala-i-Martin, and Gil (2003) ask, "Do democracies have different public policies than nondemocracies?" If their question is taken literally, the answer is surely yes—the real question is whether the policies are "substantially" different. This point raises the question of what is learned from the test of a hypothesis that is almost certainly false. As Giere (1972, p. 173) puts it, "We know when we start that the null hypothesis is false. If our test fails to reject it, that only tells us we did not take a sample large enough to detect the difference, not that there is none. So why bother testing in the first place?"

As with the first criticism, there is disagreement on this issue. Some observers, such as Tukey (1991), maintain that all or almost all point null hypotheses are false. Others maintain that many or most point null hypotheses are true: for example, Sterne and Davey-Smith (2001, p. 227) estimate that about 90% of the null hypotheses tested in epidemiology are correct. The answer is likely to differ by field of study, but it is safe to say that many of the null hypotheses that are tested in the social sciences could be rejected as a matter of common sense without any statistical test.

2.3.3 Ranking of Models

A test of a point hypothesis can be regarded as a method for choosing between two models. The model represented by the null hypothesis can be regarded a special case of a larger model, and the null hypothesis involves the restriction that some of the parameters of the larger model have specific values. However, when more than two models are involved, a hypothesis test does not always lead to a clear decision in favor of one of them. This point was discussed in Section 1.3, using the example of the the regression

$$y = \alpha + \beta_1 x_1 + \beta_2 x_2 + e$$

The full model may be tested against three alternative models, one imposing the restriction $\beta_1 = 0$, another imposing the restriction $\beta_2 = 0$, and the third imposing the restriction $\beta_1 = \beta_2 = 0$. It is possible that both $\beta_1 = 0$ and $\beta_2 = 0$ can be accepted while $\beta_1 = \beta_2 = 0$ is rejected. In this case, it would seem reasonable to say that there is no strong basis for preferring the model with $\beta_1 = 0$ over the model with $\beta_2 = 0$, but a researcher might nevertheless want to make a tentative choice. Conventional hypothesis tests do not provide a means to do this.

As a slightly more complex example, suppose that we are comparing two ways of representing social position: a single numerical measure of socio-economic status (SES) and a set of five class categories. Hypothetical data for this situation are shown in Table 2.1. The column labeled p gives the number of independent variables (not counting the constant), and D represents the deviance. A test of the null hypothesis that the coefficients for the class dummies are all zero when SES is included gives a chi-square statistic of 3.0 with

TABLE 2.1. Hypothetical Fit Statistics from Alternative Definitions of Social Position

Model	p	D
Both	5	75.0
SES	1	78.0
Class dummies	4	78.0
Neither	0	100.0

4 degrees of freedom, for a p-value of .56. A test of the null hypothesis that the coefficient for SES is zero when class is included gives a chi-square of 3.0 with 1 degree of freedom ($p = .084$). Therefore, neither the class nor the SES model can be rejected in favor of the "full" model including both class and SES at the 5% level.

In this case, common sense suggests that the SES model is superior on the grounds that it fits equally well while using fewer parameters. The SES and class dummies models cannot be tested against each other using standard tests, because they are not nested. If a non-nested hypothesis test were used, neither model could be rejected against the other at the 5% level. One could say that the SES model should be preferred on the grounds that, in a test against the full model, the class model can be rejected at the 10% level and the SES model would not, but it is difficult to say how much evidence this amounts to.

As this example illustrates, conventional hypothesis tests do not produce a complete ranking of potential models. A model that cannot be rejected against any of the others can be regarded as acceptable, but often there will be more than one acceptable model. The example in Table 2.1 is a very simple one: as more parameters are considered, the chance of having more than one "acceptable" model will tend to increase. Moreover, the classification of models as acceptable or unacceptable will differ depending on the significance levels used to make the decisions, adding another level of ambiguity.

2.3.4 Flexible versus Inflexible Interpretation of Significance

The p-value is a continuous measure, and figures slightly above and below conventional standards of statistical significance represent almost the same

amount of evidence: as Rosnow and Rosenthal (1989, p. 1277) put it, "Surely God loves the .06 almost as much as the .05." This point suggests that the standards should be treated flexibly—for example, it would be reasonable to regard a p-value of .06 as providing *some* evidence against the null hypothesis. However, other observers recommend strict adherence to conventional levels on the ground that it reduces the influence of the investigator's hopes and expectations on conclusions. Allowing room for judgment in the interpretation of p-values introduces a bias in favor of conclusions that support prior beliefs, and rigid adherence to a conventional level of significance prevents such "gamesmanship" (Bross, 1971, p. 508).

2.3.5 Arbitrary Nature of Significance Levels

The general idea behind conventional tests is that a hypothesis should be rejected if the observed data would be unlikely if the hypothesis were true. Although this principle seems reasonable, it is not clear where to draw the line between "likely" and "unlikely." In the early development of hypothesis testing, a number of different conventions were proposed. At one time, a t-ratio of 3 (equivalent to an α level of about .0025) was often taken as the standard. According to one textbook (Waugh, 1943, p. 257), "Some call a statistical result 'significant' if it would arise by chance only once in 100 times. . . . Our point, three standard errors, errs if at all in requiring too much before the possibility of chance is ruled out. It is, however, the most commonly accepted point among American statisticians." A debate between Ross (1933) and Peters (1933) in the *American Journal of Sociology* involves the use of 3 standard errors as the standard for significance and anticipates some of the points made in later debates over the interpretation of "nonsignificant" results. A somewhat later textbook (Hagood and Price, 1952, pp. 323–324) reported that "in certain fields of research it has become conventional to use the '5-percent level of significance,' . . . in others to use the 'one-percent level of significance' . . . and still others to use the 'one tenth of one-percent level of significance.'" As time went on, the convention of 5% became firmly established across a variety of fields (see Leahey, 2005, for a historical account of this process in sociology).

Some observers argue that the widespread convergence on the 5% level

shows that it is not arbitrary. Bross (1971, p. 507) argues that the .05 standard has come to dominate because it works well in practice. For example, a level of 0.1% "is rarely attainable in biomedical experimentation. . . . From the standpoint of communication the level would have been of little value and the evolutionary process would have eliminated it." Cowles and Davis (1982, p. 557) maintain that early statisticians had adopted something close to the 5% level of significance as a standard even before the development of the theory of hypothesis testing, and they suggest that it represents a widespread disposition: "People, scientists and nonscientists, generally feel that an event which occurs 5% of the time or less is a rare event."

However, regardless of the merits of these arguments, the 5% convention is certainly not derived from statistical theory. Lehmann (1959, p. 61) observed that "it has become customary to choose for α one of a number of standard values such as .005, .01, or .05. There is some convenience in such standardization since it permits a reduction in certain tables needed for carrying out various tests. Otherwise there appears to be no particular reason for selecting these values." Yule and Kendall (1950, p. 472) were more direct: "It is a matter of personal taste."

2.3.6 Effects of Sample Size

Many observers have noticed that it is often easy to reject null hypotheses when the number of cases is large. In a sufficiently large sample, researchers who use hypothesis tests to guide model selection are often led toward complicated models containing many parameters that seem unimportant or difficult to interpret. In Berkson's (1938, pp. 526–527) frequently cited words: "I make the following dogmatic statement, referring for illustration to the normal curve: 'If the normal curve is fitted to a body of data representing any real observations whatever of quantities in the physical world, then if the number of observations is extremely large—for instance, on an order of 200,000—the chi-square p will be small beyond any usual limit of significance.'" This issue is sometimes referred to as a distinction between "statistical" and "substantive" significance—in a large sample, effects that are too small to be of practical or scientific interest may be statistically significant.

In itself, this point is not an argument against the use of hypothesis tests. In the approach described in Section 1.2, if the null hypothesis is

rejected the investigator looks at the size of the parameter estimate. At this stage, some statistically significant parameter estimates may be set aside as being too small to be worth further discussion. Researchers who omitted the hypothesis test and immediately looked at parameter estimates would put themselves at risk of "explaining" effects that do not actually exist. As Wallis and Roberts (1956, p. 480) observed, "It is futile to speculate on practical significance unless the finding is statistically significant."

The connection between sample size and statistical significance does raise a more serious problem, however. There are two kinds of errors—rejecting a true null hypothesis (Type I error) and accepting a false null hypothesis (Type II error). If one uses a constant standard of statistical significance, the chance of Type II errors declines as the sample size increases, but the chance of Type I errors remains the same. Yet, if both types of error are important, it is desirable to make the chances of both decline. This would mean using a generous standard for statistical significance in small samples and making the standard increasingly stringent as the number of cases increases. Many observers have called for such adjustments: for example, Wolfowitz (1967/1980, p. 440) says that "the use of the conventional levels of significance (.05, .01, .001) without any regard for the power of the test is an absurdity which has been pointed out in many places." Yet there are no generally accepted principles for doing this: Kadane and Dickey (1980, p. 246) observe that "after all these years there is no satisfactory theory of how to decide what level of test to set, and most practitioners continue to use .05 or .01 in an automatic way, without justification." Sometimes ad hoc adjustments are made, such as using .10 as the standard for significance in a "small" sample, but these are open to the same objection as the flexible interpretation of statistical significance discussed in the previous section: they let researchers adjust the standards to increase the chance of reaching the conclusion that they prefer.[3]

---

[3]Hendry (1995, p. 490) proposes setting α equal to $1.6N^{-0.9}$, asserting that the rule strikes "a reasonable balance between the costs of Type I and Type II errors when the actual cost of either mistake cannot be assigned." However, he does not offer a theoretical argument for the formula; he merely says that it seems to match common practice. Even if his judgment is accurate on this point, it raises the question of whether common practice is correct.

2.3.7 Lack of Symmetry

Conventional hypothesis tests are asymmetrical: they cannot produce evidence in favor of the null hypothesis, only evidence against it. As Fisher (1937, p. 19) put it, "The null hypothesis is never proved or established. . . . Every experiment may be said to exist only in order to give the facts a chance of disproving the null hypothesis."

Whether the inability to produce evidence in favor of the null hypothesis should be regarded as a drawback is open to debate. Some observers see asymmetry as desirable or necessary. Tukey (1960, p. 426) proposes that a basic question in scientific research is whether or not we *can* reach a conclusion, and that in this sense "asymmetry can be essential." A nonsignificant test statistic tells us that we cannot reach a conclusion about whether a parameter is positive, negative, or zero. Popper (1959) offers a different argument for asymmetry: he holds that, as a matter of principle, scientific theories can never be confirmed, only refuted. However, in a conventional hypothesis test, the alternative hypothesis cannot be refuted: even if the parameter estimate is exactly zero, that result is compatible with the proposition that it has a small positive or negative value. Therefore, Popper's approach implies that the null hypothesis should represent the theoretical prediction.

Other observers see scientific research as a contest among competing explanations (e.g., Chamberlin 1890/1965; Anderson, 2008; Burnham and Anderson, 2002). This view implies that a test should be able to provide evidence in favor of one alternative over the others. If a test gave the relative odds of two models in light of the evidence, then a ratio of 1:1 is clearly the dividing line. Observers might disagree about whether a given ratio, say 3:1, should be regarded as weak, moderate, or strong evidence, but they could not disagree about the direction of the evidence. Thus, in contrast to conventional hypothesis tests, the standards for evaluating the test would not be completely arbitrary. Informally, researchers using conventional tests sometimes interpret large *p*-values as evidence in favor of the null hypothesis, but the choice of any specific level above which the *p*-value should count as evidence in favor of the null hypothesis is at least as arbitrary as the choice of a level for statistical significance, and no standard convention has been adopted.

From either point of view, using classical tests when theoretical proposi-

tions are represented by the alternative hypothesis means that a theory cannot be refuted, and so it may not be abandoned even after repeated failures to confirm its predictions. A theory that predicts the sign could be refuted by statistically significant estimates with the "wrong" sign, but as Merton (1945, p. 464) points out, many "theories" in the social sciences "indicate types of variables which are somehow to be taken into account rather than specifying determinate relationships between particular variables." In essence, they are claims that a certain class of factors is an important influence on an outcome. General claims of this kind can often be interpreted to accommodate parameter estimates with either sign, so that they can never be refuted by classical hypothesis tests (see Jackson and Curtis, 1972, for discussion of an example). In fact, the possibility of being among the first to find empirical support for a well-known theory will give researchers an incentive to keep trying, and given enough attempts, a few are likely to produce "significant" results simply by chance. As a result, a theory may endure in a sort of limbo—neither strongly supported nor clearly refuted.

2.3.8 Likelihood Principle

A p-value represents the probability that a test statistic would be greater than or equal to the observed value if the null hypothesis were true.[4] That is, it takes account of the probability of events that did not occur—values of the test statistic greater than the one that was observed. Some observers regard this as illogical: they hold that conclusions should be based only on the probability of the event that actually occurred. As Jeffreys (1961, p. 385) put it in a widely cited remark: "What the use of P[-values] implies . . . is that a hypothesis that may be true may be rejected because it has not predicted observable results that have not occurred. . . . On the face of it the fact that such results have not occurred might more reasonably be taken as evidence for the law, not against it." Similar passages appear in several of his other writings (Jeffreys, 1938, p. 194; 1980, p. 453), suggesting that he considered it to be an important point.

This idea that conclusions should be based only on the observed data has come to be known as the "principle of likelihood" (Savage et al., 1962,

---

[4]With a two-tailed t-test, the test statistic should be understood as $|t|$.

p. 17). In a large sample, the probability that a test statistic will have *any* specific value approaches zero, so the principle of likelihood implies that a test must be based on a comparison of models. The principle of likelihood raises complex issues, and is not universally accepted. However, it has an obvious intuitive appeal, so the fact that conventional hypothesis tests violate it is cause for concern.

2.4 IMPLICATIONS OF THE CRITICISMS

In recent years, many of the criticisms of conventional hypothesis testing have coalesced around a central point: that the conventional .05 standard is too weak, and consequently a large fraction of "statistically significant" results are spurious. If R is the ratio of true to false null hypotheses, then the odds that a test statistic that is significant at the .05 level represents a real relationship cannot be greater than 20:R. For example, suppose that, out of 1,000 null hypotheses, 100 are false and 900 are true, so that $R = 9$. We can expect to reject 45 (.05 × 900) true null hypotheses. Even if all 100 of the false null hypotheses are rejected, about 30% (45 of 145) of the rejected null hypotheses will actually be true. Realistically, we will not always reject the null hypothesis when it is false, so the proportion of spurious "findings" will be higher. If statistically significant results are more likely to be published, and investigators have some flexibility to select the most impressive results (e.g., reporting only specifications in which the parameter of interest is statistically significant), the proportion will be higher still. Ioannidis (2005; see also Young and Kerr, 2011) presents a model of the research and publication process in which *most* published findings of statistically significant relationships are spurious. These concerns have been particularly prominent in medical research and in social psychology, where it has become common to speak of a "crisis of replication," but researchers in other fields—for example, Hauser (1995) in sociology—have expressed similar concerns.

If this diagnosis is accepted, the obvious response would be to raise the bar for statistical significance; for example, to use the .01 level as the standard. However, as discussed in Section 2.3.5, there is no obvious way to decide on a specific alternative, so any choice will be somewhat arbitrary and open to objection. In addition, one could argue that the standard should

depend on sample size, but as discussed in Section 2.3.6 there is no accepted rule for making an adjustment. Finally, because conventional hypothesis tests cannot produce evidence for the null hypothesis, it would still not be possible to dispose of ideas that had not been supported. For these reasons, some observers hold that the problem goes beyond the .05 standard and involves the basic logic of conventional hypothesis tests.

Another criticism of standard hypothesis testing is that it has a detrimental effect on the development of theory. If a theory predicts that a parameter has a particular sign, a significant parameter estimate with the expected sign can be claimed as favorable evidence. As a result, researchers have no incentive to develop theories that offer predictions about the exact value of a parameter; in fact, they have an incentive *not* to, since offering a precise prediction would make it easier for the theory to be refuted. The result is a proliferation of vaguely specified theories (Meehl, 1978).

This line of criticism could be seen as directed at the state of theorizing in the social sciences rather than at the procedure of testing. If a theory offered a precise prediction about the magnitude of a parameter, that prediction could be treated as the null hypothesis (see Section 2.3.7). Accepting the null hypothesis would mean that the theory had survived a challenge, and rejecting it would suggest that the theory needed to be revised. Therefore, one response is that theories should go beyond predicting the direction of association and offer more precise claims about magnitude or functional form. As Tukey (1969/1986, p. 728) put it, if "elasticity had been confined to 'When you pull on it, it gets longer!,' Hooke's law, the elastic limit, plasticity, and many other important topics could not have appeared." However, few theories in the social sciences offer precise predictions or appear to have much potential to be developed to the point of offering precise predictions in the near future, leaving open the question of how best to evaluate the kind of theoretically based hypotheses that we actually have.

2.5 ALTERNATIVES TO CONVENTIONAL TESTS

Several alternatives to conventional hypothesis tests have been proposed, but two are particularly popular. Both are "penalized likelihood criteria" of the form:

$$D + p\, f(N)$$

where p is the number of parameters estimated in the model and $f(N)$ is a nondecreasing function of sample size. Statistics of this kind impose a penalty for increased complexity, which is understood as the number of parameters in the model. Unlike conventional hypothesis tests, penalized likelihood criteria provide a complete ranking of all of the models that are applied to a given set of data. Akaike (1974/1998) proposed making $f(N) = 2$, yielding the AIC. Schwartz (1978) proposed making $f(N) = \log(N)$, yielding the BIC. A number of other model selection criteria have been proposed, but most of these are asymptotically equivalent to either the AIC or the BIC (Teräsvirta and Mellin, 1986).

As the name suggests, the BIC is based on Bayesian principles (although not all Bayesians accept it, for reasons that will be discussed in Chapter 4). The general idea of the Bayesian approach to hypothesis testing is to obtain a statistic representing the weight of evidence in favor of one model over the other, known as the "Bayes factor." Although many observers find the idea of a statistic representing the weight of evidence appealing in principle, direct calculation of Bayes factors is usually difficult. The attraction of the BIC is that it offers a simple way of calculating an approximate Bayes factor. If the BIC for Model 1 is $B1$ and the BIC for Model 2 is $B2$, then the Bayes factor favoring Model 2 over Model 1 is $e^{(B1-B2)/2}$. For example, if $B1$ is 100 and $B2$ is 90, then the corresponding Bayes factor is $e^5 \approx 148$. This means that the observed data are 148 times more likely under the assumption that Model 2 is true. A Bayes factor is distinct from the prior probabilities of the models: two observers who disagreed about whether Model 2 was plausible in principle might nevertheless agree on the Bayes factor.

There is no single Bayes factor; instead, different definitions of the hypotheses will lead to different Bayes factors. This point will be discussed in detail in Chapter 4, but in this chapter attention will be confined to the BIC, which is much more widely used than other Bayesian tests. This is not simply because it is easy to calculate; advocates argue that the BIC can be justified as a default choice (Kass and Raftery, 1995).

The BIC and AIC imply very different standards for the inclusion of extra parameters. The AIC implies that a parameter should be included if the absolute value of its t-ratio is greater than $\sqrt{2}$, which is equivalent to using a

p-value of about .15 in a two-tailed test. As a result, if parameters are added or removed one at a time, more complex models will be chosen when the AIC is used as a criterion than when conventional hypothesis tests are used. The BIC implies that a parameter should be included if the absolute value of the t-ratio is greater than $\sqrt{\log(N)}$. If $N = 100$, this is about 2.15, slightly higher than the conventional critical value for a two-tailed test at the .05 level. If $N = 1,000$, the value is 2.63, and if $N = 10,000$, it is 3.03. As a result, the BIC tends to favor simpler models than conventional hypothesis tests or the AIC, especially when the sample size is large. Moreover, unlike conventional hypothesis tests, it can provide evidence in favor of the null hypothesis. This is part of the attraction of the BIC for some observers: by raising the bar for statistical significance and allowing for evidence in favor of the null hypothesis, it seems to offer a solution to the "crisis of replication" (Hauser, 1995; Wagenmakers, 2007).

For both the AIC and the BIC, the "break-even" value increases in proportion to the degrees of freedom. In a conventional chi-square test, the critical value increases at a decreasing rate: for example, the 5% critical values for 1, 5, and 10 degrees of freedom are 3.84, 11.1, and 18.3, respectively. Therefore, as the number of degrees of freedom in a test increases, the α corresponding to the AIC break-even point declines toward zero. For example, in a test with 7 degrees of freedom, the break-even value for the AIC will be approximately equal to the .05 critical value; in a test with 16 degrees of freedom, it will be approximately equal to the .01 critical value. The "conservatism" of the BIC relative to standard hypothesis tests is enhanced in tests with multiple degrees of freedom. As a result, model selection using conventional hypothesis tests, the AIC, and the BIC can lead to very different conclusions. The examples considered in the next section will illustrate these differences.

2.6 EXAMPLES

This section will consider the application of conventional hypothesis tests, the AIC, and the BIC to four examples. No small group of examples can adequately represent the whole range of research in the social sciences, but these datasets are quite diverse and use hypothesis tests for a number of different purposes.

2.6.1 Economic Growth

The first example involves the selection of control variables through the use of data on economic growth in 88 nations between 1960 and 1996 compiled by Sala-i-Martin, Doppelhofer, and Miller (2004). The dataset includes measurements of 67 variables that have been suggested as influencing economic growth. The goal of their research was to give an overview, ranking each variable in terms of the strength of evidence that it had some effect on growth. However, for this example, I will focus on one variable—"ethnolinguistic fractionalization," or the probability that two randomly selected members of the nation will not speak the same language—and treat the others as merely potential control variables. Some observers have argued that fractionalization reduces economic growth, either by leading to political unrest or by making it more difficult to organize economic activity (Alesina, Devleeschauwer, Easterly, Kurlat, and Wacziarg, 2003). The values of the fractionalization measure range from zero in South Korea to 0.89 in Tanzania. The dependent variable is average annual growth in per-capita GDP, which ranges from –3.18% (Zaire) to 6.91% (Singapore).

Table 2.2 shows selected statistics from seven models.[5] The first model includes all potential control variables, while the others use stepwise regression to decide on the control variables. Models 2–4 begin with only the measure of fractionalization and use levels of .05 (Model 2), .10 (Model 3), and .15 (Model 4) to add or remove control variables. Models 5–7, like Models 2–4, use standards of .05, .10, and .15, respectively, but they begin by including all independent variables. The estimated effects of fractionalization differ widely among the models, ranging from 0.30 in Model 7 to –1.14 in Model 2. The estimate in Model 2 is statistically significant by conventional standards ($p = .012$), while the estimate in Model 3 is in the range that is sometimes treated as significant ($p = .055$). Given the range of the independent and dependent variables, an estimate of –1.14 is certainly large enough to be of interest: it would imply that the difference in fractionalization between Korea

---

[5]The figures for the AIC and BIC given here are $N \log(SSE) + 2p$ and $N \log(SSE) + p \log(N)$. The likelihood of a model with normally distributed errors depends on the variance of the error distribution, which is unknown and has to be estimated from the data. This formula uses the maximum likelihood estimate of the variance—a formula using the unbiased estimate would give somewhat different figures.

TABLE 2.2. Estimated Effects of Fractionalization on Economic Growth

Model	Estimate	Standard error	p	df	R^2	MSE	AIC	BIC
1	−0.02	1.41	67	20	.913	1.362	−779.7	−613.7
2	−1.14*	0.44	10	77	.788	0.868	−814.7	−789.9
3	−0.90	0.46	11	76	.792	0.862	−814.5	−787.2
4	−0.02	0.50	17	70	.837	0.734	−823.9	−781.7
5	−0.24	0.47	13	74	.824	0.749	−825.2	**−793.0**
6	0.19	0.49	15	72	.839	0.702	**−829.3**	−792.1
7	0.30	0.56	27	60	.876	0.650	−828.1	−761.2

Note. Bold type indicates the best fitting model according to that criterion.
*Indicates that the estimate is significantly different from zero at the .05 level.

and Kenya produced a difference of about 1% in annual growth rates, which would come to about 50% over the whole period. However, the estimates in the other models are not statistically significant—the t-ratios are all well under 1.0. Thus, conclusions about the relationship, or absence of a relationship, between fractionalization and growth depend on the choice of control variables.

The AIC chooses Model 6 as the best, while the BIC chooses Model 5. However, the difference between the BIC statistics for Models 5 and 6 is only 0.9, implying odds of only about 1.5:1 in favor of Model 5 over Model 6. When using conventional hypothesis tests, the decision depends on the prior choice of a standard of significance. Although .05 is the usual standard, it is possible to make arguments for a less stringent level. First, the sample is relatively small, so it may be difficult to reject a false null hypothesis. Second, if the goal is to estimate the effect of fractionalization on economic growth, the potential of bias from omitting a relevant variable might be regarded as more serious than the loss of efficiency from including an irrelevant one. However, neither of these arguments is definitive, so individual judgment plays a role.

A second issue in the standard approach is how to choose between models using the same level of significance but different starting points. For example, if we adopt a standard of .05, then it is necessary to decide between Models 2 and 5. The models are not nested, but it is possible to fit a model that includes all independent variables that appear in either model. With respect to Model 2, the hypothesis that the coefficients of the additional variables in the larger model are all zero can be rejected ($p = .004$); with respect

to Model 2, the hypothesis that all of the additional coefficients are zero cannot be rejected ($p = .12$). Therefore, Model 5 could ultimately be chosen over Model 2.

In a general sense, all three approaches yield the same conclusion: the data do not provide clear evidence for the claim that ethnolinguistic fractionalization influences economic growth. However, there is a difference in the conclusions suggested by the BIC and those of classical tests. Using conventional hypothesis tests, the ultimate conclusion is that the data do not contain enough information to tell us much about the relationship between fractionalization and economic growth. In Model 5, the confidence interval for the coefficient ranges from −1.16 to +0.68; that is, it ranges from a substantial negative effect to a substantial positive effect. The BIC, in contrast, leads to a more definite conclusion. The difference in BIC values between Model 5 and a model omitting ethnolinguistic fractionalization can be computed by using the t-ratio and sample size: $\left(\frac{.24}{.47}\right)^2 - \log(88) = -4.2$. This difference gives odds of $e^{(4.2/2)} = 8.2$ in favor of the model that omits fractionalization. That is, the BIC implies that we have fairly strong evidence in favor of the null hypothesis that ethnolinguistic fragmentation has *no effect whatsoever* on economic growth.

An important point that applies to all three methods of model selection is that conclusions depend on the models that are considered. For example, if we limit attention to the three models that were obtained by starting from the regression of growth on fractionalization (that is, Models 2–4), then the BIC would choose Model 2. The t-ratio for ethnolinguistic fractionalization in that model is 2.59, implying odds of about 3:1 in favor of the proposition that fractionalization affects economic growth.[6] This point means that when it is not practical to estimate every possible model it is necessary to think about the strategy of searching for models.

2.6.2 Development and Fertility

The second example also relates to a comparison of nations, but it involves only two variables, the total fertility rate and scores on the Human Development Index (HDI), which is a combination of measures of health, education, and per-capita GDP. In 2005, the HDI ranged from 0.3 to 0.97, with a mean

---

[6]The break-even t-value for 88 cases is 2.11.

of 0.71. It has long been known that higher levels of development go with lower levels of fertility. Myrskylä, Kohler, and Billari (2009), however, argue that this relationship is not monotonic—that, after development exceeds a certain point, further increases in development are associated with increases in fertility. This hypothesis goes beyond saying that the relationship between development and fertility is nonlinear: it holds that there is a reversal of direction that occurs within the range of development found among nations today. At the same time, it does not imply a precise model for the relationship. Thus, the question is one of primary structure; that is, choosing a model in order to estimate theoretically meaningful parameters.

Table 2.3 shows fit statistics from several models of the relationship. The first is a linear regression, which can be taken as a baseline. The second is the spline model proposed by Myrskylä et al. (2009), in which there are two distinct linear relationships, one that holds when the HDI is less than or equal to 0.85, another that applies when the HDI increases beyond 0.85. Because the value of 0.85 was chosen after examination of the data, it should be regarded as another parameter rather than as a constant. The model therefore involves three parameters (excluding the intercept): the two slopes and the point dividing the range in which each slope applies. The third and fourth models are polynomials including powers of the HDI. Model 5 is a nonlinear regression given by

$$y = \alpha + \beta_1 x + \beta_2 x^\gamma + e; e \sim N(0, \sigma^2)$$

It is clear that the relationship between fertility and development is non-linear: all criteria favor at least one of the nonlinear models over the linear

TABLE 2.3. Models for the Relationship betweeen Development and Fertility

Model	Form	R^2	p	df	MSE	AIC	BIC
1	Linear	.783	1	138	0.585	614.36	620.22
2	Spline (.85)	.810	3	136	0.519	599.81	611.54
3	Quadratic	.807	2	137	0.524	600.14	**608.94**
4	Cubic	.810	3	136	0.519	599.80	611.54
5	$\alpha + \beta_1 x + \beta_2 x^\gamma$	.811	3	136	0.515	**598.73**	610.46

Note. Bold type indicates the best fitting model according to that criterion.

regression. However, the lowest value of the AIC occurs for the nonlinear regression (Model 5), while the lowest value of the BIC occurs for the quadratic polynomial (Model 3). More precisely, according to the BIC the evidence favors Model 3 over Model 5 by $\exp[(610.46 - 608.94)/2] = 2.1$. These models have very different implications on the point of theoretical interest. In the quadratic model, the relationship between development and fertility is negative over the entire range of HDI values. At HDI = 0.96, the estimated value of $\partial y \partial x$ is about −3. In Model 5, the relationship changes direction for HDI values above 0.915, and $\partial y \partial x$ is equal to about 0.9 at HDI = 0.96. Thus, conclusions about the Myrskylä, Kohler, and Billari hypotheses differ, depending on whether one uses the AIC or BIC.

In the classical approach, the linear model can be rejected against the quadratic model. The quadratic model cannot be rejected against the cubic model at conventional levels of significance (the t-ratio for the cubed term is 1.51, giving a p-value of .13). The quadratic model is a special case of Model 5, implying the restriction $\gamma = 2$. An F-test involving Models 3 and 5 gives a value of 3.39 (1, 136 df), which has a p-value of .068. This is in the gray area that might be treated as weak support for Model 5 or as grounds for accepting the quadratic model. The spline model cannot easily be tested against any of the others, but it has a larger mean square error than Model 5 and the same number of degrees of freedom, so there is no reason to prefer it.

To summarize, if the AIC is used as the model selection criterion, the results support the proposition that the effects of development on fertility change direction; if conventional hypothesis tests are used, they are ambiguous; and if the BIC is used, they count against it. None of the approaches can be interpreted as strongly favoring one model over the others, so it could be said that all agree in the sense of suggesting that more evidence is needed before we can offer a firm conclusion. Nevertheless, they lead to different conclusions about the most fundamental point—the direction of the evidence provided by the data.

2.6.3 Comparative Social Mobility

The third example involves social mobility in the United States and Britain (Long and Ferrie, 2013). The data are tables of father's occupation by own occupation for samples of 19th-century British men, 20th-century British

men, 19th-century American men, and 20th-century American men. Occupation is classified into five categories: higher white-collar, lower white-collar, farmer, skilled and semiskilled manual, and unskilled manual.[7] The sample includes 9,304 men. The table can be analyzed using what Erikson and Goldthorpe (1992; see also Xie, 1992) call a "uniform difference" model:

$$\log(\hat{n}_{ijk}) = \beta_{ik} + \beta_{jk} + \phi_k \gamma_{ij} \qquad (2.5)$$

where i represents father's occupation, j represents own occupation, k represents the combination of nation and time, and n is the number of cases that have a given combination of characteristics. For example, n_{111} is the number of 19th-century American men with professional jobs whose fathers also had professional jobs. The observed values of n are assumed to follow a Poisson distribution with parameter $\hat{n}$. The β parameters represent the marginal totals of men in different occupations at each time and place. The association between occupations is represented by the product of the γ_{ij} parameters, which represent the pattern of assocation between different occupations, and the ϕ_k parameters, which represent the strength of the association.

An appealing feature of this model is that it makes it possible to describe differences in mobility in simple terms: a higher value of ϕ means a stronger association, or less mobility. It is possible that the model will not hold; that the pattern of association will differ in more complex ways over times or places. In terms of the classification in Section 2.2, this means that one of the purposes of model selection in this example is to decide on primary structure.

Table 2.4 shows fit statistics from several models. The column headed "*df*" gives the number of degrees of freedom remaining after fitting the model; the number of parameters in each model is $100 - df$. Model 3 represents the model in Equation 2.5: a common pattern but different amounts of mobility. The estimated values of ϕ are 1.48 for 19th-century Britain, 1.26 for 20th-century Britain, 0.61 for 19th-century America, and 0.90 for 20th-century America. The basic conclusion is that the gap between the nations

---

[7]Long and Ferrie considered several different classifications. The data used here are taken from Long and Ferrie (2008, Tables A-2-1 and A-2-2).

**TABLE 2.4. Fit Statistics for Models of Social Mobility
in the United States and Britain**

Model	Association	Deviance	df	AIC	BIC
1	No association	1,747.3	64	1,819.3	2,076.3
2	No differences in association	268.9	48	372.9	744.1
3	Different amounts	108.1	45	218.1	**610.7**
4	Amount by nation, pattern by time	48.1	30	**188.1**	687.8
5	Amount by time, pattern by nation	69.0	30	209.0	708.7
6	Different patterns	0	0	200.0	913.8

Note. Bold type indicates the best fitting model according to that criterion.

became smaller in the 20th century, mostly because of increased inheritance of status in the United States. This is the best fitting model according to the BIC.

The AIC, however, favors Model 4, in which the *pattern* of mobility differs between the 19th and 20th centuries. In terms of Equation 2.5, this means that there are two sets of γ parameters, one for the 19th century and one for the 20th. Within each century, it is possible to compare the nations: as with Model 4, social mobility is greater in the United States in both the 19th and 20th centuries, but the national differences are smaller in the 20th century. However, this model does not allow one to say that social mobility increased or decreased over time; all one can say is that the pattern of mobility changed. Using conventional hypothesis tests, only Model 6 can be accepted at the .05 level of significance. This is a "saturated" model, fitting one parameter for every data cell, so that it reproduces the data perfectly but leaves no degrees of freedom. In this example, it can be understood to mean that each nation at each time has a qualitatively different pattern of social mobility. The *p*-value for Model 4 is about .02, so some investigators might argue in favor of accepting it, particularly given the large sample size. Model 3 can be rejected at any reasonable level of significance against both Models 4 and 6.

In the first two examples, the BIC and classical tests agreed that there was room for doubt about which model should be preferred. In this case, however, the conclusions are completely different. According to the BIC, the odds in favor of Model 3 against Model 6 are $e^{\frac{913.8-610.7}{2}}$, or about 10^{64}, although the *p*-value of Model 3 is about .00000004. The odds in favor of Model 3 against Model 4 are also very strong, about 10^{17}. As a result, the BIC implies that, if one of these models is correct, it is almost certainly Model 3.

The difference reflects two features of the data: first, the sample is large, and second, the tests involve multiple degrees of freedom. Both of these factors increase the divergence between the BIC and classical tests. In a sample of 139 cases, like the fertility example, an additional parameter must reduce the deviance by at least 4.93 in order to reduce the BIC; in a sample of 9,304, it must reduce the deviance by at least 9.14. For tests of a single parameter, these figures correspond to t-ratios of about 2.2 and 3.0, or p-values of about .03 and .004. The differences grow as the number of degrees of freedom increase: with a sample of 9,304, a model including three extra parameters must reduce the deviance by at least 27.4 to reduce the BIC, which corresponds to a p-value of about 5×10^{-6}.

Putting statistical issues aside, this example illustrates a feature of the BIC that many researchers find appealing (Hauser, 1995; Xie, 1999). In some cases, the BIC favors a model with a straightforward interpretation, while classical tests lead to a much more complex model. In this case, Model 3 permits a direct answer to questions about whether there is more or less mobility in different societies; Model 6 tells us that there are differences in the patterns of mobility but does not give any guidance on how they should be described.

2.6.4 Race and Voting Choices

The final example involves the 2004 U.S. presidential election, using data from the Edison–Mitofsky election day exit poll. The models are binary logistic regressions of the choice between the two major candidates, George W. Bush and John Kerry. In contrast to the first three examples, which all focus on specific hypotheses, this example involves an inductive or exploratory analysis. The general question is whether there are interaction effects involving race.[8] The survey contains information on a number of other potential influences on vote: age, family income, gender, marital status, state of residence, and size of community. More information on the variables is provided in Table 2.5. Although the exit poll does not contain as many demographic

---

[8]The race variable is a dichotomous division between blacks and all others. For convenience, I will sometimes refer to the nonblack group as "whites."

TABLE 2.5. Description of Variables, 2004 Exit Poll

Variable	Values
Categorical variables	
Race	Black
	Nonblack
Community	City over 500,000
	City 50,000–499,999
	Suburb
	City 10,000–49,999
	Rural
Sex	Male
	Female
Marital status	Married
	Not married
State	
Covariates	
Family income	1 = under $15,000 . . . 8 = $200,000 or more
Age	1 = 18–24 . . . 9 = 75 and over

variables as some other election surveys, its large sample size provides more power to detect any interactions that might exist.

The baseline model includes the main effects of all variables but no interaction effects. Adding interactions between race and all of the other independent variables adds 47 parameters and reduces the deviance by 166.0. The 5% critical value for a chi-square distribution with 47 degrees of freedom is 64, and the 0.1% critical value is 82.7, so the hypothesis that the effects of all variables are the same among blacks and whites can be definitively rejected.

The next step in an investigation using conventional tests is to consider intermediate models in which there are interactions involving some subset of the independent variables. Table 2.6 shows the relevant parameter estimates and standard errors from the model including interactions (estimates involving state differences are omitted to save space).

The estimates for income and marital status are almost the same among blacks and whites, and the null hypothesis can obviously be accepted. This conclusion, however, does not mean that there is positive evidence that the effects are the same or even that any differences are "small." Examination of the standard errors shows that there is a wide range of uncertainty: it is cer-

tainly possible that the effects are the same, but it is also possible that they are substantially larger or smaller among blacks—that is, there is not enough evidence to make any strong claim one way or the other. The BIC, however, gives very different conclusions: odds of about 100:1 in favor of the hypothesis of no difference.

The estimated effects of gender are considerably smaller for blacks than for whites, but the hypothesis of no difference cannot be rejected using conventional tests—the t-ratio is about 1. The BIC finds strong evidence in favor of the hypothesis of no difference (odds of 70:1).

Table 2.7 shows fit statistics from a number of models. Models 3–5 consider state, community, and age interactions assuming that the effects of income, gender, and marital status do not differ by race. The difference in deviance between Models 3 and 4 is 2.8, which is in between the 5% and 10%

TABLE 2.6. Selected Parameter Estimates and Standard Errors from Model 2

	Nonblack	Black	Difference
Male	.258***	.061	.197
	(.042)	(.195)	(.199)
Age	−.020*	−.100*	.080
	(.010)	(.051)	(.052)
Income	.094***	.096	−.002
	(.013)	(.064)	(.065)
Married	.490***	.473*	.017
	(.047)	(.212)	(.217)
Community			
Large city	−.500***	−1.659**	
	(.096)	(.576)	
City	−.283***	.119	
	(.082)	(.433)	
Suburbs	−.146*	−.186	
	(.071)	(.438)	
Town	.067	−.347	
	(.103)	(.393)	
Rural	.000	.000	

Note. Standard errors in parentheses. Statistical significance is indicated by * = .05; ** = .01; *** = .001.

TABLE 2.7. Fit Statistics for Models of Democratic versus Republican Vote, Interactions with Race

Model	Association	Deviance	df	AIC	BIC
1	None	13,902.9	56	14,014.9	14,428.2
2	State, community, income, age, sex, married	13,736.9	103	13,942.9	14,703.2
3	State, community, age	13,738.0	100	**13,938.0**	14,676.1
4	State, community	13,740.8	99	13,938.8	14,669.5
5	State	13,752.8	95	13,942.8	14,644.0
6	State (nonblack only)	13,843.2	56	13,955.2	**14,368.5**

Note. N = 11,862 for all models. Bold type indicates the best fitting model according to that criterion.

critical values. The difference in deviance between Models 4 and 5 is 12.0, which falls in between the 5% and 1% critical values for a chi-square distribution with four degrees of freedom. The difference in deviance between Models 1 and 5 is about 150 with 39 degrees of freedom, which is well beyond the 0.1% critical value. Thus, a researcher using a 10% level would choose Model 3, a researcher using a 5% level would choose Model 4, and a researcher using a 1% level would choose Model 5. However, most researchers do not strictly follow a single significance level, so the usual conclusion would be that there is weak evidence that the effects of age differ by race, reasonably strong evidence that the effects of community differ, and strong evidence that the effects of state differ.

The lowest value of the AIC occurs for Model 3, followed closely by Model 4. Thus, researchers using the AIC and standard hypothesis tests would come to similar conclusions. The BIC, however, strongly favors a model including no interactions (Model 1) over Models 2–5.

The final alternative, Model 6, holds that there are differences by state in the voting choices of nonblacks, but not among blacks. The relationships among Models 1, 5, and 6 can be understood by considering β_j and γ_j, the set of parameters representing the effects of state among blacks and nonblacks. Model 5 imposes no restriction on the values of these parameters. Models 1 and 6 are both nested in this model: Model 1 imposes the restriction $\beta_j = \gamma_j$ for all j, while Model 6 imposes the restriction that $\beta_j = 0$ for all j. As seen previously, Model 6 can be rejected against Model 5: they differ by 90.4 in deviance and 39 in degrees of freedom, and the 0.1% critical value for a chi-

square distribution with 39 degrees of freedom is 72.0. The BIC, however, strongly favors Model 6 over Model 5.

This example, like the preceding one, illustrates the tendency of the BIC to favor simpler models than conventional hypothesis tests and the AIC, particularly when the number of cases is large. The example also illustrates a more subtle point—the ambiguity in the meaning of "a simple model." In terms of the number of parameters, Models 2 and 6 are equally complex. However, Model 2 contains only main effects, while Model 6 involves an interaction between state and race, so in some sense Model 2 might be regarded as simpler. Investigators analyzing this kind of data often do not even consider possibilities like Model 6.

2.7 SUMMARY AND CONCLUSIONS

This chapter has described the various purposes for which hypothesis tests are used and the major criticisms that have been made against that practice. It introduced two alternatives to conventional tests, the AIC and the BIC, and illustrated their application to four examples. The examples show that the different methods of model selection can lead to very different conclusions. This difference was particularly evident in the social mobility example: the BIC strongly supported the hypothesis that all four cases had the same pattern of mobility, while conventional tests strongly rejected that hypothesis. Even in cases where the methods favored the same model, their implications could differ in important ways. In the economic growth example, the BIC implies fairly strong evidence against the proposition that ethnolinguistic fractionalization affects growth, while a classical test merely says that we cannot rule out the possibility of no effect.

As a result, the strategy of using both the BIC and conventional hypothesis tests, as advocated by Xie (1999), is not viable. In many cases, when two alternative statistics have been proposed, it is informative to consider both. To take a simple example, the mean and median are both measures of central tendency; if there is a substantial difference between them, that tells us something about the distribution of the variable. However, the AIC, the BIC, and classical tests do not provide different information about the fit of the model;

rather, they all involve a comparison of deviance to degrees of freedom and simply propose different standards for interpreting the same information. Therefore, it is necessary to examine the rationale for each criterion in detail and to decide which is most persuasive.

RECOMMENDED READING

Cohen, J. (1994). The earth is round (p < .05). *American Psychologist, 49,* 997–1000. —One of the best known of recent critiques of conventional significance testing.

Cox, D. R. (1982). Statistical significance tests. *British Journal of Clinical Pharmacology, 14,* 325–331. —Gives a clear account of conventional significance tests and argues that they are useful in scientific research.

Giere, R. N. (1972). The significance test controversy. *British Journal for the Philosophy of Science, 23,* 170–181. —A review of Morrison and Henkel (1970) that provides a useful guide to the issues debated in that book.

Ioannidis, J. P. A. (2005). Why most published research findings are false. *PLoS Medicine, 2,* 696–701. —Provides a model of the research and publication process that suggests that a majority of statistically significant "findings" are spurious.

Krantz, D. H. (1999). The null hypothesis testing controversy in psychology. *Journal of the American Statistical Association, 44,* 1372–1381. —Discusses the different uses of hypothesis tests and concludes that "we need a foundational theory that encompasses a variety of inferential goals."

Morrison, D. E., & Henkel, R. E. (Eds.). (1970). *The significance test controversy.* Chicago: Aldine. —Collects a variety of articles from the 1940s through the 1960s. The ones by Lipset, Trow, and Coleman; Kendall; Davis; Morrison and Henkel; Lykken; Meehl; and Berkson are particularly informative.

Nickerson, R. (2000). Null hypothesis significance testing: A review of an old and continuing controversy. *Psychological Methods, 5,* 241–301. —A balanced review of the controversy over significance testing, with many references to the literature.

Savage, L. J. (1972). *The foundations of statistics* (2nd ed., Chap. 16). New York: Dover. —Discusses the question of testing null hypotheses that are almost certainly false.

Wolfowitz, J. (1967/1980). Remarks on the theory of testing hypotheses. In *Selected papers.* New York: Springer-Verlag. (First published in *New York Statistician, 18,* 1–3.) —Criticizes the practice of hypothesis testing; especially noteworthy because Wolfowitz was an important contributor to the theory.

3

The Classical Approach

This chapter discusses the "classical" approach to hypothesis testing. It begins by considering the relationship between random sampling and hypothesis tests. Next, it distinguishes between two different classical approaches to testing: in the first a hypothesis test is seen as a way to assess the fit of a single model, while the second sees the test as a rule for deciding between two models. The chapter outlines the classical interpretation of confidence intervals and discusses methods of choosing a significance level, giving examples. The chapter concludes by assessing the criticisms of conventional hypothesis testing described in Chapter 2 and offering recommendations for practice.

3.1 RANDOM SAMPLING AND CLASSICAL TESTS

Nearly all textbook discussions of classical hypothesis testing involve random samples from a definite population. In that situation, we can imagine taking repeated samples from the same population and observing the relative frequency of various outcomes. The same logic can be applied to processes that can be repeated under identical circumstances such as plays in games of chance, since the observed data can be regarded as a random sample from a hypothetical population of possible outcomes.

However, much of the data used in the social sciences does not involve random samples or repeated processes. Data on organizations or political units often are what Berk, Western, and Weiss (1995, p. 422) call an "appar-

ent population," in which "the data on hand are all the data there are. No additional data could be collected, even in principle." For example, in the analyses of fertility discussed in Section 2.6.2, the units of observation were nations for which the data were available. The data could be regarded as a complete population, but from that point of view there is no basis for hypothesis testing, since the population parameters can be calculated exactly. The data could be regarded as a sample from the population of nations that have existed, or from a hypothetical population of nations that might have existed, but they are not random samples from those populations. Many observers hold that classical tests cannot reasonably be used for such data (see Section 2.3.1).

There is, however, an alternative interpretation of classical hypothesis tests, which Cox (2006, p. 178) calls the "model-based" approach. This interpretation regards hypothesis tests as a comparison between the observed data and the data that could be generated by a probability model. The investigator attempts to "construct hypothetical probability models from which it is possible, by random drawings, to reproduce samples of the type given by 'Nature' " (Haavelmo, 1944, p. 52). If it is not possible to distinguish between the observed data and data generated by the model, then the model is adequate in a statistical sense—whether it should be regarded as adequate in a more general sense depends on substantive knowledge and the purposes of the investigator. Note that the random drawings do not involve the actual data but rather the data generated by the hypothetical probability model. From this point of view, "The logic for tests of significance without random sampling is a logic of ignorance" (Johnstone, 1989, p. 448). The random component in a probability model represents the part of the outcome that cannot be predicted using the measured variables. This part may reflect sampling, but it might also reflect measurement error, the effects of other variables, or some deterministic process that is too complex to specify. As Bartlett (1940, p. 13) put it, "The practical statistician will hope to apply theory wherever he has reason to believe that a complex of causes is operating to produce an unavoidable element of chance variation in his material."

To illustrate the difference between the sampling and model-based approaches, suppose we use ordinary least squares to fit a regression including a single independent variable to data representing an "apparent population":

$$y_i = \alpha + \beta x_i + e_i \qquad (3.1)$$

If we regard the data as a complete population, the resulting coefficient for β is a population parameter: the value that minimizes the sum of the squared errors. There is no need to make assumptions about the error distribution, because the actual values of e_i can be calculated, given the values of y_i, x_i, α, and β. However, one might ask why we should be interested in the value of β that minimizes the sum of squared errors rather than the value that minimizes some other criterion, or in the regression containing x rather than a regression containing a different set of predictors. The sampling-based approach does not provide answers to these questions. That is, although the parameters of the model can be calculated exactly, the choice of a model becomes arbitrary.

In contrast, the model-based approach requires some assumptions about the distribution of the error term. These assumptions guide the choice of a method of estimation—for example, if the errors are normally distributed with constant variance and are uncorrelated with x, then ordinary least squares estimates will be efficient. Moreover, the validity of the assumptions can be tested using the observed data. Residuals can be computed from the actual values of x and estimates of α and β; statistical inference can be applied to decide if the distribution of the residuals is consistent with the assumptions of the model. For example, it is possible to test the hypothesis that the residuals are normally distributed. If that hypothesis is rejected, the model can be modified in an appropriate way, such as by transforming the dependent variable. There is no definitive test that can establish the validity of a model, but a model that has survived a number of tests can be regarded as acceptable.

In the model-based interpretation, random sampling still brings some important advantages. For example, if the data are not from a random sample, estimates of the parameters of interest may be affected by "sample selection bias" (Heckman, 1979), which produces a correlation between the error term and the independent variables. Even if specification tests show no evidence of such bias, one can never be *certain* of its absence. With a random sample, selection bias can be ruled out in principle. At the same time, random sampling does not eliminate the possibility of all kinds of misspecification: for example, it does not guarantee that the relationship between two variables

is linear. Regardless of whether or not the data are from a random sample, the goal of hypothesis testing is to find a model that is consistent with the observed data. Random sampling is merely a useful device that reduces the range of models that need to be considered.

3.2   TWO APPROACHES TO HYPOTHESIS TESTS

There are two major classical approaches to testing. The first, which was developed by R. A. Fisher, attempts to assess the fit of a single model. The second, which was developed by Jerzy Neyman and Egon Pearson, explicitly compares the fit of two models representing the "null" and "alternative" hypotheses. Fisher's approach is often referred to as "significance testing." There is no generally accepted term for the second approach, so I will simply refer to it as the "Neyman–Pearson approach."[1] In most cases, the two approaches use the same test statistics, but they offer somewhat different interpretations.

3.2.1   Significance Tests

Significance tests address the question of whether a given model can plausibly account for the observed data. Given a model and hypothetical values for the parameters of that model, it is possible to calculate the probability (or likelihood) of obtaining the data. If that probability is low—that is, if the observed outcome would be unlikely if the model were true—that suggests that the model is false. However, given a large amount of data, the probability of *any* specific outcome, even the most likely one, is usually very small. For example, suppose that we have 10,000 independent observations of a binary outcome, and 5,000 are "successes." The data are obviously consistent with the hypothesis that the probability of success is 0.5, but the probability of getting exactly 5,000 cases of success in 10,000 trials is only .008. Thus, the problem is to define an "unlikely" outcome. Significance tests accomplish this by combining the probability of a range of outcomes including the

---

[1]Some authors, such as Kempthorne (1976), limit the term "hypothesis testing" to the Neyman–Pearson approach, but this usage has not been generally adopted. I will use "hypothesis testing" as a general term covering Fisherian, Neyman–Pearson, and Bayesian approaches.

observed one. If the outcome is a continuous variable, the probability of any specific outcome is zero, but it is possible to integrate the likelihood over some range. In effect, this means considering the probability of observing outcomes "similar" to the one actually observed.

Fisher proposed using the probability that a test statistic would have a value greater than or equal to the observed value. This quantity, known as the p-value, has a uniform distribution over the $(0, 1)$ interval if the model representing the null hypothesis is correct. If the p-value is small, the investigator has a choice between two conclusions: "Either the hypothesis is untrue, or the value of [the test statistic] has attained by chance an exceptionally high value" (Fisher, 1958, p. 80). Any convention about which values should be regarded as "exceptional" is somewhat arbitrary since the p-value is fundamentally a matter of degree: for example, a value of .009 is only slightly less "unusual" than a p-value of .011.

Moreover, it is not necessary to reduce the p-value to "significant" or "nonsignificant": there could be an intermediate zone in which results are regarded as suggestive or deserving of further investigation but not definitive. Many early discussions of significance testing proposed a division into three or more regions. According to Fisher (1958, p. 80), if the p-value is greater than .1, "there is certainly no reason to suspect the hypothesis tested. If it is below .02 it is strongly indicated that the hypothesis fails to account for the whole of the facts. . . . A value . . . exceeding the 5 per cent. point is seldom to be disregarded." Barnard (1947, p. 659) said that the accumulation of research results had made it necessary to develop "rules for dividing experimental results into three classes: (a) those fit for the waste-paper basket, (b) those which should be put on file, and (c) those that were worth following up immediately. The conceptions of five per cent significance for class (b), and one per cent significance for class (c) were exceedingly valuable in this connection." Similarly, Cramér (1955, p. 202) proposed calling p-values between .05 and .01 "almost significant" and reserving "significant" for p-values under .01.

"Accepting" a hypothesis on the basis of a significance test does not mean positive support for the hypothesis—it simply means that the observed data are consistent with that hypothesis. One could say that the null hypothesis is given the benefit of the doubt: accepted unless there is reasonably strong evidence that it is incorrect. For example, if 43 successes were observed in

100 trials, the value of the chi-square statistic given the hypothesis that the probability of success is 0.5 would be 1.96. For a chi-square distribution with 1 degree of freedom, $F(1.96) = 0.832$, so the p-value is approximately 0.168 and the hypothesis of equal frequencies would be accepted using the conventional standards, even though the data are obviously also consistent with many other propositions about the probability of success—most obviously, that it is 0.43.

One might ask why we should give either hypothesis the benefit of the doubt rather than beginning from a position of neutrality (Berk and Brewer, 1978). The practical reason is that the proposition that a parameter does *not* have a specified value is consistent with any observed outcome, so beginning from a position of neutrality between $\theta = k$ and $\theta \neq k$ could never lead to a decision in favor of $\theta = k$. Even if $\hat{\theta}$ were exactly equal to k, the data would be almost equally consistent with the possibility that θ was very slightly larger or smaller than k. The theoretical answer is that the null hypothesis is chosen to represent a value of special interest. The standard null hypothesis $\theta = 0$ represents a simpler model, in the sense that the parameter can be omitted. The widely accepted principle of "Occam's razor" holds that when there is room for doubt a simpler model should be preferred over a more complex one.[2]

If the null hypothesis specifies the values of several parameters, the logic of significance testing is the same: accept the null hypothesis unless the p-value of the null hypothesis falls below some conventional level. However, if the null hypothesis is rejected, the alternative is that *at least one* of the statements making up that hypothesis is false. For example, rejecting $\theta_1 = \theta_2 = \theta_3$ is equivalent to saying that either $\theta_1 \neq \theta_2$ or $\theta_2 \neq \theta_3$, or both. To choose among these alternatives, it is necessary to conduct additional tests.

3.2.1.1 Significance Tests and Model Comparison

Fisher (1958, pp. 80–81) maintained that both high and low p-values should count as evidence against the null hypothesis: "values [of p] over .999 have sometimes been reported. . . . [In] these cases the hypothesis considered is as definitely disproved as if P had been .001." In effect, with a very high

---

[2]This principle will be discussed in greater detail in Chapter 8.

p-value, the match between the data and the model is "too good to be true." Other observers argued that data which are entirely consistent with a model cannot reasonably be regarded as evidence against that model (Stuart, 1954). Cochran (1952, p. 337) took an intermediate position, suggesting that in the case of "very high P's, say those greater than 0.99," one should "give the data further scrutiny before regarding the result as evidence in favor of the null hypothesis."

The controversy has been largely forgotten, and today high p-values are almost universally treated as simply "not significant." However, it raises an important question of principle: Why should *any* particular values be singled out as unusual? If the null hypothesis is true, the p-value will be approximately uniformly distributed so that in some sense all values are equally "exceptional." Howson and Urbach (1994, p. 48) assert that this point invalidates the fundamental logic of significance testing: "The dichotomy ["hypothesis is untrue" or "exceptionally high value"] has no force: all it says is that the null hypothesis is either true or false."

If we think in terms of comparing models, however, there is a clear case for treating small p-values as evidence against the null hypothesis. For example, the common problem of deciding whether to include an independent variable in a regression equation can be regarded as a choice between two models:

$$y = \alpha + \beta_1 x_1 + \beta_2 x_2 \ldots + \beta_{k-1} x_{k-1} + e; \ e \sim N(0, \sigma^2) \qquad (3.2)$$

$$y = \alpha + \beta_1 x_1 + \beta_2 x_2 \ldots + \beta_{k-1} x_{k-1} + \beta_k x_k + e; \ e \sim N(0, \sigma^2) \qquad (3.3)$$

If the p-value for the estimate of β_k is very small, that means that there are some values of β_k that make Equation 3.3 considerably more likely than Equation 3.2. As Barnard (1967, p. 33) says, the basic principle behind the interpretation of small p-values as evidence against a model is "our disposition to prefer that hypothesis which makes more probable what we know to be true."

Less obviously, the same disposition explains why p-values close to 1 might sometimes be regarded as evidence *against* the null hypothesis. Some assumptions, particularly those involving correlated errors, make large p-values more likely than they are under the null hypothesis. For example, Fisher

(1958, pp. 58–60) gives an example of an experiment in which there was a remarkably good fit between predicted and observed values because the variation among samples had been artifically suppressed.

The kind of departures from the null model that would make high p-values more likely can sometimes be ruled out in principle: for example, if the data are a sample of individuals from a large population, there is no possibility of substantial correlation among the errors for different cases. Therefore, it would not be reasonable to follow a general rule of rejecting the null hypothesis when the p-value is high, but under some circumstances large p-values can be a sign of a problem with the model.

3.2.2 The Neyman–Pearson Approach

The implicit comparison of models in significance tests is made explicit in the Neyman–Pearson approach. According to Pearson (1939, p. 242), the "idea which has formed the basis of all the . . . researches of Neyman and myself . . . is the simple suggestion that the only reason for rejecting a statistical hypothesis is that some other hypothesis explains the observed events with a greater degree of probability."

Neyman and Pearson proposed that a hypothesis test should be regarded as a rule for deciding between the null and alternative hypotheses. The performance of different rules can be evaluated by the expected rates of Type I errors (rejecting the null hypothesis if it is true) and Type II errors (accepting the null hypothesis if it is false). It is not possible to minimize the chance of both types of errors at once: for example, using a .01 rather than a .05 standard for rejecting the null hypothesis will reduce the chance of Type I errors but increase the chance of Type II errors. Neyman and Pearson suggested that one should begin by fixing an acceptable rate of Type I errors (which they called α) and choose the test that minimizes the rate of Type II errors, given that constraint.

This principle provides a way to evaluate proposed tests and leads to interesting problems for statistical theory, such as establishing the conditions under which "most powerful" tests exist and resolving various paradoxes and anomalies that arise in particular applications. It also provides a basis for "power analysis" in the design of studies (Cohen, 1988). The rate of Type II errors is a function of the significance level, the true parameter

value, and the standard error of the parameter estimate, so a researcher who specifies a significance level and a value of interest for the parameter can calculate the sample size necessary to reduce the rate of Type II errors to some target level.

However, the Neyman–Pearson approach has little immediate practical impact on the analysis of observational data. The general procedure is the same as that for significance tests: accept or reject the null hypothesis depending on whether the test statistic is below or above the critical value for the α level. The most important difference is that in the significance testing approach, the division of the p-value into categories is merely a convenience, whereas in the Neyman–Pearson approach the division into exactly two categories is fundamental. Thus, in practical terms, the most important difference is that the Neyman–Pearson approach focuses attention on the choice between accepting and rejecting the null hypothesis.

3.3 CONFIDENCE INTERVALS

A confidence interval is an interval (c_a, c_b) that has a given probability of including the true parameter value. In contrast to an interval hypothesis, the endpoints of the interval are not specified in advance but rather depend on the data. In the classical approach, the parameter is an unknown constant, not a random variable, so it is not possible to speak of the probability that a specific confidence interval constructed from the observed data includes the true value. For example, a statement like $0.3 < \theta < 0.6$ is simply true or false. However, the endpoints of the intervals computed from different samples are random variables, so before the data are observed one can speak of the probability that the as-yet unknown confidence interval will contain the true parameter value. Although this distinction raises interesting philosophical questions, it is of little importance for practical purposes. For example, an investigator who followed a rule of stating that the parameter value is in the 95% confidence interval could expect to be correct 95% of the time. In a strict sense, the probabilities involve the correctness of statements, but in an every-day sense it would be entirely reasonable for a user of classical hypothesis tests to say that the parameter was "probably" in (c_a, c_b).

There are many ways to construct an interval that will have a given

probability of including the true parameter value, so in order to obtain a unique solution it is necessary to add additional conditions. One appealing approach is to choose the shortest interval including the unbiased estimate of the parameter, which will be centered at $\hat{\theta}$. However, there are cases in which this approach leads to paradoxes. Jaynes (1976) offers a simple example: suppose that y is a failure time given by $\theta + x$, where x is a random variable following a standard exponential distribution and the observed values of y are 12, 14, and 16. The shortest 90% confidence interval including the unbiased estimate of θ is (12.15, 13.83). Yet, because the minimum value of the standard exponential distribution is zero, we know that in this case θ must be less than or equal to 12, which is the smallest observed value of y. Therefore, in this case we can be sure that the shortest unbiased 90% confidence interval does *not* include the parameter value. Such cases are by definition unusual: if the same rule were used to construct confidence intervals for other samples from the same population, 90% of them would include the parameter value. However, statements about what would happen in other samples would not be useful to an investigator who was trying to draw conclusions from the observed data. ·

An alternative approach that avoids problems of this kind is the "likelihood-based" confidence interval. In this definition, the $100 \times (1 - \alpha)$ confidence interval includes all values θ_c for which the hypothesis $\theta = \theta_c$ cannot be rejected at the α level using a likelihood ratio test.[3] That is, the confidence interval could be said to represent parameter estimates that are consistent with the data. By definition, a likelihood-based confidence cannot include parameter values that are impossible given the observations: in the example proposed by Jaynes, the 90% confidence interval is (11.55, 12).

In addition to making a clear link between hypothesis testing and confidence intervals, this approach also has an important implication for the interpretation of hypothesis tests. To say that the hypothesis $\theta = 0$ is rejected at the α level is equivalent to saying that all values in the $(1 - \alpha)$ confidence interval have the same sign. Under this interpretation, a hypothesis test is meaningful even if the null hypothesis $\theta = 0$ is not credible: rejecting the null hypothesis means that we can be reasonably confident about the sign of the

---

[3]This method of constructing a confidence interval is sometimes called "inverting" hypothesis tests (Barnard, 1967, p. 34).

parameter, while accepting it means that we do not (Cox, 1982, p. 327). However, it is not possible to specify the degree of confidence precisely, since that involves a conditional probability: the probability that θ is in the interval, given that all of the interval is positive. In order to make an exact statement about the probability that θ is positive, it is necessary to make some assumptions about the actual distribution of parameter values—that is, to take a Bayesian approach.

3.4 CHOOSING A SIGNIFICANCE LEVEL

Neyman and Pearson generally followed Fisher in using the conventional .05 or .01 levels of significance. However, they observed that "in certain cases we attempt to adjust the balance between the risks [of Type I and Type II errors] to meet the problem before us" (Neyman and Pearson, 1933/1967, p. 191). This point was developed by Wald (1950), who proposed considering the probabilities and "costs" of different kinds of errors in order to decide on the optimal decision rule for each case. Although Wald focused on general theory, several authors followed his lead and proposed methods of choosing α that could be applied in empirical work. None of those methods have been widely adopted, but they help to illuminate several important issues with hypothesis testing. Therefore, this section features a detailed discussion of the methods suggested by Lindley (1953) and Lehmann (1958).[4]

Figure 3.1 shows the relationship between the rate of Type I and Type II errors given a simple regression

$$y = \alpha + \beta x + e$$

where x and e are both normally distributed with a variance of 1, and the value of β is 0.1. The three lines represent samples of 50, 200, and 500. At the standard .05 level of significance, the rate of Type II errors is about 89% in a sample of 50, 71% in a sample of 200, and 39% in a sample of 500.

Because the rate of Type II errors depends on the value of the parameter,

---

[4]Arrow (1960/1984) proposed a variant of Lehmann's method, while Quandt (1980) and Das (1994) independently proposed methods similar to Lindley's. Leamer (1978, pp. 93–99) also contributes some relevant discussion.

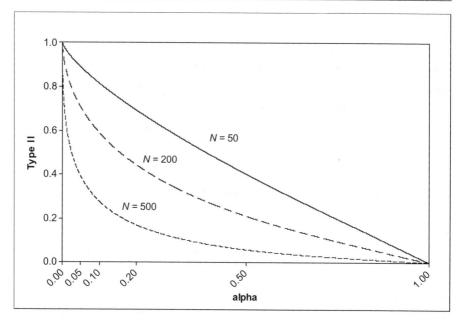

FIGURE 3.1. Examples of the relationship between Type I and Type II errors.

a calculation of the "balance of risks" must begin by specifying a value of interest. Then the power of the test can be calculated under the assumption that $|\theta| = \delta$, where δ is the smallest value considered "important" from a practical or theoretical point of view. If $|\theta| > \delta$, then the rate of Type II errors will be lower. Of course, if $|\theta| < \delta$, the rate of Type II errors will be higher, but a Type II error might then be regarded as a matter of indifference, or even as the preferable decision. Therefore, calculations based on the assumption that $|\theta| = \delta$ can be regarded as conservative if we are interested in the possibility that $\theta \geq \delta$.

Given a value for $|\delta|$, we can consider rules for balancing the two kinds of errors. Lindley (1953) suggested assigning relative weights and choosing the value of α that makes the weighted sum of the errors as small as possible.[5] That is, the α level is chosen to minimize the function $w\alpha_1 + \alpha_2$, where

---

[5]Lindley later became a prominent advocate of the Bayesian approach and emphasized the difference between Bayesian and classical hypothesis tests. However, when he made this proposal, he thought that it was possible to reconcile the two approaches.

α_1 and α_2 are the rates of Type I and Type II errors, respectively.[6] If one is willing to think of the hypotheses as having prior probabilities, w is the product of the relative prior probability and "cost" of that kind of error, and minimizing $w\alpha_1 + \alpha_2$ is equivalent to minimizing the expected loss from the decision. Type I errors are conventionally regarded as more serious than Type II errors (Neyman, 1977, p. 104), suggesting that w should be at least 1, but the exact value could differ, depending on the nature of the problem and the purpose of the investigation.

For illustration, Table 3.1 shows the α-values implied in this example at different sample sizes when w has the values of 20, 10, 5, 2, and 1. When the two kinds of errors are given equal weight, the α level is inversely related to sample size. It approaches .316 (corresponding to a t-ratio of 1.00) as N goes toward zero and approaches zero as N goes to infinity. When w is greater than 1, the relationship is more complex: below a certain sample size, the standard for significance becomes more stringent as N becomes smaller. For example, when $w = 10$, α is .000005 when $N = 50$. As a result, it can be very difficult to reject the null hypothesis in a small sample. In this case, the critical value of the t-statistic would be about 4.5, corresponding to a parameter estimate of 0.63; the probability of a Type II error assuming $\theta = 0.1$ is about .9999. This apparently paradoxical relationship between sample size and the α level will be discussed in the following section.

The figures in Table 3.1 should *not* be understood as a general rule for choosing the α level according to sample size. Rather, the optimal level of α is a function of w and δ/σ, where σ is the standard error of the parameter estimate. Given a value for δ and an estimate of the standard error $\hat{\sigma}$, the figures can be applied outside of the context of this example. For example, if Type I and Type II errors are weighted equally, the optimal α level is always .278 when $\delta/\sigma = 1$, and .017 when $\delta/\sigma \approx 4.5$.

The rule can be represented in a graphical form, as shown in Figure 3.2. The figure corresponds to the case in Table 3.1 for which $N = 500$ and $r = 2$. The points on the downward-sloping line represent combinations of α_1 and α_2 for which the loss function $2\alpha_1 + \alpha_2 = .47$. The curve represents the relationship between the rates of Type I and Type II errors when $N = 500$. A point

---

[6]Neyman and Pearson used β for the rate of Type II errors, but this symbol is now commonly used for regression coefficients, so I will use α_2.

TABLE 3.1. Relation of α Values to Sample Size, Minimum Cost

N	Standard error	δ/σ	w = 20	w = 10	w = 5	w = 2	w = 1
50	.141	0.71	<.00001	.000005	.00032	.024	.297
100	.100	1.00	.00003	.00047	.005	.063	.278
500	.0445	2.25	.0057	.014	.032	.082	.152
1,000	.0314	3.18	.0060	.011	.021	.043	.070
2,000	.0225	4.44	.0023	.0038	.0206	.0113	.017
3,000	.0182	5.49	.00063	.00099	.0061	.0027	.0030
5,000	.0141	7.09	.00005	.00007	.00011	.00018	.00027

of tangency occurs when $\alpha_1 = .082$ and $\alpha_2 = .306$. This is the smallest possible loss that can be obtained given these conditions.

Lehmann (1958) proposed adjusting the α level by keeping a constant ratio of the rate of Type I to Type II errors: $r = \alpha_2/\alpha_1$.[7] For simple hypotheses, this rule minimizes the maximum "loss" (Lehmann, 1958, p. 1172; Leamer, 1978, p. 96). The principle that Type I errors are more important suggests that the ratio would be greater than or equal to 1, that is, we should be willing to accept a higher chance of the less important kind of error.

Table 3.2 shows the α levels implied by Lehmann's approach or this example using different ratios. As the sample size goes to zero (i.e., the standard error of the parameter estimate goes to infinity) the α level approaches $1/(r + 1)$. For example, if $r = 19$, then the limiting value of α is .05. Of course, in this case the test would have no power to discriminate between the two hypotheses: the chance of rejecting the null hypothesis when it is true will be equal to the chance of rejecting it when $\theta = \delta$.

Lehmann's rule can also be represented in graphical form, as shown in Figure 3.3. A constant ratio of the two types of errors is represented by a line starting at the origin and going upward and to the right, with the slope given by $y = rx$. The figure corresponds to the case in which $N = 500$ and the desired ratio of Type II to Type I errors equals 5. The line representing that ratio intersects the curve representing the tradeoff between the two types of errors at $\alpha = .068$ (see Table 3.2).

---

[7] Arrow (1960/1984) proposed specifying the value of δ that would make Type I and Type II errors equally undesirable and using a ratio of 1.0.

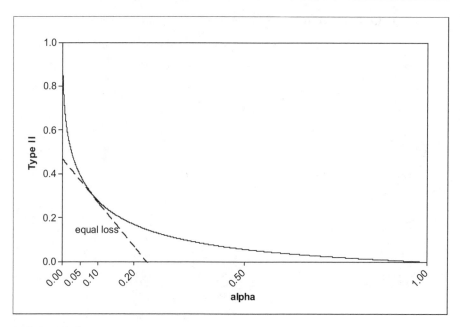

FIGURE 3.2. Example of choosing an optimal α level.

3.4.1   One-Tailed Tests

Until this point, it has been assumed that both positive and negative deviations from the value specified by the null hypothesis are of interest. However,
sometimes we are concerned only with deviations in a particular direction.
For example, if one is comparing a new technique to an existing one, the
question of interest is whether the new one is *more* effective. The critical
value for a one-tailed test at the α level is equal to the two-tailed critical

**TABLE 3.2. Example of Relation of α Values to Sample Size,
Constant Ratio**

N	Standard error	δ/σ	r = 20	r = 10	r = 5	r = 2	r = 1
50	.141	0.71	.045	.084	.150	.296	.448
100	.100	1.00	.042	.077	.136	.264	.402
500	.0445	2.25	.025	.042	.068	.121	.181
1,000	.0314	3.18	.012	.020	.031	.053	.077
2,000	.0225	4.44	.0033	.005	.008	.013	.018
3,000	.0182	5.49	.0008	.0012	.0018	.003	.004
5,000	.0141	7.09	.00006	.00008	.00012	.00019	.00026

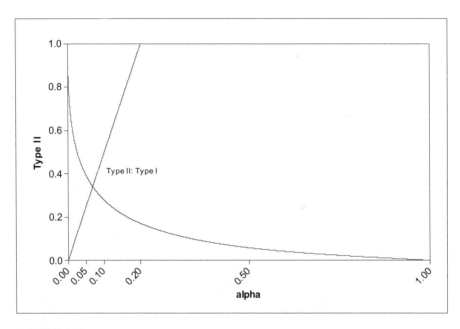

FIGURE 3.3. Example of choosing an α level by ratio of errors.

value at the 2α level; for example, saying the α parameter is significant at the 5% level using a one-tailed test is equivalent to saying that it is significant at the 10% level using a two-tailed test. Thus, when using a standard level for statistical significance, the use of one-tailed or two-tailed tests is essentially just a matter of convention.

The rules for choosing α proposed by Lindley and Lehmann can be applied to one-tailed tests. As in a two-tailed test, the rate of Type II errors is calculated assuming $\theta = \delta$, where δ is the minimum value of interest. Performance under the null hypothesis $\theta \leq 0$ is calculated at $\theta = 0$, since that is the value that is closest to δ.[8] Therefore, the distribution of the test statistic under the null hypothesis is the same as in a two-tailed test, but the Type I error rate is only half as large. The Type II error rate is $F_1(c)$, where F_1 is the cumulative distribution function of the test statistic if $\theta = \delta$ and c is the critical value.

---

[8]The discussion assumes that interest centers on positive parameter values, but the same α-values apply regardless of the direction of interest.

Table 3.3 shows the optimal α levels for one-tailed tests in this example using Lindley's standard of minimum cost. At small values of N, the optimal one-tailed α is larger than the corresponding two-tailed value. That is, the one-tailed test sets a considerably lower critical value for parameter estimates in the expected direction. For example, when counting both types of errors equally, the critical values of the t-statistic are ±1.08 with a two-tailed test and 0.50 in a one-tailed test. If both kinds of errors are counted equally, the α for a one-tailed test approaches .5 as N approaches zero; that is, the test amounts to simply accepting $\theta \leq 0$ if the parameter estimate is negative and $\theta \geq 0$ if it is positive.

When Type I errors are counted more heavily, the α levels for a one-tailed test are also larger than those for a two-tailed test in small samples. However, the one-tailed test still sets a high bar for rejecting the null hypothesis. For example, in a sample of 100 with $r = 5$, the critical value of the t-statistic is ±2.80 in a two-tailed test and 2.11 in a one-tailed test.

Table 3.4 shows the α-values for a one-tailed test calculated using Lehmann's rule. As with two-tailed tests, the α level falls as the sample size and desired ratio of Type II to Type I errors increases. The critical values for one-tailed tests are somewhat larger than those for two-tailed tests. For example, using a ratio of 5:1, the critical values for one-tailed tests are 1.12 in a sample of 50, 1.99 in a sample of 1,000, and 3.16 in a sample of 5,000; the corresponding critical values are 1.47, 2.16, and 3.84 for a two-tailed test.

Neither approach gives a simple relationship between the α levels of one-tailed and two-tailed tests, as there is when using a fixed level of significance.

TABLE 3.3. Relation of α Values to Sample Size in One-Tailed Test, Minimum Cost

N	Standard error	w = 20	w = 10	w = 5	w = 2	w = 1
50	.141	<.00001	.00016	.00435	.091	.361
100	.100	.00024	.0025	.0175	.116	.309
500	.0445	.0070	.016	.033	.076	.131
1,000	.0314	.0057	.010	.018	.035	.056
2,000	.0225	.0019	.003	.0049	.0087	.013
3,000	.0182	.00004	.00077	.0011	.0020	.0030
5,000	.0141	.00001	.00005	.00008	.00013	.0002

TABLE 3.4. Example of Relation of α Values to Sample Size in One-Tailed Test, Constant Ratio

N	Standard error	$r = 20$	$r = 10$	$r = 5$	$r = 2$	$r = 1$
50	.141	.042	.076	.131	.245	.361
100	.100	.039	.069	.116	.211	.308
500	.0445	.021	.034	.053	.091	.131
1,000	.0314	.0099	.015	.023	.039	.056
2,000	.0225	.0025	.0038	.0056	.0092	.013
3,000	.0182	.0006	.00089	.00124	.0021	.003
5,000	.0141	.00004	.00006	.00009	.00014	.00020

That is, if the significance level is chosen for the particular problem, the decision to treat it as a one-tailed or two-tailed test is consequential rather than merely conventional.

3.4.2 Tests with Multiple Degrees of Freedom

It is difficult to apply the rules for balancing different types of errors to multi-parameter hypotheses. For example, suppose that we want to test the overall significance of a regression with two independent variables:

$$y = \alpha + \beta_1 x_1 + \beta_2 x_2 + e \tag{3.4}$$

It would be possible to specify minimum important values of both parameters, find the distribution of the test statistic if the parameters were equal to those values, and choose an α level according to Lindley's or Lehmann's principles. However, this procedure would produce a test of the null hypothesis against the alternative that *both* β_1 and β_2 are nonzero. To test the alternative that *at least one* of the parameters is nonzero, it would be necessary to calculate the distribution of the test statistic under two conditions: $\beta_1 = \delta_1$, $\beta_2 = 0$ and $\beta_1 = 0$, $\beta_2 = \delta_2$. The distributions under the two conditions would not normally be identical, raising the problem of which one (or which combination of the two) to use to represent the alternative hypothesis. Even if we agree on an answer to that question in principle, the amount of effort involved in specifying the optimum α level would soon become excessive as the number of degrees of freedom increases. Thus, when a test involves multiple degrees

of freedom, there is no practical alternative to relying on conventional levels of significance.

3.5 COMPARISON TO CONVENTIONAL PRACTICE

In conventional practice, ad hoc adjustments to the α level are sometimes made in unusually large or small samples, but these usually stay inside a range of about .10 to .001. Both Lindley's and Lehmann's approaches imply that adjustments should go well beyond this range. For example, in the example of Table 3.1, a two-tailed test in a sample of 5,000 should have an α level of .00027 if the two types of errors are counted equally. This would correspond to a t-ratio of about 3.65. If $w = 10$, meaning that Type I errors are considered much more important than Type II errors, the α level for a sample size of 5,000 is .00007, which corresponds to a t-ratio of about 3.9. In this sense, choosing the α level for the specific problem can set a much higher standard than conventional practice.

However, as discussed in Section 1.2, after establishing that a parameter estimate is significant at conventional levels, a researcher may ask whether it is "substantively significant." In this example, in a sample of 5,000 the parameter estimate required to reach the critical value is .051 if the two kinds of errors are counted equally and .056 if $r = 10$. Suppose that the observed parameter estimate was .056: then the 95% confidence interval would be about (.028, .084), so if δ was taken as the minimum value for "substantive significance," the conventional approach would yield a clear conclusion that the parameter was greater than zero but not "substantively significant." Thus, the conventional two-stage approach is arguably *more* conservative than procedures that set the α level by balancing the risk of both kinds of errors.

The reason for the difference is that the approach of using a fixed α level and then considering the size of $\hat{\theta}$ allows a conclusion of "nonzero but small," while the methods described in this section force a choice between zero and "large enough to be important." If it is necessary to make a choice between $\theta = 0$ and $\theta = \delta$, then the common-sense choice is whichever one is closer to the observed parameter estimate: choose the null hypothesis when $\hat{\theta} < \delta/2$ and the alternative when $\hat{\theta} > \delta/2$. If both kinds of errors are counted equally, both methods converge on this simple rule as N goes to infinity.

In principle, there is usually no reason that conclusions should be limited to zero and "large." The parameter value may actually be small. In fact, this possibility is often more plausible than the hypothesis that the parameter is exactly zero. When the confidence interval is entirely within the range of "small" values, the obvious conclusion is that the parameter is actually small. Therefore, the methods for choosing α are not generally necessary when the standard error of the parameter estimate is small.

3.5.1   Hypothesis Tests in Small Samples

The methods for choosing an α level are more likely to be useful in "small" samples, that is, when both large, small, and zero parameter values are all at least somewhat consistent with the data. In such cases, it might be desirable to focus on the possibilities of large and zero values even if small values cannot be ruled out. For example, suppose that θ represents the effect of some proposed new program. If $\theta = 0$—that is, if the program is completely ineffective—it should clearly not be implemented. If δ is chosen to represent the smallest value at which the program would definitely be worthwhile, then values between 0 and δ constitute a gray area where it is not clear whether the benefits outweigh the costs. If it is necessary to decide whether or not to implement the program, then the values 0 and δ are of primary interest. That is, we would want to avoid the mistakes of implementing the program if $\theta = 0$ or failing to implement the program if $\theta = \delta$. If $0 \leq \theta \leq \delta$, it is not clear which would be the correct decision and which would be a mistake, so those values would be of little interest in terms of making decisions.

The same general point applies in purely scientific investigations. For example, suppose that a value of δ would be a success for some theory and a value of 0 would be a clear failure, while values between 0 and δ would be ambiguous. Even if it were not possible to reach a definitive conclusion, it would be desirable to offer a judgment about whether the observed results were basically favorable or unfavorable to the theory. This kind of judgment cannot easily be made by using a significance test but can be made by choosing the α level, using one of the methods described above.

To say that large, small, and zero parameter values are all consistent with the data is equivalent to saying that the standard error of the parameter

estimate is large relative to δ. In this situation, a parameter estimate may be "substantively significant" while falling short of conventional standards of statistical significance. For example, suppose that δ and the standard error of the parameter estimate are both 0.10 ($N = 100$ in Tables 3.1–3.4). Then a parameter estimate of 0.15, although considerably larger than δ, would not be statistically significant at even the 10% level. If both kinds of errors were counted equally, Lindley's method would produce a judgment in favor of the alternative hypothesis: the critical value for the t-statistic is only 1.08 for a two-tailed test and 0.50 for a one-tailed test. Using Lehmann's approach and a ratio of 1:1, the critical values are 0.803 for a two-tailed test and 0.501 for a one-tailed test. Thus, if we begin from a position of neutrality between the null and alternative hypotheses, both approaches imply that we should accept the alternative hypothesis.

However, the situation changes if Type I errors are counted more heavily than Type II errors. In Lindley's approach, if Type I errors are given twice as much weight as Type II errors, the critical value rises to 1.86 in a two-tailed test and 1.16 in a one-tailed test. If Type I errors are regarded as five times as important, the critical values are 2.80 and 2.10, so an estimate of 0.15 with a standard error of 0.10 would lead to a decision in favor of the null hypothesis even with a one-tailed test. Using Lehmann's approach of keeping a constant ratio of errors, when the ratio is 5:1, the critical values in a two-tailed test rise to 1.49 in a two-tailed test and 1.19 in a one-tailed test. With a ratio of 20:1, they rise to 2.03 in a two-tailed test and 1.76 in a one-tailed test.

There is necessarily a subjective element in the choice of a value for δ and weights for the two kinds of errors, so the methods for choosing α levels cannot give a single answer that would be accepted by all observers. However, they are useful in giving a sense of the strength of evidence provided by a test. One can consider the decisions that result with a particular range of values for δ and degrees of preference for the null hypothesis.

3.6 IMPLICATIONS OF CHOOSING AN α LEVEL

One important implication is that although a test statistic that is statistically significant at the .05 level may provide some evidence against the null hypothesis, it does not provide *strong* evidence. Table 3.1 shows that in a

two-tailed test, if we use a minimum cost standard and count Type I errors five times as heavily as Type II errors, a p-value of .05 will always lead to acceptance of the null hypothesis, regardless of the value of δ or its standard error. With weights of 5:1, the α level chosen will be no greater than .032. That is, if we begin with a moderate preference for the null hypothesis (whether because of a belief that it is more plausible or because the practical consequences of mistakenly rejecting it are more serious), then a p-value of .05 will not be enough to overcome that.

A second important implication is that it is important to consider the size of the parameter under the alternative hypothesis *before* carrying out a hypothesis test. The usual procedure is to ask if the parameter estimate is statistically significant at conventional levels and then to consider its size. However, if the standard error of the estimate is large, then the parameter estimate must be large in order to be statistically significant, and the usual procedure provides no new information.

Gelman and Weakliem (2009) discuss a study by Kanazawa (2007) that found a large and statistically significant relationship between the physical attractiveness of parents and the probability of having a daughter.[9] They observed that there was a good deal of previous research on sex ratios and that any effects had been very small: 1% or less. The standard error of Kanazawa's parameter estimate was equivalent to about 4%, so the ratio of δ to the standard error was only about 0.25. In a case like this, the distribution of the test statistic is very similar under the assumptions that $\theta = \delta$ and $\theta = 0$, so almost no outcome can provide strong evidence in favor of the alternative hypothesis. For example, if $\theta = \delta$, there is only about a 5.7% chance that the t-ratio will be greater than the 5% critical value, and about a 0.14% chance that it is greater than the 0.1% critical value. Therefore, the fact that the parameter estimate is significant at the 5% or even the 0.1% level provides little evidence in favor of the alternative hypothesis.

Of course, if we assume a larger value of δ, exceeding the critical value will provide stronger evidence; for example, if δ is equal to 8%, there is about a 50% chance that the t-value will exceed the 5% critical value if $\theta = \delta$. Therefore, if one is willing to argue that a large effect is reasonable in principle, the

---

[9]Gelman and Weakliem (2009) argued that when properly calculated the estimate should fall somewhat short of the conventional standards of statistical significance. However, the general point applies regardless of which estimate is preferred.

result can be interpreted as stronger evidence for the alternative hypothesis. What is a reasonable size of δ is a substantive issue rather than a statistical one, but the value of the procedures for choosing an α level is that they make it necessary to confront this issue.

3.7 OTHER KINDS OF ERRORS

If the null hypothesis is rejected, researchers almost always go on to say something about the sign and magnitude of the parameter. As a result, the Type I and Type II errors that are considered in the Neyman–Pearson theory are not the only issues that matter to researchers. One important concern is the risk of what Gelman and Tuerlinckx (2000) call a "Type S" error: rejecting the null hypothesis $\theta = 0$ when the sign of $\hat{\theta}$ differs from that of θ. This type of error has been given a number of names, such as "Type III" error (Kaiser, 1960), but "Type S" has the advantage of being easy to remember. In terms of the Neyman–Pearson theory, this is not an error at all but rather a correct decision to reject the hypothesis that $\theta = 0$ in favor of the alternative $\theta \neq 0$. In terms of science or policy, however, a Type S error is certainly an error, since it means that the researcher will come to an inaccurate conclusion about the direction of the effect; in fact, it would usually be regarded as worse than a Type I or Type II error. A second issue is the average magnitude of the parameter estimate when the null hypothesis is correctly rejected. If $\hat{\theta}$ is much larger than θ, then substantive conclusions may be misleading even though the correct model is chosen. With a sufficiently large difference between $\hat{\theta}$ and θ, the model with $\theta = 0$ might be regarded as preferable to the true model as estimated. This would depend on the purpose for which the model was being used. For example, if the goal was to establish the sign of θ, overestimation would not be a problem; if the goal were prediction, it would be.

Table 3.5 compares the results from two-tailed tests using the .05 significance level and an α level chosen according to the standard of minimum cost with both types of errors counted equally. The leftmost column shows the ratio of the true value of the parameter to the standard error of the parameter estimate. The next three columns show the probabilities of different outcomes of the test when $\theta = \delta$: Type II errors, rejection of the null hypothesis with the "correct" sign, and Type S errors. The next column shows the ratio

TABLE 3.5. Performance of Tests by α Level for Different Parameter Values

θ/σ	α	Type II	Correct	Type S	C/S	$\hat{\theta}/\theta$
0.5	.307	.63	.30	.064	4.7	3.32
	.05	.92	.07	.006	10.4	4.82
1.0	.278	.52	.47	.018	25.0	1.85
	.05	.83	.16	.0015	110.0	2.49
1.5	.233	.38	.62	.004	175	1.40
	.05	.68	.32	.0002	1,194	1.74
2.0	.179	.26	.74	.0004	1,801	1.21
	.05	.48	.52	—	—	1.39
2.5	.127	.16	.83	—	—	1.12
	.05	.29	.71	—	—	1.20
3.0	.083	.10	.90	—	—	1.07
	.05	.29	.71	—	—	1.09

of rejections with the correct sign to Type S errors. The last column shows the mean value of $\hat{\theta}/\theta$ when the null hypothesis is rejected with the correct sign.

When the ratio of δ to the standard error of the parameter estimate is greater than about 2.0, the risk of Type S errors is small, even at the higher α levels selected by the standard of minimum cost. However, when the ratio is small, there is a substantial chance that a significant parameter estimate will represent a Type S error. When the ratio is 0.5, about a tenth of the estimates that are significant at the 5% level will have a sign opposite to that of θ. With the minimum cost α level of .307, the proportion is more than one in five.

Moreover, when δ is small relative to the standard error of the parameter estimate, statistically significant estimates with the correct sign are typically much larger than the true value of the parameter. At a ratio of 0.5, estimates that are significant using an α of .307 are, on the average, more than three times as large as the true value. Using a .05 level of significance, significant estimates average more than four times the true value. The reason is that when the true value of the parameter is small relative to the standard error, the estimate must be much larger than the true value in order to reach significance. The lower the α level, the greater the difference between the value of the significant estimates and the true parameter value. On the other hand, a higher α level increases the risk of Type S errors.

The major implication of Table 3.5 is that when the true parameter value is small relative to the standard error, the risk of misleading inferences goes beyond the obvious possibility of Type II error. First, if a false null hypothesis is rejected, there is a good chance that the estimate will have the "wrong" sign. Second, even if a false null hypothesis is rejected and the parameter estimate has the correct sign, it will be much larger than the actual parameter value. The overall conclusion is that looking for small effects in an "underpowered" sample is problematic, regardless of the α level that is used.[10]

3.8 EXAMPLE OF CHOOSING AN α LEVEL

The minimum cost and constant ratio methods can be illustrated using the voting example discussed in Chapter 2. There is clearly no evidence that the effects of income and marital status differ by race—the p-values are over .9. The difference in the estimated effect of gender is substantial, but the t-ratio is only 0.99, and as seen in Table 3.1, t-ratios of less than 1.0 can never justify rejection of the null hypothesis when using the minimum cost method. For age, however, the t-ratio of the difference in the estimated effects for blacks and nonblacks is 1.54, giving a p-value of .12. Here there is a real question of whether we should interpret the results as evidence that the effect of age differs by race.

The first step in carrying out a hypothesis test is to specify the minimum value of interest for the parameter. Because there are eight age categories, a coefficient of about .10 would produce a difference of 0.7 in the logit scale between the predicted values for the lowest and highest categories, which corresponds to a change from a 50% chance to about a 67% chance of voting in favor of a given party. Thus, it seems safe to say that a difference of 0.10 would be regarded as important. The estimates are −0.02 for whites and −0.10 for blacks, for a difference of .08, or somewhat less than this value.

The standard error of the difference in parameter estimates is .052, so if we take .10 as the minumum important difference, the ratio of δ to the

---

[10]Lindley's method of calculating optimal significance levels can easily be extended to take account of the risk of "Type S" errors. Although there is a subjective element in assigning the cost of each type of error, this analysis could be useful when it is necessary to use an underpowered sample.

standard error is about 2.0, a little smaller than the ratio when $N = 500$ in Table 3.1. The minimum cost α level if the two kinds of errors are counted equally is .179. Since the observed p-value is below this level, we reject the null hypothesis that the effects of age are the same in both groups. However, if Type I errors are regarded as twice as important as Type II errors, then the α level is .091, so we should accept the null hypothesis. Given δ and the values for the parameter estimates, the ratio of Type II to Type I errors is almost exactly 2.0, so with Lehmann's rule we could reject the null hypothesis if the desired ratio is less than 2. Putting these results together, if we regard the two types of errors as being about equally important, we should conclude that there is an "important" difference—that is, a difference of at least 0.10—in the effects of age, but if we begin with even a mild preference for the null hypothesis, we should conclude that there is no difference.

Carrying out these kinds of calculations has the advantage of forcing the investigator to notice the magnitude of the standard errors. A sample of almost 15,000 would usually be regarded as "large," and perhaps even as calling for the use of a stricter standard for statistical significance. However, only about 10% of the sample is black, and only about 10% of the black respondents supported the Republican candidate, so the sample does not provide much power to test hypotheses about interactions involving race and the other independent variables. An investigator who simply noted the p-values and the sample size might feel unwarranted confidence in concluding that there was no evidence of an important difference between blacks and whites.

3.9 EVALUATION OF CRITICISMS

We can now return to the criticisms of conventional hypothesis testing discussed in Chapter 2 and assess their validity.

3.9.1 Sampling

The claim that conventional hypothesis tests are meaningful only when the data are a random sample from a definite population is incorrect. They can be used whenever the dependent variable is influenced by factors that are unpredictable from the point of view of the observer.

3.9.2   Credibility of Point Null Hypotheses

Even if the null hypothesis is not credible in principle, a conventional hypothesis test provides meaningful information. If the null hypothesis θ = 0 is rejected at the α level, all values in the $1 - \alpha$ confidence interval have the same sign. Therefore, rejecting the null hypothesis means that we can be fairly sure about the sign of the parameter, while accepting the null hypothesis means we cannot be sure. This interpretation is useful for parameters of theoretical interest, for which the sign is usually of fundamental importance.

   With parameters involving control variables or issues of primary and secondary structure, the major question is not whether they are exactly zero but whether they can safely be treated as zero. The hypothesis θ = 0 can be regarded as approximating a test of the hypothesis that θ is small relative to the parameter estimate, for example, that $|\theta| < .01|\hat{\theta}|$. In such cases, treating the parameter as zero might be better than treating it as equal to $\hat{\theta}$.

3.9.3   Ranking of Models

As discussed in this chapter, classical hypothesis tests envision a choice between two alternatives. Most contemporary research, however, involves a large number of models. The fertility example discussed in Section 2.6.2 provides an example of the ambiguity that can arise when classical tests are used to choose among models. The spline model and the nonlinear regression $\alpha + \beta_1 x + \beta_2 x^\gamma$ (Models 2 and 5 in Table 2.3) can both be accepted at the .05 level when tested against a larger model including both as special cases. Although those models agree in the general conclusion that the effect of development on fertility reverses at high levels of development, they provide different estimates of the extent of change. In the nonlinear regression, predicted fertility rises from a minimum of 1.6 to about 1.8 at the highest levels of development observed in the sample, while in the spline model the predicted increase is only about half as large. Because the nonlinear model has a higher R^2 and the same number of parameters, it seems clear that it should be preferred to some degree, but classical tests do not tell us how strongly it should be preferred.

3.9.4 Flexible versus Rigid Interpretation of Significance Levels

In Fisher's approach, the p-value is the fundamental quantity: conventional levels of significance are just an aid in interpreting p-values. Therefore, significance levels should be used in a flexible manner; for example, there is no justification for treating the difference between .051 and .049 as more important than the difference between .049 and .047.

If a hypothesis test is regarded as a rule for making decisions and the α level is chosen to produce optimal decisions, then it should be followed strictly—that is, any departure from the rule will produce inferior decisions. However, even from this point of view, it is reasonable to ask whether a particular decision was obvious or a close call. There will almost always be some room for disagreement about the value chosen for δ and the degree of preference for the null hypothesis, and so there will be a gray area in which the null hypothesis might be accepted under some reasonable choices and rejected under others. Therefore, in practice both classical approaches to hypothesis tests imply that levels of significance should be treated in a flexible fashion: a test statistic that is just short of the critical value casts some doubt on the null hypothesis, and one that is just over the critical value does not rule it out.

3.9.5 Arbitrary Nature of Significance Levels

In the Neyman–Pearson approach, it is possible in principle to decide on an optimal significance level using the methods discussed in this chapter. These methods require the exercise of some judgment about the minimum parameter that should be regarded as "important." Therefore, they may be useful for parameters of theoretical interest but cannot be applied to all issues of model specification. When making decisions about a large number of parameters, it is necessary to have some all-purpose standard. As seen in the economic growth example, the standard used can make a substantial difference to conclusions about the parameters of interest, so the lack of a defnite justification for conventional significance levels is a matter of concern.

3.9.6 Effects of Sample Size

This issue can be addressed using the methods for choosing an α level discussed in this chapter. If these methods are used, the chance of both Type I

and Type II errors will approach zero as the sample size increases. However, these methods are not based on sample size alone but rather on a minimum value of interest for the parameter and the standard error of its estimate. Therefore, they cannot be applied in an automatic fashion, that is, it is not possible to replace a fixed α level by some simple function of sample size.

3.9.7 Lack of Symmetry

Significance tests using a standard level of significance are asymmetrical in that it is possible to get more or less evidence against a point null hypothesis but not to get evidence *in favor of* one. In contrast, when the critical value is chosen by methods such as those of Lindley (1953) or Lehmann (1958), the test is symmetrical: accepting the null hypothesis means that the hypothesis $\theta = 0$ is in some sense better than the alternative $|\theta| \geq \delta$. Putting the question in this way means ignoring the possibility that θ is nonzero but "small," but when data are limited this may be a useful simplification.

3.9.8 Likelihood Principle

The likelihood principle holds that a test should be based only on the likelihood of the observed data. Classical tests violate this principle, since they consider the chance of more extreme values of the test statistic. Some observers hold that this has important consequences in practice. For example, Raftery (1995a) discusses the case of a model with deviance of 150.2 and 16 degrees of freedom. Although the p-value is essentially zero, the BIC favors this model over the saturated model. Gelman and Rubin (1995, p. 168) ask, "How can the BIC select a model that does not fit the data over one that does?" Raftery (1995b, p. 188) replies that the p-value involves the probability of "data as extreme or more so," while the BIC involves "the probability of observing the data at hand; there is no 'or more so.' And that makes all the difference."

   To evaluate this issue, it is necessary to consider specific examples. Suppose that the test statistic is a t-ratio and the sample is large enough that its distribution is approximately normal. Table 3.6 shows several standard p-values and the corresponding values of the likelihood. The p-value is $2 - 2F(t)$ and the likelihood is $f(t)$ where $F(t)$ and $f(t)$ are the cumulative distribution function and density function for a normal distribution, respectively.

TABLE 3.6. p-Values and Normal Likelihood at Standard Levels of Statistical Significance

t	p-value	$f(t)$	p-value/$f(t)$
1.44	.15	.142	1.06
1.65	.10	.103	0.97
1.96	.05	.058	0.86
2.33	.02	.027	0.74
2.58	.01	.014	0.71
3.29	.001	.0018	0.56

Lower p-values go with lower values of the likelihood, so there is no conflict between the general principles of rejecting the null hypothesis when the p-value is small and rejecting it when the likelihood of the observed t-statistic is low. Moreover, the p-values are roughly proportional to the likelihood. As the last column shows, they are not exactly proportional: for example, the likelihood corresponding to $p = .10$ is only about 57 times as large as the likelihood corresponding to $p = .001$. However, p-values are usually interpreted in qualitative terms: rather than saying that the evidence is 100 times as strong when $p = .001$ as when $p = .10$, one would say something like "$p = .001$ provides much stronger evidence." The difference in the likelihoods is certainly consistent with a characterization of this kind.

Returning to the question raised by Gelman and Rubin (1995), the density function for a chi-square distribution with 16 degrees of freedom is about 3×10^{-24} at a value of 150.2. The maximum value of the density function is about .075, so the value at 150.2 is about 4×10^{-23} times its maximum, which could be regarded as "unlikely" by any reasonable standard. As this example shows, although the likelihood principle raises difficult issues for theory, it does not make much practical difference in standard situations: a model that does not fit according to the p-value will not fit well according to the likelihood.[11]

3.10 SUMMARY AND CONCLUSIONS

One implication of the discussion in this chapter is that standard errors or confidence intervals should always be shown for parameters of theoretical

---

[11]Christensen (2005) gives some examples in which p-values and the likelihood principle lead to different conclusions.

interest. This point has been made many times, but it is worth repeating. A confidence interval is more informative than an indication of significance, which reduces the information provided by the interval to a smaller number of categories (Barnard, Jenkins, and Winsten, 1962, pp. 331–332). p-values are more informative than indications of significance, and standard errors can be calculated from the p-values. However, for the convenience of readers, standard errors or confidence intervals are clearly the best choice.

A second implication is that the expected magnitude of the parameter should be considered when interpreting hypothesis tests. The standard approach is to ask whether statistically significant estimates are large enough to be of substantive importance. This is useful when the standard error of the parameter estimate is small; however, when the standard error of the parameter estimate is relatively large, a statistically significant estimate will necessarily be large. In this situation, it is necessary to discuss the *credibility* of the parameter estimates. When the observed estimate is too large to be credible, as in Kanazawa's (2007) study of the relationship between parental attractiveness and the sex ratio, the evidence is weaker than the p-value suggests. Conversely, when parameter estimates are "large" but not significant at conventional levels, the methods of selecting an α level proposed by Lindley (1953) and Lehmann (1958) can be used to understand the conditions under which the results would justify at least a tentative decision in favor of the alternative hypothesis.

A third implication is that the different uses of hypothesis tests call for different approaches. Hypothesis tests based on standard levels of significance do not add any information beyond that contained in confidence intervals, so when dealing with parameters of theoretical interest it would be possible to simply show a confidence interval. This would not lead to different conclusions, but it would be more understandable and would direct attention to the range of uncertainty rather than fixing attention on the point estimate. If a definite choice between hypotheses was required, the α level for a test could be chosen in order to achieve the desired balance of errors. However, for questions involving control variables or model specification, it is necessary to make decisions, and it is impractical to choose an α level for each test. Therefore, some standard α level is required, but classical theory does not give any guidance on what it should be—for example, .10, .05, .01, or something else?

RECOMMENDED READING

Anscombe, F. J. (1963). Tests of goodness of fit. *Journal of the Royal Statistical Society, Series B, 25,* 81–94. —Makes a case for the value of significance tests even in the absence of a well-defined alternative.

Fisher, R. A. (1929). The statistical method in psychical research. *Proceedings of the Society for Psychical Research, 39,* 189–192. —A good short summary of Fisher's views on the logic of significance testing.

Fisher, R. A. (1958). *Statistical methods for research workers* (13th ed. [1st ed. 1925]). New York: Hafner. —Gives examples of Fisher's use and interpretation of significance tests.

Gelman, A. and Weakliem, D. L. (2009). Of beauty, sex, and power. *American Scientist, 97,* 310–316. —Discusses the problems of making inferences about small effects in small samples.

Johnstone, D. (1987). On the interpretation of hypothesis tests following Neyman and Pearson. In R. Viertl (Ed.), *Probability and Bayesian Statistics* (pp. 267–277). New York: Plenum. —Argues that Neyman took a strict frequentist and behaviorist view, but that Fisher (and Pearson) saw hypothesis tests as measures of evidence.

Johnstone, D. J. (1989). On the necessity for random sampling. *British Journal for the Philosophy of Science, 40,* 443–457. —Provides a careful discussion of the topic and concludes that hypothesis tests are appropriate even if the data are not from a random sample.

Leamer, E. E. (1978). *Specification searches* (Chap. 4). New York: Wiley. —Outlines the logic of hypothesis testing and the problem of balancing the risks of Type I and Type II errors in choosing an α level.

Lehmann, E. J. (2011). *Fisher, Neyman, and the creation of classical statistics.* New York: Springer. —Compares the views of Fisher, on the one hand, and Neyman and Pearson, on the other, with many extracts from their writings.

Lindley, D. V. (1953). Statistical inference. *Journal of the Royal Statistical Society, Series B, 15,* 130–176. —Proposes choosing an α level in order to maximize utility, and makes connections between the Bayesian approach and classical decision theory. More difficult.

Wilson, E. B. (1952). *An introduction to scientific research* (Chaps. 4 and 10). New York: McGraw-Hill. —A clear and nontechnical discussion of the logic of hypothesis testing.

4

Bayesian Hypothesis Tests

The chapter begins with a review of Bayes's rule and Bayesian estimation. It then provides a detailed discussion of the Bayesian approach to hypothesis testing. A "Bayes factor" represents the weight of evidence provided by the data in favor of one model against another. Different ways of representing the hypotheses produce different Bayes factors, and I conclude that the assumptions that correspond to the BIC are not reasonable. The only defensible objective standard for a Bayes factor is the one that is most favorable to the alternative hypothesis. By this standard, a t-ratio of about 2 provides some evidence against the null hypothesis, although not strong evidence. The chapter then discusses the interpretation of Bayes factors for multiparameter hypotheses: they are comparisons of specific models, not goodness-of-fit tests. In general, Bayes factors should be applied only to hypotheses involving single parameters or parameters that are intrinsically connected.

4.1 BAYES'S THEOREM

The foundation of Bayesian statistics is a simple formula known as Bayes's theorem or Bayes's rule. When written in terms of odds, it is

$$\frac{P(A_1 \mid B)}{P(A_2 \mid B)} = \frac{P(B \mid A_1)}{P(B \mid A_2)} \frac{P(A_1)}{P(A_2)}$$

There is no question about the mathematical validity or usefulness of the theorem. For example, it plays an important role in medical diagnosis (Ledley and Lusted, 1959). Suppose that A_1 is the event of a person having a disease, A_2 is the event of the person not having the disease, and B is the event in which a test for the disease gives a positive result. If the proportion of the population that has the disease is .01, the conditional probability that the test will be positive when a person has the disease is .98, and the conditional probability that the test will be positive when a person does not have the disease is .01, Bayes's theorem can be applied to find the odds that a person who has a positive test result has the disease:

$$\frac{.98}{.02} \frac{.01}{.99} = \frac{.0098}{.0099} = .99$$

The odds can be converted into a probability by $\frac{.99}{.99+1}$ = .497. In this example, although the test is highly accurate, the disease is rare, so most of the people with positive test results do not have the disease.

The foundation of Bayesian statistics is the principle that degrees of belief can be treated as probabilities. Given this premise, Bayes's theorem can be used as a rule for revising beliefs in light of new evidence. For example, suppose that we have two hypotheses, A_1 and A_2. Then $\frac{P(A_1)}{P(A_2)}$ represents a person's beliefs about the relative odds of the two hypotheses before observing the data, $P(B|A_1)$ represents the likelihood of the data under the assumption that A_1 is true, and $P(B|A_2)$ represents the likelihood under the assumption that A_2 is true. Given these elements, Bayes's theorem can be used to calculate $\frac{P(A_1|B)}{P(A_2|B)}$, the relative odds of the two hypotheses, given the data.

In a general sense, scientific investigation necessarily involves combining prior beliefs and the evidence from new observations to reach some kind of conclusion. Advocates of a Bayesian approach argue that Bayes's theorem provides the *only* logically consistent method of doing this and thus provides the best foundation for statistical analysis, or scientific investigation more generally. However, these general issues do not need to be addressed here. Many observers who do not accept a thoroughgoing Bayesian approach agree that some techniques derived from Bayesian principles are useful. For example, Cox (comment on Lindley, 2000, p. 324) states, "I want to object to the practice of labelling people as Bayesian or frequentist. . . . I want to be both and can see no reason for not being, although if pushed . . . I regard the

frequentist view as primary." For their part, Bayesians hold a variety of views on hypothesis testing, and some, like Gelman and Rubin (1995), hold that it is rarely appropriate. Therefore, the techniques described in this chapter do not stand or fall depending on the adoption of the Bayesian philosophy.

4.2   BAYESIAN ESTIMATION

Suppose that an investigator begins with some ideas about the values that a parameter is likely to have. Of course, in most cases these ideas do not take the form of a fully developed probability distribution, but rather of statements like "$|\theta|$ is probably between 0.1 and 0.5, and unlikely to be much greater than 1.0." However, if the ideas can be refined into a probability distribution, it is possible to use Bayes's theorem to reach conclusions that combine the prior beliefs and the evidence provided by the data.

To take a simple example, suppose that we have independent binomial trials with the same probability of success and that prior beliefs about the probability of success can be represented by a normal distribution with a mean of 0.5 and a standard deviation of 0.1. This distribution implies that the investigator begins by thinking that there is about a 67% chance that the probability of success is between .4 and .6, and about a 95% chance that the probability is between .3 and .7. Suppose that 10 trials are observed, of which 7 are successes. Applying Bayes's theorem gives:

$$f(b|x) = p(x|b)f(b)k$$

In this equation, f is the probability density function representing prior beliefs about values of the binomial parameter b. The right-hand side of the equation is the product of the probability of observing 7 successes in 10 trials given a value of the parameter, the distribution representing initial beliefs about the probability that the parameter is equal to that value, and a normalizing constant.

When comparing the value of $f(b|x)$ at different values of b, the normalizing constant can be ignored. For example, the value of the initial density function $f(b)$ is 3.99 at $b = 0.5$ and 0.54 at $b = 0.7$. The likelihoods $p(x|b)$ are .117 at $b = 0.5$ and .267 at 0.7. The products are then about 0.47 and 0.14.

Before observing the data, the probability that $b = 0.5$ is about seven times as large as the probability that $b = 0.7$; after observing the data, the probability that $b = 0.5$ is only about three times as large as the probability that $b = 0.7$. The functions $f(b)$ and $f(b|x)$ are known as the "prior" and "posterior" density functions. The prior and posterior density functions for this example are displayed in Figure 4.1.

The maximum value of the posterior distribution $f(b|x)$ occurs at 0.558, and the cumulative posterior density function reaches .025 when $b = 0.394$ and .975 when $b = 0.722$. Therefore, .558 could be called the Bayesian estimate of b, and (0.394, 0.722) could be called a Bayesian 95% confidence interval (sometimes known as the "credible interval"), although Bayesians hold that singling out a single value as "the estimate" is misleading and that the posterior distribution as a whole is of primary interest. In this case, the classical maximum-likelihood estimate is 0.7 and the likelihood-based 95% confidence interval is (0.394, 0.915). The Bayesian estimates and confidence intervals can be thought of as a compromise between prior beliefs and the evidence suggested by the data. Because the proportion of successes observed

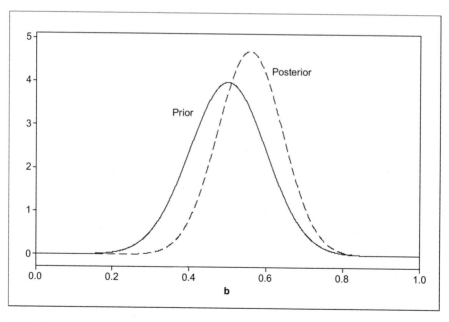

FIGURE 4.1. Prior and posterior distributions, binomial example.

in the data was larger than expected, beliefs about the likely value of *b* shifted upward.

The strength of prior beliefs is represented by the variance of the prior distribution. The extreme case in which the prior belief is a conviction that cannot be altered by evidence corresponds to a variance of zero. The prior distribution is then a single value and the posterior distribution is that same value. However, as long as the variance of the prior distribution is greater than zero, the posterior distribution will shift in the direction suggested by the observed data. As more data are observed, they have more influence on the posterior distribution. For example, if we begin with a normal prior distribution with mean 0.5 and standard deviation 0.1 and observe 700 successes out of 1,000 trials, the Bayesian estimate is .696 and the 95% confidence interval is (0.667, 0.723), almost equal to the classical estimate of .7 and 95% confidence interval of (0.671, 0.728). As the sample goes to infinity, the Bayesian estimates and confidence intervals converge to the classical ones because the information in the sample comes to dominate the information in the prior distribution.

In some cases, an investigator may begin with little or no idea of the likely value of a parameter. If the parameter has a limited range, a natural way to represent the absence of any definite prior beliefs is by a uniform distribution over that range. Given a uniform prior distribution, the posterior distribution will be exactly proportional to the likelihood function, so the Bayesian estimate will be exactly equal to the classical maximum-likelihood estimate and the Bayesian confidence interval will be exactly equal to the classical likelihood-based confidence interval. When the parameter has no inherent limits, the uniform distribution is not defined. However, if the prior distribution is approximately uniform over all parameter values for which the likelihood $p(x|b)$ is substantially above zero, the posterior distribution will be approximately proportional to the likelihood function. This can be accomplished simply by choosing any standard distribution with a sufficiently large variance, known as a "diffuse" prior distribution. Thus, from a Bayesian point of view classical estimates and confidence intervals can be regarded as special cases that apply when an investigator has no prior information about the parameter values.

4.2.1 Accuracy of Bayesian and Classical Estimates

As discussed in Chapter 3, there is a $1 - \alpha$ chance that θ will be in a classical $1 - \alpha$ confidence interval for $\hat{\theta}$. If the prior distribution is not diffuse, Bayesian estimates and confidence intervals will generally be different from classical ones. Therefore, the chance that the true value of the parameter will be in the corresponding Bayesian confidence interval may be greater than $1 - \alpha$ or may be less. If the prior distribution represents accurate information, the Bayesian estimates will typically be more accurate than the classical ones; if it represents misinformation or prejudice, the Bayesian estimates will typically be less accurate. As Herman Rubin (quoted in Good, 1983, p. 139) put it, a "good Bayesian does better than a non-Bayesian, but a bad Bayesian gets clobbered."

The Bayesian approach can be defended more generally as giving the optimal way to learn from experience. In Rubin's terms, after observing enough data, a "bad Bayesian"—that is, one who starts out with prior distributions that are far from the truth—will eventually become a "good Bayesian." However, in any specific situation, some Bayesian estimates can be expected to be superior to classical estimates, and others to be inferior. Therefore, the fact that an estimate is Bayesian does not, in itself, tell us anything about how accurate it might be: in order to say anything on this point, it is necessary to consider the specific prior distribution that produced the estimate.

4.3 BAYES FACTORS

The fundamental idea of the Bayesian approach to hypothesis testing is to apply Bayes's theorem to the choice between models. Specifically,

$$\frac{p(M0 \mid x)}{p(M1 \mid x)} = \frac{p(x \mid M0)}{p(x \mid M1)} \frac{p(M0)}{p(M1)}$$

In this equation, $\dfrac{p(M0)}{p(M1)}$ represents initial beliefs—before the data are observed—about the relative probability that each model is true. Values greater than 1 mean that M0 is thought to be more likely, values less than 1 mean that M1 is more likely, and a value of 1 means that they are equally likely. The values $p(x|M0)$ and $p(x|M1)$ are the likelihoods of the observed data under Models 0 and 1. If the ratio is greater than 1, that means that the observed data are more likely under the hypothesis that Model 0 is true; if it

is less than 1, they are more likely under the hypothesis that Model 1 is true. Using Bayes's theorem, the product of $\frac{p(x\,|\,M0)}{p(x\,|\,M1)}$ and $\frac{p(M0)}{p(M1)}$ gives the ratio of the probabilities of $M0$ and $M1$ after observing the data.

The ratio $\frac{p(M0)}{p(M1)}$ is purely a matter of prior knowledge or beliefs, but $\frac{p(x\,|\,M0)}{p(x\,|\,M1)}$ depends on the data: it can be thought of as a measure of the strength and direction of the evidence provided by the observations. Jeffreys (1961 [first editon 1938]) proposed using this ratio as a hypothesis test. He used K as a symbol for the ratio, but did not give it a name; Good (1950) called it the "Bayes factor," and this name has since been widely adopted. Since the null hypothesis is the numerator and the alternative hypothesis is the denominator, values greater than 1 indicate support for the null hypothesis and values less than 1 indicate support for the alternative. However, the designation of null and alternative hypotheses is merely a convention, and Bayes factors are not limited to nested models: they can be used to compare any two models.[1] The value of 1 provides an objective dividing line, and the strength of evidence is given by the odds. Therefore, there is no need for conventional dividing lines, as there is with p-values: the Bayes factor stands on its own.[2]

The BIC statistic is closely related to a Bayes factor. Specifically, the difference in the BIC between two models can be used to calculate a Bayes factor: $BIC_1 - BIC_0 \approx 2\log(K)$. For example, suppose that we are testing the linear regression against the quadratic regression in the development and fertility example discussed in Section 2.6.2. The BIC statistics are 620.2 for the linear regression and 608.9 for the quadratic, giving a difference of -11.3. Therefore K is approximately $e^{-11.3/2} = .0035$, or about $1/284$; that is, the observed data are several hundred times more likely under the quadratic model than under the linear model.

If the two models involved both specify exact values for the parameter, then the Bayes factor is simply the ratio of likelihoods at the two hypothetical values θ_0 and θ_1. However, the usual form of hypothesis test compares a

---

[1] When discussing non-nested models, I will add subscripts: for example, K_{AB} is a Bayes factor with Model A in the numerator and Model B in the denominator.

[2] Jeffreys (1961, p. 432) offered guidelines for translating Bayes factors into descriptive terms for the strength of evidence. Kass and Raftery (1995, p. 777) proposed a modified version that is more widely used today. These guidelines were intended as a way to calibrate Bayes factors against conventional standards of statistical significance; this point will be discussed in Chapter 8.

point null hypothesis $\theta = \theta_0$ to the alternative $\theta \neq \theta_0$, so in order to calculate a Bayes factor for a hypothesis of this kind it is necessary to decide how to represent the alternative hypothesis. Jeffreys (1961) proposed that the alternative hypothesis should be understood as a probability distribution—that is, not just saying that parameter values other than θ_0 are possible, but specifying how likely each value is. The likelihood under the alternative hypothesis could then be calculated as $\int p(x|b)f(\theta)$, that is, essentially a weighted average of the likelihoods at the values of θ that are possible under the alternative hypothesis. If a theory suggests a likely range of values, specifying $f(\theta)$ is straightforward in principle. However, often researchers do not have a clear alternative hypothesis, but merely want to consider the possibility that θ does *not* equal zero. Whether Bayes factors can be usefully applied to these situations is a more difficult question.

4.3.1   Bayes Factors for General Alternative Hypotheses

To understand the application of the Bayes factor to the general alternative hypothesis $\theta \neq \theta_0$, it is useful to begin with the simple but important problem of testing a hypothesis about the probability of "success" in a binary outcome. The Bayes factor was originally developed in connection with this question—specifically, with the problem of verifying a proposed law of the form "all ravens are black" from a finite number of observations (Jeffreys, 1977, p. 95). Suppose that 540 successes are observed in 1,000 trials and we want to test the null hypothesis that $b = 0.5$. The chi-square statistic for the hypothesis that $b = 0.5$ is 6.4, with 1 degree of freedom, for a p-value of .012, so according to classical tests the hypothesis would be rejected at the 5% level but not at the 1% level.

The Bayes factor is the ratio of the probabilities of 540 successes in 1,000 trials under the null and alternative hypotheses. The probability for a given value of b is easily calculated from the formula for a binomial distribution: for $b = 0.5$, it is about .001. If we began with no clear ideas about the possible values of b and merely wanted to consider the possibility that it has some value other than 0.5, an obvious candiate for $f(b)$ would be a uniform distribution over all values other than 0.5. Given a uniform distribution, the likelihood under the alternative hypothesis is .001, and the Bayes factor $p(x|M1)/p(x|M0)$ is about 0.97. Thus, the data provide essentially no evidence either way: the

observation of 540 successes in 1,000 outcomes is almost equally likely (or unlikely) under the null and alternative hypotheses. The BIC is $6.4 - \log(500)$ = 0.185, giving a Bayes factor of $\exp(-.185/2) = 0.90$, quite close to the exact Bayes factor.

With 54 successes in 100 trials, the chi-square statistic is 0.64, for a p-value of .42. The Bayes factor produced by a uniform distribution is about 5.9, and the BIC is $0.64 - \log(50) = -3.27$, giving a Bayes factor of about 5. In the most general way, classical hypothesis tests and Bayes factors could be said to produce the same conclusion in this case: both imply that the null hypothesis should be accepted. However, there is an important difference between them. In the classical approach, we could not claim positive support for the null hypothesis. In fact, the 95% confidence interval for b is about (0.4, 0.68), which could not reasonably be interpreted as justifying even a conclusion that b was "close" to 0.5. All that could be said is that there is no compelling evidence against the hypothesis that $b = 0.5$. According to the Bayes factors, however, the data provide evidence *in favor* of the hypothesis that the probability of success is exactly 0.5 against the alternative that $b \neq 0.5$.

With the same proportion of successes in 4,000 trials (2,160 successes), the chi-square statistic is 25.6, for a p-value of about 4×10^{-7}. The Bayes Factor from a uniform prior distribution is about 0.00014; that is, the evidence strongly favors the alternative hypothesis. The BIC is $25.6 - \log(4,000) = 17.3$, giving a Bayes factor of about 0.0001.

At all of the sample sizes considered, the Bayes factors are more favorable to the null hypothesis than are classical tests. In a sample of 100, where classical tests merely accept the null hypothesis, the Bayes factor suggests positive evidence in favor of the null hypothesis. In a sample of 500, where a classical test rejects the null hypothesis, the Bayes factor is neutral between the null and alternative hypotheses. In a sample of 4,000, both the classical test and the Bayes factor strongly favor the alternative hypothesis, but there is still a difference of degree: the p-value is less than 1 in a million, while the Bayes factor in favor of the alternative hypothesis is about 7,000 to 1.

4.3.2 Prior Distributions and Bayes Factors

In the binomial example, there is an obvious candidate for a "neutral" prior distribution. This is not the case in the more usual situation in which the

possible values of the parameter are unbounded. However, it seems reasonable that the hypothesis $\theta \neq \theta_0$ should be represented by a symmetrical unimodal distribution centered at θ_0, and within this class the normal distribution is a convenient choice.[3] Given this choice, the remaining issue is to decide on the dispersion of the distribution. Figure 4.2 shows the relationship between the standard deviation of a normal prior distribution and the resulting Bayes factor for t-values of 2.0 and 2.5; the standard error of the parameter estimate is assumed to be 1.0. As the figure shows, the Bayes factor does *not* converge to a finite value as the standard deviation increases; rather, it increases without limit, meaning stronger evidence in favor of the null hypothesis. For large values of the standard deviation, the Bayes factor is

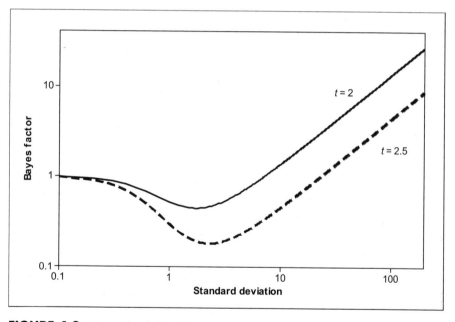

FIGURE 4.2. Example of the relationship between the dispersion of the prior distribution and Bayes factors.

---

[3]Jeffreys proposed using a Cauchy distribution, which gives results that are somewhat more favorable to the null hypothesis, but there are no strong arguments of principle in favor of one distribution over the other, so the familiarity of the normal distribution gives it an advantage.

proportional to the standard deviation. For example, with a standard deviation of 50, a t-ratio of 2.0 gives a Bayes factor of about 6.8, and with a standard deviation of 100 it gives a Bayes factor of about 13.5.

The relationship between the dispersion of the distribution representing the alternative hypothesis and the Bayes factor can be understood by noting that for many values of θ the likelihood of the observed data will be almost zero. The likelihood is noticeably greater than zero only if θ is within about 3 standard errors of the maximum-likelihood estimate; for example, if $\hat{\theta} = 2$ with a standard error of 1, the "effective" range is about –1 to 5. As the standard deviation of the prior distribution representing the alternative hypothesis increases, this range constitutes a smaller part of the probability. For example, in a normal distribution with mean zero and standard deviation 5, about 42% of the probability is between –1 and 5; with mean zero and standard deviation of 50, this falls to 4.8%, and with a standard deviation of 100, to 2.4%. The same relationship holds regardless of the specific distribution used to represent the alternative hypothesis: as the dispersion increases, the share of prior probability near the maximum-likelihood estimate declines toward zero and the Bayes factor rises toward infinity.

A consequence of this relationship was noted by Lindley (1957) and has come to be known as "Lindley's paradox": regardless of the p-value, a Bayes factor can be found that gives any specified degree of evidence in favor of the null hypothesis. This can be accomplished simply by increasing the dispersion of the prior distribution (Startz, 2014a).[4] The implication of Lindley's paradox is that the distribution representing the alternative hypothesis cannot be chosen arbitrarily: it must have some positive justification.

4.3.3 Influence of Sample Size on Bayes Factors

The preceding section considered the effect of changes in the dispersion of the prior distribution given the sample size. This section will consider the effect of changes in the sample size given the prior distribution. The gen-

---

[4]Sometimes the paradox is put in terms of sample size: for a given p-value and prior distribution, there is a sample size beyond which the Bayes factor will favor the null hypothesis (e.g., Hubbard and Lindsay, 2008, pp. 75–76). However, this formulation is less illuminating, since it is not in the investigator's power to hold a p-value constant while increasing the sample size.

eral relationship can be understood by considering the BIC. The difference between the BIC statistics for two models that differ by one parameter has two components, the difference in deviance $D1 - D0$ and $\log(N)$. The first component has a noncentral chi-square distribution, which has a mean of $1 + \lambda$, where λ is the noncentrality parameter. The noncentrality parameter is equal to θ^2/σ_θ^2.

If the null hypothesis is true, $\theta = 0$ and the noncentrality parameter is zero, so the expected value of the difference in deviance is 1 at all sample sizes. The "penalty" term $\log(N)$ will increase without limit as the sample size increases. Therefore, $BIC_1 - BIC_0$ will increase without limit, and the Bayes factor will tend to show steadily stronger evidence for the null hypothesis.

If the null hypothesis is false, λ will be proportional to N because the standard error of the parameter estimate (σ_θ) is inversely proportional to N. Therefore, the expected value of the difference in deviance will be $1 + kN$, where k is a constant. Until N reaches $1/k$, $\log(N)$ will increase more rapidly than $1 + kN$; after N reaches $1/k$, $1 + kN$ will increase more rapidly than $\log(N)$. As N increases, the expected value of $BIC_0 - BIC_1$ will first increase, and then decline without limit. Therefore, the Bayes factor will initially tend to show increasing evidence in favor of the null hypothesis, before turning to show increasingly strong evidence in favor of the alternative hypothesis (Atkinson, 1978).

As an example, suppose we have a simple regression

$$y = \alpha + \beta x + e \qquad (4.1)$$

in which both x and e are normally distributed with a variance of 1. Then $\sigma(\beta) = 1/\sqrt{(N)}$, and $k = .01$. The miniumum expected value of the BIC occurs when $N = 100$: $2 - \log(100) \approx -2.6$, corresponding to a Bayes factor of about 3.7. The expected value of the BIC is approximately zero, corresponding to no evidence in either direction, when $N = 530$. When $N = 1,000$, the expected value of the BIC is about 4, corresponding to 7.4:1 odds in favor of the alternative hypothesis. If $\beta = .01$, then the minimum expected value of the BIC occurs when $N = 10,000$. This value is about -8.2, corresponding to a Bayes factor of about 66.7. That is, when the value of β is smaller, the maximum odds in favor of the null hypothesis are stronger.

Table 4.1 shows the Bayes factors for the example in Equation 4.1 produced by several different prior distributions at selected sample sizes. The true value of β is assumed to be 0.1, and the prior distributions for β are all normal with mean zero, differing only in their standard deviations.[5] The table shows that the differences among the Bayes factors produced by different distributions do not disappear as the sample size increases; rather, the ratios of the Bayes factors are approximately the same at all sample sizes. For example, in a sample of 50, the Bayes factor resulting from a distribution with a standard deviation of 10 is 9.85 times as large as the Bayes factor resulting from a distribution with a standard devation of 1.0; in a sample of 2,000 the ratio is 9.94.

If $\beta \neq 0$, as the sample goes to infinity the Bayes factor will eventually favor the alternative hypothesis regardless of the prior distribution. In this sense, Bayes factors are similar to classical hypothesis tests using a fixed significance level. However, a classical test using a fixed level of significance will always have a chance of a Type I error; that is, it may reject the null hypothesis if it is true. In contrast, as the sample size increases, the "break-even" value of the t-ratio for the Bayes factor increases without limit so that the chance of favoring the alternative hypothesis over a true null hypothesis also goes to zero. The probability of favoring the correct model goes to 1 as

TABLE 4.1. Example of the Relationship between the Sample Size and Bayes Factors

		Standard deviation of prior					
N	t	0.2	0.5	1	2	5	10
50	0.71	1.47	2.91	5.59	11.06	27.55	55.08
100	1.00	1.50	3.15	6.13	12.16	30.34	60.66
500	2.24	0.42	0.94	1.85	3.68	9.18	18.36
1,000	3.16	0.05	0.11	0.21	0.43	1.07	2.13
2,000	4.47	0.00046	0.0010	0.0020	0.004	0.010	0.020

---

[5]The calculations assume that the maximum-likelihood estimate in the sample is equal to the true parameter; allowing for sampling variation in $\hat{\beta}$ produces only minor changes.

the sample size goes to infinity, a property known as "consistency."[6] As seen in Chapter 3, consistency can be achieved in the framework of classical hypothesis testing by adjusting the significance level as the sample becomes larger; whereas with Bayes factors the adjustment is built into the calculations.

Although Bayes factors are consistent, in a finite sample the Bayes factor based on a given prior distribution may have a substantial probability of favoring the wrong model. For example, if $\theta = 0.2$, $\sigma(\theta) = 0.1$, and $N = 10,000$, the Bayes factor calculated from the BIC will have an 85% chance of favoring the null hypothesis and a 55% chance of favoring the null hypothesis by odds of more than 10:1. That is, consistency provides no assurance about the performance of a Bayes factor in a finite sample, even a "large" one. Moreover, a given increase in sample size may make performance worse rather than better. For example, in Table 4.1, an increase from 50 to 100 results in stronger odds in favor of the incorrect null hypothesis for all of the distributions shown.

The general implication is that the point about the relative accuracy of Bayesian and classical estimates (see Section 4.2.1) also applies to Bayes factors and classical hypothesis tests. Bayesian techniques can do better than classical ones, in the sense of having a higher chance of yielding correct conclusions, but they also can do worse. Which will be the case depends on the prior distribution.

4.4 BAYESIAN CONFIDENCE INTERVALS AND BAYES FACTORS

In the classical approach, confidence intervals and hypothesis tests present the same information in different ways: the confidence interval is the range of parameter values that cannot be rejected at a given level. In the Bayesian approach, the relationship is more complex. As the dispersion of the prior distribution increases, the Bayesian confidence interval approaches the classical one, but the Bayes factor shows increasingly strong evidence in favor of the null hypothesis. That is, increasing the dispersion of the prior distribution

---

[6]This should not be confused with the property of consistency in parameter estimation.

makes classical and Bayesian confidence intervals converge, while classical tests and Bayes factors diverge. Alternatively, one could say that the conclusions suggested by Bayesian confidence intervals and Bayes factors diverge.

The resolution of this paradox is that Bayes factors implicitly assume that there is a mass of probability at $\theta = 0$, that is, a definite probability that the null hypothesis is exactly true. This point can be illustrated by an example from Table 2.6. The estimated effect of being male rather than female on support for George W. Bush is .258 among whites and .061 among blacks, for a difference of .197, with a standard error of .199. The confidence interval for the difference is (−.193, .587). Using a classical hypothesis test, the null hypothesis would be accepted. However, the confidence interval indicates that there is a good deal of uncertainty about the value: it would not be reasonable to conclude that any difference is small. With a diffuse prior distribution, the Bayesian confidence interval would be the same as the classical one, and the basic conclusion would be the same: positive, negative, and zero parameter values are all possible.[7]

The BIC statistic for the hypothesis that there is no difference in the effect of gender is $\left(\frac{.197}{.199}\right)^2 - \log(11{,}862) = -8.4$, implying odds of about 67:1 in favor of the hypothesis of no difference. Thus, there appears to be a dramatic difference in conclusions. According to classical and Bayesian confidence intervals, the data are consistent with a wide range of parameter values; according to the BIC, the data strongly suggest that the parameter is exactly equal to zero. However, as discussed in Section 4.3, the posterior odds in favor of $M0$ are a product of the Bayes factor and the prior odds. With a continuous distribution, the prior probability that θ will be *exactly* equal to any specific value is zero, so the posterior probability that $\theta = 0$ is also zero. Therefore, a Bayes factor is not meaningful unless it is assumed that there is a mass of probability at $\theta = 0$.

It could be objected that the hypothesis $\theta = 0$ can be understood as an approximation for the interval hypothesis that $|\theta| < \delta$, where δ is a value

---

[7]As Lindley (1965) observed, this equivalence means that classical hypothesis tests using a fixed significance level can be given a Bayesian interpretation. From this point of view, a test asks if the null hypothesis is consistent with the observed data. However, this interpretation raises the question of why the value suggested by the null hypothesis should be singled out for special treatment rather than just regarded as one of many values that are consistent with the data—see Chapter 8 for more discussion of this point.

regarded as small. The prior probability that the parameter value falls in an interval is greater than zero, so if the null hypothesis is meant as an approximation it will be meaningful to compute a Bayes factor. Table 4.2 considers this interpretation for this example, assuming a normal prior distribution with a mean of 0 and a standard deviation of 21.7.[8] If "approximately zero" is understood as the range (−0.01, 0.01), the prior probability that θ is approximately zero is 0.0004 and the posterior probability is 0.0246. The posterior probability is 66.7 times as large as the prior, matching the Bayes factor implied by the BIC. The Bayes factor is correct in the sense that data increase support for the proposition that the parameter is approximately zero. However, it would be misleading to summarize the analysis by simply giving the Bayes factor, since the posterior probability that θ is approximately zero is very small.

In contrast, suppose that 5% of the prior probability is in the range (−0.01, 0.01), while the remaining 95% has a normal distribution with mean 21.7. In that case, after observing the data we could conclude that the parameter probably was approximately equal to zero. However, putting even 5% of the prior probability in the range (−0.01, 0.01) would create a discontinuity in which the probability density within that range was about 100 times as great as the density just outside of that range. That is, the distribution would be "highly spiked" around zero (Bayarri, comment on Greenhouse and Wasserman, 1996, p. 59).

TABLE 4.2. Prior and Posterior Probabilities, Differences in Effects of Gender

Range	Description	Prior probability	Posterior probability	Posterior/ prior
Greater than 0.5	Large	.4908	.0639	0.1302
0.1 to 0.5	Medium	.0074	.6231	84.6
0.01 to 0.1	Small	.0017	.1393	84.1
−0.01 to 0.01	Approximately zero	.0004	.0246	66.7
−0.1 to −0.01	Small	.0017	.0813	49.1
−0.5 to −0.1	Medium	.0074	.0676	9.2
Less than −0.5	Large	.4908	.0002	0.0005

[8]This prior distribution provides a Bayes factor that matches the one implied by the BIC. See Section 4.6 for more discussion.

4.5 APPROACHES TO BAYESIAN HYPOTHESIS TESTING

One conclusion that can be drawn from the points discussed in the preceding section is that Bayes factors are not generally useful; in most cases, a Bayesian analysis should simply give the posterior distribution. This conclusion is based on the premise that it is usually not reasonable to assume a mass of probability at any particular point, or even a highly spiked distribution around a particular point. It may be reasonable to think that small parameter values are more likely than large ones, but in that case Bayesian confidence intervals can be calculated using a prior distribution that represents this belief—for example, a normal distribution with a mean of zero. That is, a Bayesian analysis can generally do without hypothesis tests: rather than making decisions to include some parameters and omit others, one can estimate all parameters using a combination of prior information and the evidence in the data (Gelman and Rubin, 1995).

Other Bayesians, however, hold that it is reasonable to think of a mass of probability at or near a specific point. According to Jeffreys (1961, p. 245), the purpose of a hypothesis test is to answer the question "In what circumstances do observations support a change of the form of the law itself?" He adds that "this question is really logically prior to the estimation of the parameters, since the estimation problem presupposes that the parameters are relevant." In that case, it is necessary to decide on a distribution to represent the alternative hypothesis. The "subjectivist" position is that the distribution must represent the actual prior beliefs of some observer concerning that particular parameter (Dickey and Lientz, 1970). Of course, different observers are likely to have different beliefs, but then the investigator should compute Bayes factors from a variety of distributions representing the range of beliefs held by informed observers. In this approach, the appropriate prior distributions must be chosen separately for each problem based on theory and substantive knowledge; that is, it is much like the calculation of an optimal α level for a classical test. "Objectivists," in contrast, attempt to specify prior distributions that can be used as a general baseline in all situations (Jeffreys, 1961). A distribution of this kind cannot represent *complete* ignorance; as discussed in Section 4.3.2, increasing the dispersion of θ means that the Bayes factor will inevitably favor the null hypothesis.

Jeffreys observed (1961, p. 251) that "the mere fact that it has been sug-

gested that [a parameter] is zero corresponds to some presumption that it is fairly small." Therefore, he suggested that the standard should be a distribution that represents a minimal amount of knowledge rather than complete ignorance. In effect, it would represent the views of an observer who agrees that it is reasonable to test the hypothesis $\theta = 0$ but has no additional information about possible values of θ. Kass and Raftery (1995, p. 791) suggest that the resulting Bayes factor is "well suited for summarizing results in scientific communication," since it does not rely on any assumptions that are specific to the situation.

4.6   THE UNIT INFORMATION PRIOR

Jeffreys proposed that the goal of representing a minimal amount of knowledge could be accomplished by using a distribution that was equivalent to the average information in a single observation from the data, or what Kass and Wasserman (1995) call a "unit information prior." With a single parameter, the unit information prior is approximately equal to a normal distribution with mean $\hat{\theta}$ and standard deviation $s_{\hat{\theta}} \sqrt{N}$. Kass and Wasserman (1995) show that the Bayes factor implied by the BIC is very close to the Bayes factor produced by a unit information prior.

In a strict sense, the unit information prior cannot represent actual prior beliefs, since $\hat{\theta}$ is not known until the parameter estimates are observed. The natural way to represent the hypothesis $\theta \neq 0$ would be with a distribution symmetrical around zero, but using a normal distribution with mean of zero rather than $\hat{\theta}$ usually produces very similar results. The differences are substantial only if the mean is large relative to the standard deviation, which is the case only if the sample is very small or the value of $\hat{\theta}$ is very large. It would be possible to "correct" the BIC to make it correspond to a prior distribution with mean zero, but the difference from the standard BIC is usually of little practical importance.

4.6.1   An Example of the Unit Information Prior

The example in Section 2.6.4 involved racial differences in voters' choice between Bush and Kerry in 2004. In the parameter for differences in gender effects, the unit information prior implies a standard deviation of 0.199 ×

$\sqrt{11,862}$ = 21.67. Is this distribution a reasonable representation of prior beliefs? The parameter in question involves the logarithm of an odds ratio. Suppose that among whites, Bush received 99.9% of men's votes and only 0.1% of women's votes, and that among blacks the pattern was reversed: Bush received 0.1% of men's votes and 99.9% of women's. The logarithm of the odds ratio representing the interaction between race and gender would then be $\log\left(\frac{.999 \times .999}{.001 \times .001}\right)$ = 13.8. In a normal distribution, about half of the probability falls within two-thirds of one standard deviation from the mean, so the unit information prior implies that there is about a 50% chance that the interaction will be *at least as strong* as this. While there is certainly room for differences of judgment how best to represent the hypothesis that $\theta \neq 0$, it is hard to defend the implied distribution in this example as reasonable—in that using the unit information prior amounts to saying that if there is *any* interaction, it will probably be so large as to be overwhelmingly obvious without using any statistical test.[9]

In the case of a binomial parameter, the Bayes factors that result from the unit information prior closely match those derived from the obvious "neutral" prior, the uniform distribution (see Section 4.3.1). However, with the binomial parameter, there is a minimum to the information that can be provided by a representative observation. This minimum corresponds to the maximum standard deviation for binomial outcomes, which occurs when half of the observations are successes. In most other situations, there is no minimum on the amount of information that can be provided by one observation. To illustrate this point, consider a test for independence in a two-by-two frequency table. Table 4.3 gives two hypothetical examples, both with 100 cases. The odds ratio representing the association is somewhat larger in the second frequency table than in the first: $\frac{82 \times 2}{8 \times 8}$ = 2.56 versus $\frac{30 \times 30}{20 \times 20}$ = 2.25. The deviance for a model of independence is 4.03 for the first table and 1.02 for the second, and the Bayes factors implied by the BIC are about 1.3 and 6. That is, although the observed association is stronger in the second table, the

---

[9]Startz (2014b) shows that the BIC is also a close approximation to the Bayes factor given by a uniform prior distribution centered at θ = 0 with width $s_\theta \sqrt{2\pi N}$. In this case, the width of the uniform distribution is about 54, also implying about a 50% chance of an odds ratio greater than 13.8.

TABLE 4.3. Two Hypothetical Frequency Tables Illustrating the Effect of Marginal Distributions on the Unit Information Prior

30	20	50
20	30	50
50	50	100

82	8	90
8	2	10
90	10	100

Bayes factor produced by the unit information prior indicates considerably stronger evidence *in favor* of the hypothesis of no association.

The reason is that the unit information prior implies a standard deviation of 2.0 in the first table and 4.4 in the second table, that is, the prior distribution in the second table is more diffuse. The standard deviations are different because a representative observation from the second table provides less information about the degree of association than does a representative observation from the first table. The second table, however, does not provide a lower limit; as the marginal distributions become more unequal, the amount of information in a representative observation will approach zero, and the standard deviation implied by the unit information prior will increase without limit.

This point is particularly relevant to the voting example in Section 4.4. Blacks make up only about 11% of the sample, and only about 11% of blacks voted for Bush. The uneven marginal distribution helps to explain the large standard deviation implied by the unit information prior in this example. In terms of the BIC, one could say that the large value of N in the penalty term is misleading, because an average observation provides very little information about interactions involving the effect of race on voting choices.

4.6.2 Evaluation

The fundamental problem with the unit information prior is that "the information in a representative observation" does not have a definite meaning, but rather it differs depending on the measurement and distribution of the

variables. For example, in a discrete-time survival analysis of factors affecting the human lifespan, changing the time units from the year to the month would multiply the number of cases by 12 without substantially increasing the amount of information in the data. Therefore, the information contained in a representative case is smaller when the unit is the month. Using the BIC amounts to saying that the ideas of a "neutral" observer about the possible values of the parameters will differ depending on the units that are used.

Berger and Pericchi (1996) propose an alternative to the unit information prior: a prior equivalent to the information in a "minimal training sample" containing the smallest number of observations needed to produce estimates for all parameters in the model. In the simplest version of this approach, the minimal sample is simply equal to the number of parameters in the model. More sophisticated versions calculate the number of observations from random subsamples of the data that would be required in order to estimate the model. These versions overcome some of the problems discussed above. For example, in order to estimate the parameters of a model with a binary outcome, it is necessary to have observations for both of the outcome categories. In a study of human mortality, if the time unit were changed from a year to a month, the minimal training sample would be approximately 12 times as large, so the penalty in a BIC-type expression would remain about the same. In Table 4.3, the expected value of the minimal training sample for the first frequency table is about 8, while the minimal training sample for the second table is about 50. Given these prior distributions, the Bayes factors for both tables show weak evidence—odds of less than 2:1—against the null hypothesis.

One drawback of the minimal training sample approach is that the calculations become much more complex. There is no general formula—the minimal training sample must be specially calculated for each model.[10] A more fundamental limitation can be illustrated by a simple example. Suppose we have a linear regression:

$$y = \alpha + \beta_1 x_1 + \beta_2 x_2 + e; \ e \sim N(0, \sigma^2) \tag{4.2}$$

---

[10]Usually the calculations would be done by repeated sampling (as was done to get the figures for Table 4.3) rather than analytically. Berger and Pericchi (1996) recommend using the distribution of minimal training samples rather than just the expected value, making the calculation of the Bayes factor more complicated.

A reasonable prior distribution clearly cannot be defined in terms of the values of the regression coefficients—for example, whether a coefficient of 1.0 should be regarded as large or small depends on the units in which the variables are measured. Jeffreys (1961) made the prior distribution independent of the units by defining it in terms of the covariances of the regression coefficients, but this means that it depends on the distribution of the independent variables. For example, if the variance of x_1 differs in two samples, then the distribution corresponding to the unit information prior will differ as well. When considering either β_1 or β_2, it is possible to adjust for such differences by the minimal training sample approach: for example, a sample with a smaller number of cases and another sample with a larger number of cases may contain the same amount of information about β_1. However, in general the adjustments will have to be different for different parameters: for example, a given sample may provide a precise estimate of β_1 but only an imprecise estimate of β_2. Therefore, it is not possible to characterize a sample as "large" or "small" (that is, informative or uninformative): a sample may be highly informative for some purposes and much less informative for others. Rather than applying a general penalty based on sample size—that is, saying that the prior distribution is equal to some number of observations—one must consider each parameter individually.

Advocates of the unit information prior have given almost no attention to this question. For example, Kass and Wasserman (1995, p. 933) merely assert that the unit information prior is "intuitively reasonable," while Greenhouse and Wasserman (1996, p. 47) say that it "seems intuitively reasonable but could certainly be questioned." One of the few discussions that goes deeper is provided by Box and Tiao (1973, p. 58), who propose that a "small" amount of knowledge should be understood in a relative sense: "The phrase 'knowing little' can only have meaning relative to a specific experiment. The form of a noninformative prior thus depends upon the experiment to be performed, and for two different experiments, each of which can throw light on the same parameter, the choice of 'noninformative' prior can be different." They suggest that the prior distribution should "represent . . . an amount of prior information which is small *relative* to what the particular projected experiment can be expected to provide" (p. 44). This argument is plausible

when the data are obtained from an experiment focusing on a single parameter, because the size and design of the experiment would implicitly reflect the investigator's prior knowledge or expectations.[11] However, in most observational studies, the design is given by "nature" rather than chosen by the investigator. From the point of view of the investigator, the amount of information that an average observation provides about a particular parameter is essentially a matter of chance.

In conclusion, the unit information prior does not provide a constant standard: it amounts to making the prior distribution vary in an arbitrary fashion. Moreover, no modified or "corrected" version of the BIC can provide a constant standard. It is possible to defend it on pragmatic grounds—that the BIC usually produces "reasonable" conclusions, but the same claim has been made for classical hypothesis tests using conventional significance levels (Bross, 1971). Judgments about what is a reasonable conclusion differ so widely that they cannot provide a convincing argument for any criterion.

4.7 LIMITS ON BAYES FACTORS

A different form of the "objectivist" approach to Bayesian hypothesis tests considers limits on Bayes factors. Although there is no limit to how strongly a Bayes factor can favor the null hypothesis, there are limits on how strongly a Bayes factor can favor the alternative hypothesis. The absolute limit is $\exp(-t^2/2)$, which would occur when the alternative hypothesis is defined as the point hypothesis $\theta = \hat{\theta}$; this would mean that a t-ratio of 2.0 would give a Bayes factor of about 0.14. Of course, this is not a reasonable way to represent the standard alternative hypothesis $\theta \neq \theta_0$, so the practical limit is higher. Edwards et al. (1963) proposed that the standard alternative hypothesis $\theta \neq 0$ should be represented by a symmetric unimodal distribution, and they found limits for one distribution of this kind, the normal. Berger and Sellke (1987) extended the work of Edwards et al. by showing that the limit for the uniform distribution was more favorable to the alternative hypothesis than was

---

[11]However, their argument might be taken to suggest that the prior distribution should be equivalent to a fixed fraction of the data rather than a fixed number of observations. That is, a decision to collect a large amount of data suggests that a small parameter value was expected. See Section 5.7 for more discussion.

the limit for other symmetric unimodal distributions. Table 4.4 shows the maximum odds in favor of the alternative hypothesis (i.e., $1/K$) for selected values of t when the alternative hypothesis is represented by normal, logistic, and uniform distributions. The limits suggest that a p-value of .10 is almost completely uninformative and a p-value of .05 provides no more than weak evidence against the null hypothesis. Even a p-value of .01 provides odds of no more than about 6 or 8 to 1.

In order to go beyond these negative statements, it is necessary to consider a range of distributions. Figure 4.3 provides more information on the sensitivity of Bayes factors to assumptions about the prior distribution. Like Figure 4.2, it examines the relationship between the standard deviation and the Bayes factor, assuming that the alternative hypothesis is represented by a normal distribution centered at zero. The difference is that Figure 4.3 is limited to a smaller range of standard deviations. As in Figure 4.3, the standard deviation of $f(\theta)$ is set to equal the standard error of the parameter estimate so that the prior distribution can easily be translated into the expected t-ratio. The horizontal axis gives the standard deviation of the prior distribution, and the vertical axis represents the odds in favor of the null hypothesis (that is, the reciprocal of the Bayes factor).

There are two curves, one representing a t-ratio of 2.0, the other a t-ratio of 2.5. As the standard deviation goes to zero, the odds resulting from both t-ratios decline to 1.0, indicating neutrality between the two hypotheses. The reason is that, as the standard deviation approaches zero, the alternative hypothesis converges to the null hypothesis. In effect, when the standard deviation is small, the null hypothesis is that $\theta = 0$, and the alternative is that

TABLE 4.4. Maximum Odds in Favor of Alternative Hypothesis, Normal, Logistic, and Uniform Prior Distributions

p	t	Normal	Logistic	Uniform
.32	1.00	1.0	1.0	1.0
.15	1.44	1.2	1.2	1.3
.10	1.65	1.4	1.4	1.6
.05	1.96	2.1	2.0	2.5
.01	2.58	6.6	6.2	8.2
.003	2.97	16.8	15.8	21.9
.001	3.29	41.3	38.7	55.4
.0001	3.89	301.2	281.4	421.2

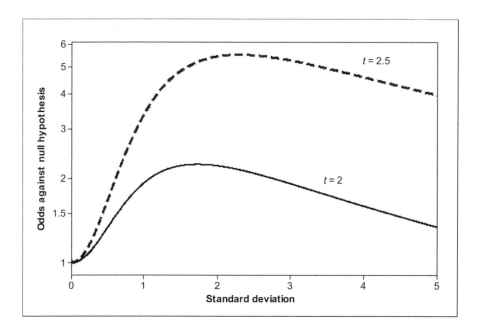

FIGURE 4.3. Examples of odds against the null hypothesis provided by Bayes factors.

θ is almost equal to zero. As the standard deviation increases, the resulting odds in favor of the alternative hypothesis increase to a maximum and then decline toward zero. For a *t*-ratio of 2, the odds in favor of the alternative hypothesis are greater than 1.5 for all standard deviations between about 0.65 and 4.3 and fall to 1:1 when the standard deviation is 6.7. For a *t*-ratio of 2.5, the odds in favor of the alternative hypothesis are greater than 5 for standard deviations between about 1.6 and 3.4, and fall to 1:1 when the standard deviation is about 19.8.

A normal distribution with a standard deviation of 0.65 implies that if the alternative hypothesis is true there is about a 88% chance that θ will have an absolute value of less than 1 and only about a 0.2% chance that θ will have an absolute value of more than 2. Therefore, a substantial *t*-ratio would be surprising under *both* the null and alternative hypothesis. This situation would represent a severely "underpowered" analysis, such as the study by Kanazawa (2007) discussed in Chapter 3. A standard deviation of 4.3 would imply about a 50% chance that θ will have an absolute value of more than

3 and about a 25% chance that it will have an absolute value of more than 5. Under the alternative hypothesis, a t-ratio of 2 or 2.5 would be somewhat smaller than expected. A situation of this kind would generally be regarded as giving ample power, probably more than is usual in the social sciences for active research questions. Therefore, it seems that in most cases a reasonable choice of standard deviation would give odds of at least 1.5:1 in favor of the alternative hypothesis when the t-ratio is 2. Although these calculations are based on a normal distribution, Table 4.4 shows that the maximum evidence for the alternative hypothesis is not very sensitive to the specific distribution chosen: the maximum is almost exactly the same, given a normal and logistic distribution, and not much larger, given a uniform distribution.

Another approach to deciding on a prior distribution for the alternative hypothesis is to use Bayes factors. As discussed in Section 4.3, it is possible to compute a Bayes factor for any two distinct distributions. For example, in Table 2.6, the estimated effect of age on support for George Bush is −.02 among whites and −.10 among blacks. The difference is .08 with a standard error of .052, for a t-ratio of 1.54. The limits in Table 4.4 show that under the most favorable normal distribution a t-ratio of 1.54 would give odds of about 1.3:1 in favor of the hypothesis of a difference in the effect of age by race, or a Bayes factor of about 0.8. The Bayes factor implied by the unit information prior is about 33. If we call the hypothesis that θ has the distribution that gives the most favorable Bayes factor $H1A$ and the hypothesis that θ follows the unit information prior $H1B$, then

$$\frac{p(H0 \mid x)}{p(H1A \mid x)} = 0.8$$

$$\frac{p(H0 \mid x)}{p(H1B \mid x)} = 33$$

Therefore,

$$\frac{p(H1A \mid x)}{p(H1B \mid x)} = \frac{33}{0.8} = 41.3$$

The observed data strongly support the most favorable prior over the unit information prior. Therefore, unless we begin with a strong theoretical rationale for representing the alternative hypothesis in a particular way, the logic of Bayesian hypothesis testing suggests choosing a distribution that gives something close to the most favorable Bayes factor.

From a subjectivist point of view, decisions about how to represent the alternative have to be made on a case-by-case basis; this would depend on theory or substantive knowledge. However, if one adopts an objectivist approach, it is reasonable to use the most favorable Bayes factors as a guide to the interpretation of test statistics. If this is done, the differences in the conclusions of Bayesian and classical tests are less dramatic than when the BIC is used to produce Bayes factors. With the BIC, an estimate that is statistically significant according to classical tests can provide strong evidence in favor of the null hypothesis; with most favorable Bayes factors, any test statistic that is significant at the 5% or 10% level can reasonably be interpreted as providing *some* evidence in favor of the alternative hypothesis. However, the evidence provided by test statistics that are significant only at the 5% level is quite weak. On the basis of limits like those shown in Table 4.4, Berger and Sellke (1987, p. 120) propose the following guidelines: "$t = 2$ means only mild evidence against $H0$, $t = 3$ means significant evidence against $H0$, and $t = 4$ means highly significant evidence against $H0$." That is, t-ratios between 2 and 3 would be regarded as suggestive but inconclusive rather than as grounds for "rejecting" the null hypothesis.

4.7.1   Most Favorable Bayes Factors and Evidence for the Null Hypothesis

If the absolute value of the t-ratio is less than or equal to 1 and the alternative hypothesis is represented by a symmetric unimodal distribution, the Bayes factor will always favor the null hypothesis. The Bayes factor will approach 1 as the standard deviation approaches zero: that is, when the alternative hypothesis is that the parameter is infinitesimally different from zero. Of course, this is not an alternative hypothesis that any researcher would actually want to test, so it is reasonable to count t-ratios of less than 1 as evidence for the null hypothesis. However, with small or moderate values of the standard deviation, Bayes factors cannot produce *strong* evidence in favor of the null hypothesis. For example, if the alternative hypothesis is represented by a normal distribution with a standard deviation of 1, a t-ratio of 1.0 implies a Bayes factor of 1.1, and a t-ratio of 0 implies a Bayes factor of 1.4. With a standard deviation of 2, the Bayes factors are 1.5 and 2.2.

4.8 BAYES FACTORS FOR MULTIPLE PARAMETERS

To this point, the discussion of Bayes factors has been limited to hypotheses involving a single parameter. The direct calculation of Bayes factors for hypotheses involving multiple parameters is more difficult, since it requires multiple integration. One of the attractions of the BIC for researchers is that it can easily be applied to any hypothesis, whether it involves one parameter or many.

When multiple parameters are involved, the gap between the conclusions of the BIC and those of classical tests can become very wide. For example, with the data on social mobility, a model of quantitative differences in mobility (Model 3 in Table 2.4) gives a deviance of 108.1 with 45 degrees of freedom, while a model in which the pattern of mobility differs by time period (Model 4) has a deviance of 48.1 with 30 degrees of freedom. Using a conventional hypothesis test, the difference of 60.0 with 15 degrees of freedom is highly significant (the p-value is about 10^{-7}, so the hypothesis that the pattern of mobility remains the same over time is decisively rejected. However, the difference in BIC statistics is $60 - 15 \log(9304) = -77.1$, giving overwhelming (about 5×10^{16}) odds in favor of that hypothesis.

One reason for the difference is the large sample size: to give evidence in favor of adding a single parameter would require a reduction in deviance of 9.1. A more fundamental reason, however, is that the classical test and the Bayes factor are not testing the same hypothesis. In a classical test, the alternative hypothesis is that *at least one* parameter in a group differs from zero; in the Bayesian test, the alternative is that *all* of the parameters in a group differ from zero.

As a simple example, consider a three-way table with two rows, two columns, and two levels and frequencies (115, 85, 85, 115, 105, 95, 95, 105). A model with no row–column association at either level gives a deviance of 10.03 with 2 degrees of freedom, for a p-value of .007. If we regard the unit information prior as a reasonable representation of prior beliefs, the BIC can be used to calculate the Bayes factor. The BIC is $10.03 - 2 \log(800) = -3.34$, giving a Bayes factor of about 5.3. That is, it shows the evidence as favoring the model of no row–column association against the model of nonzero association in both levels. However, there are several possible intermediate models: association only in level 1, association only in level 2, and equal

association in both levels. The deviance, BIC, and Bayes factors against the model of association at both levels are shown in Table 4.5.

If we assume that the prior probability of each model is equal, Bayes's theorem can be used to calculate the posterior probabilities, which are shown in the final column. The posterior probability for Model i is

$$\frac{K_i}{\Sigma(K_i)}$$

where K_i is the Bayes factor for Model i against the model of different patterns of association.[12]

Although the model of no association is more likely than the model of separate association parameters, it is less likely than two of the intermediate models. Thus, an investigator who treated the Bayes factor for the model of no association against the model of separate association parameters as equivalent to a classical test and concluded that there was no need to search for intermediate models would be misled. Of course, in a simple example like this, most investigators would routinely consider the intermediate models. However, in more complex models, a strong part of the appeal of the BIC has been that it seems to make it possible to "accept" models that are convenient or theoretically appealing but are clearly rejected by classical tests. However, this practice is not justified even if the BIC is regarded as valid on its own terms, since it is not a test against the hypothesis that *some* parameters are nonzero. To investigate that possibility, one must estimate all intermediate models and compute posterior probabilities, as in Table 4.5. Edwards et al.

TABLE 4.5. Fit Statistics and Bayes Factors for Examples of Association in a 2 × 2 × 2 Table

Model	Deviance	df	BIC	K	Posterior probability
No association	10.03	2	−3.34	5.3	.16
Association, level 1	1.04	1	−5.64	16.8	.50
Association, level 2	9.03	1	2.34	0.3	.01
Equal association	2.02	1	−4.66	10.3	.31
Different association	0	0	0	1	.03

---

[12]The Bayes factor of the model against itself is 1.

(1963, p. 233) investigated limits to Bayes factors in favor of the hypothesis that some parameters are nonzero, but they found that with a large number of parameters the limits were so large as to be "of almost no practical use."

In this simple example, there were only a few reasonable intermediate models, but the number of possibilities increases rapidly as the number of parameters increases. Moreover, it may be difficult to specify the intermediate models in advance. In cases like the economic growth example, where the issue is the choice of control variables in a regression, the obvious intermediate models are simply the subsets of the class of potential independent variables. However, in cases like the social mobility example, the cells representing particular combinations of fathers' and sons' status have to be considered in the context of the whole table. In a general sense, the intermediate models would be ones that combined or arranged the categories in "reasonable" ways: for example, making a distinction between cases in which father's and son's class were the same and those in which they were different. It would be hard to draw up a comprehensive list of those models in advance.

Jeffreys (1961) held that Bayes factors should be applied only to tests of single parameters or to parameters that were intrinsically linked together. An example in which parameters are intrinsically linked is the spline model for development and fertility. The break point is not defined unless there is a difference in slopes, so it would be appropriate to use a Bayes factor to test this model against the linear model. When comparing models that differed by multiple parameters, he simply used classical tests. For example, discussing a case in which the model of independence for a cross-tabulation gave a chi-square statistic of 707 with 165 degrees of freedom, he said that "no test of significance is needed. . . . The hypothesis of independence is seriously wrong" (Jeffreys, 1961, p. 352). The BIC would have been $707 - 165 \log(8{,}047)$ $= -776$: that is, overwhelming support for the hypothesis of independence over a model with a separate parameter for each cell.[13] However, the model of a separate parameter for each cell is only one alternative, and probably not the most plausible one, and thus this conclusion would not be of much interest. The conventional goodness-of-fit test gives an answer to a different ques-

---

[13]Although the BIC had not been proposed at the time, a straightforward extension of Jeffreys's formulas for approximate Bayes factors would have yielded the same conclusion.

tion, namely, "whether agreement between this hypothesis and the data is so bad that we must begin to exercise our imaginations to try to think of an alternative that fits the facts better" (Barnard, 1972, p. 129).

4.9   SUMMARY AND CONCLUSIONS

The discussion in this chapter suggests four primary conclusions. First, a Bayes factor is meaningful only if there is a "highly spiked" prior distribution: a concentration of probability at or near zero. This does not mean merely that the parameter might be zero or approximately zero: it means that there is some kind of discontinuity in which values in a small range near zero are much more likely than slightly larger values. In effect, the prior distribution is a mix of two parts—a "spike" at or near some value and a distribution over all other values. Some Bayesians consider this to be a reasonable assumption while others do not. Because this is a question of science rather than statistical theory, it will be left until Chapter 8.

Second, Bayes factors depend on the prior distribution that represents the alternative hypothesis. The unit information prior has been offered as a general standard that could be applied to all situations, but it varies in ways that are difficult to justify, so it cannot provide a basis for Bayesian hypothesis tests. Modifications based on the idea of a "minimal training sample" can remove some, but not all, of the difficulties associated with the unit information prior. The basic problem is that a typical observation may be informative about some parameters and much less informative about others. Therefore, the idea of a general "penalty" based on the size of the sample is not reasonable.

Third, there are limits on the evidence that Bayes factors can provide for the alternative hypothesis. These limits can be used to provide an objective, although somewhat imprecise, standard for interpreting test statistics. These limits are not affected by the sample size, so in a practical sense this approach amounts to setting a higher bar for statistical significance.

Finally, Bayesian hypothesis tests are comparisons of specific models, so they are not comparable to classical tests for hypotheses involving multiple degrees of freedom. With classical tests, the alternative hypothesis is that *some* of the parameters are zero; with Bayes factors, the alternative is that *all*

are. To obtain a Bayesian parallel to the classical test, it is necessary to compute Bayes factors for all intermediate models. This normally requires a good deal of work and is sometimes impossible. Therefore, when multiple parameters are involved, it is more efficient to use p-values for preliminary screening: "When χ^2 lies far outside the range $v \pm \sqrt{2v}$ a significant departure from [the] hypothesis is clear. It is only when it is a little outside the range that a more detailed test is often needed" (Jeffreys, 1977, p. 89).

The implication of these points is to narrow the apparent gap between Bayesian and classical tests. Dramatic differences in conclusions result from a combination of unreasonable prior distributions—particularly the unit information prior—and misinterpretation of Bayes factors for tests involving multiple parameters. The major discrepancy between Bayes factors and classical tests occurs for tests of a single parameter that give t-ratios of 2 to 3. Such results are "statistically significant" by conventional standards but provide only weak evidence against the null hypothesis, according to most favorable Bayes factors. In fact, the guidelines proposed by Berger and Sellke (1987) are close to the convention of treating a t-ratio of 3 as the standard of significance that was sometimes used in the early days of hypothesis testing (see Section 2.3.5).

RECOMMENDED READING

Berger, J. O., & Delampady, M. (1987). Testing precise hypotheses. *Statistical Science, 2*, 317–352. —Extends the approach of Edwards, Lindman, and Savage to a wider range of distributions and proposes guidelines for the interpretation of *t*-ratios.

Edwards, W., Lindman, H., & Savage, L. J. (1963). Bayesian statistical inference for psychological research. *Psychological Review, 70*, 193–242. —An important article on the application of Bayesian methods in the social sciences, with an emphasis on hypothesis tests. The first to systematically consider limits on Bayes factors.

Gelman, A., Carlin, J. B., Stern, H. S., Dunson, D. B., Vehtari, A., & Rubin, D. B. (2014). *Bayesian Data Analysis* (3rd ed.). Boca Raton, FL: CRC Press. —A comprehensive and up-to-date discussion of Bayesian estimation.

Gelman, A., & Rubin, D. B. (1995). Avoiding model selection in Bayesian social research. *Sociological Methodology, 25*, 165–173. —A comment on Raftery (1995) that advocates an approach based on estimation of a general model rather than model selection.

Hubbard, R., & Lindsay, R. M. (2008). Why P values are not a useful measure of evidence in significance testing. *Theory and Psychology, 18*(1), 69–88. —Examines *p*-values from a Bayesian perspective and argues that they exaggerate the evidence against the null hypothesis.

Jeffreys, H. (1937). *Scientific Inference* (2nd ed.). Cambridge, UK: Cambridge University Press. —The "Addenda" (pp. 245–260) give an account of his views on induction and hypothesis testing.

Jeffreys, H. (1980). Some general points in probability theory. In A. Zellner (Ed.), *Bayesian analysis in econometrics and statistics* (pp. 451–453). Amsterdam and New York: North-Holland. —A short summary of Jeffreys's views on hypothesis testing.

Raftery, A. E. (1995). Bayesian model selection in social research. *Sociological Methodology, 25,* 111–163. —Criticizes conventional hypothesis tests and proposes a Bayesian approach to model selection, with emphasis on the BIC.

Startz, R. (2014). Choosing the more likely hypothesis. *Foundations and Trends in Econometrics, 7,* 1–70. —A clear discussion of Bayes factors.

Weakliem, D. L. (1999). A critique of the Bayesian information criterion for model selection. *Sociological Methods and Research, 27,* 359–397. —A detailed examination of the BIC and the unit information prior; proposes alternative models for the data considered in Raftery's article.

5

The Akaike Information Criterion

The Akaike information criterion (AIC) provides an alternative to classical and Bayesian hypothesis tests. The AIC is not intended to select the true model, but a model that is "close" to the true model. This chapter discusses the standard rationale for the AIC and its interpretation in terms of cross-validation. It also discusses an alternative interpretation of the AIC as a Bayes factor. It concludes that the AIC is most useful for the selection of control variables and the general specification of the model, rather than for conclusions about parameters of theoretical interest.

5.1 INFORMATION

Kullback and Leibler (1951) proposed a measure of what could be regarded as the distance between two probability distributions:

$$\int p(x) \log \frac{p(x)}{q(x)}$$

This measure is known as the "information" divergence between the distributions.[1] The measure of information is not symmetrical: that is, $I(p{:}q)$ is not generally equal to $I(q{:}p)$. As a result, $I(p{:}q) + I(q{:}p)$ is often used as a general measure of the divergence between p and q.

Information is closely related to maximum-likelihood estimation. For

---

[1]See Kullback (1959, pp. 1–10) for a brief history of information theory.

example, suppose that we have a count variable with a Poisson distribution. If n represents the observed frequencies and $\hat{n}$ represents the expected frequencies according to a model, then the maximum-likelihood estimation is equivalent to minimizing

$$\sum n \log \frac{n}{\hat{n}}$$

Moreover, $2I(n:\hat{n})$ will follow a chi-square distribution if the hypothesized model is true.

In itself, the idea of information does not challenge the classical approach to hypothesis testing: Kullback (1959) shows how standard tests can be interpreted in terms of information theory. However, the existence of a general measure of divergence raises the possibility of an alternative method of model selection. The goal of this approach is not to select the true model but rather a model that is "close" to the true model. Although this idea is intuitively appealing, it cannot be applied in practice without some general measure of distance. Kullback–Leibler information provides such a measure.

5.2   PREDICTION AND MODEL SELECTION

Suppose we are considering two nested regression models, one including the restriction that $\theta = 0$. The estimate of θ in the unrestricted model is chosen to maximize the fit to the observed data, so it will always have a smaller error sum of squares than the restricted model. However, when parameter estimates from the observed data are applied to produce predictions for another set of data from the same population, the restricted model may have a smaller sum of squared prediction errors.

If the restriction is true, then the predictions of the restricted model will be based on the correct assumption that $\theta = 0$, so they will clearly tend to be better than those from the unrestricted model. However, the predictions from the restricted model may be better even if the restriction is false. In that case, the value of θ assumed in the restricted model differs from the true value, but the estimate $\hat{\theta}$ in the unrestricted model will also differ from the true value because of random error. Which one is likely to produce better predictions will depend on the relative sizes of the true parameter value and the standard error of the parameter estimate. If the true parameter value

is small enough relative to the error in estimation, then the restricted model will tend to produce better predictions.

5.3 THE AIC

The practical difficulty with using predictive power as a criterion for model selection is to find data that can be used to assess the predictions. One possibility is to randomly divide the observed data into two groups, one of which is used for estimation and the other for evaluation of the estimated models. The parameter values estimated from the first group could be used to produce predictions for the second group, and the best model would be the one that had the smallest error of predictions. However, although the idea is appealing in principle, there are several problems in putting it into practice. First, it is necessary to decide how large each group should be; as Savage (Savage et al., 1962, p. 34) observed, "There seems to be little cogent advice as to what fraction of the data should be used for explanation and what fraction for confirmation." Second, the estimates and the predictive performance will differ depending on the random division into subsamples, so two investigators who began with the same data and considered the same models could come to different conclusions.

The idea of the AIC is to estimate the expected performance of predictions from the model, estimated by using the observed data in a *hypothetical* sample generated by the same model.[2] Suppose that we fit a model including one parameter θ and obtain a deviance of D_1. How well would a model using the estimated parameter values from this sample be expected to fit in another sample of the same size from the same population? To simplify calculations, we can assume that the standard error of θ is 1.0. Then the estimate of θ in any sample can be thought of as $\theta + u$; $u \sim N(0, 1)$. The expected loss of fit when the estimate from the observed sample is used to predict outcomes in a second sample from the same population will depend on the squared difference between the estimates of θ in the two samples:

$$E[(u_1 - u_2)^2] = E[(u_1)^2] + E[(u_1 u_2)] + E[(u_2)^2]$$

---

[2]Or a hypothetical sample from the same population.

The cross-product term is zero, since the two samples are independent, so the expected increase in deviance when the sample estimate of a parameter is used for prediction follows a chi-square distribution with 2 degrees of freedom. The expected value of a random variable from this distribution is 2, producing:

$$D + 2p \qquad (5.1)$$

This is an estimate of how well the model estimated from the observed data would fit additional data from the same population. Akaike (1974/1998) proposed using Equation 5.1 as a criterion for model selection. The AIC has several attractive features. First, by seeking a good approximation rather than the true model, it seems to bypass the theoretical issues involved in the Bayesian and classical hypothesis testing. Second, as discussed in Section 3.5.1, a test of the hypothesis $\theta = 0$ against $\theta \neq 0$ can yield a correct but misleading result: $\hat{\theta}$ may have the wrong sign or be much larger than the actual value of θ. Because the AIC is intended to minimize the distance between the estimate and the true value, it automatically takes account of these problems. Third, it eliminates the arbitrary or subjective element in deciding on a standard for including an additional parameter. Classical hypothesis tests require the choice of an α level, and Bayesian tests require the choice of a prior distribution to represent the alternative hypotheses. The penalty of 2 in the AIC, in contrast, follows from the principle of minimizing the expected prediction error, and in this sense is objective.

5.3.1 The AIC in Small Samples

The derivation of the AIC described above is based on asymptotic properties. Hurvich and Tsai (1989) proposed an adjusted version of the AIC for use in small samples: $D + 2(p + 1)\dfrac{N}{N - p - 1}$. The adjusted criterion, known as the AIC_c, imposes a larger penalty on additional parameters when N is small relative to the number of parameters, and it converges to the standard penalty of 2 as N increases. Several simulation studies have found that the AIC_c performs substantially better than the standard AIC when p is large relative to N (Hurvich, 1997; Burnham and Anderson, 2004, pp. 261–304).

5.3.2 The AIC and Related Criteria for Regression Models

In a regression with normally distributed errors, the deviance is $N \log(\sigma^2) + \frac{RSS}{\sigma^2}$, where RSS is the residual sum of squares and σ^2 is the error variance. The error variance σ^2 is unknown, so different estimates produce different values for the deviance. When the AIC is applied to regression models, the maximum-likelihood estimate RSS/N is usually used, so the deviance for Model k becomes $N \log(RSS_k) - N \log(N) + N$. The last two terms are constant across models, so they can be omittted, and the AIC is $N \log(RSS_k) + 2p$, where RSS_k is the residual sum of squares from Model k.

This approach means that the estimate of σ^2 differs among models. An alternative is to take a single estimate of the value of σ^2 and apply it to all models. Then $N \log(\sigma^2)$ becomes a constant, so the differences among models involve the values of RSS.

The C_p statistic (Mallows, 1973) is intended for the selection of a subset of m potential regressors. It is defined as $RSS + 2p\hat{\sigma}_m^2$, where $\hat{\sigma}_m^2$ is the mean square error from the regression including all potential regressors. This is equivalent to

$$\hat{\sigma}_m^2 \left(\frac{RSS}{\hat{\sigma}_m^2} + 2p \right)$$

The term in parentheses is equivalent to the AIC with $\hat{\sigma}_m^2$ as the estimate of the error variance. In effect, the C_p statistic takes the model including all of the independent variables as the standard, and asks if any of the smaller models provide a good approximation to that model.

In a comparison of two models, the assumption that the smaller model is true produces the following criterion (Amemiya, 1980): $RSS \frac{(N+p+1)}{(N-p-1)}$. Tukey (comment on Anscombe, 1967; see also Hocking, 1976) proposed another criterion: $\frac{RSS}{(N-p-1)(N-p-2)}$. Finally, the AIC_c can be applied to regression models by using the formula $N \log(RSS) + 2 \frac{(p+1)N}{N-p-1}$. As the number of observations goes to infinity, all of these criteria converge to a break-even value of 2 for the F-statistic involving the parameter restrictions. However, when the number of parameters is large relative to the sample size, the break-even value is greater than 2, meaning that the alternative criteria are more favorable to the null hypothesis than the standard AIC.

5.4 CONSISTENCY AND EFFICIENCY

The standard errors of parameter estimates go toward zero as the sample increases. As a result, if $\theta \neq 0$, the AIC is certain to favor the model including that parameter as the sample goes to infinity. If $\theta = 0$ there is about a 15% chance that the AIC will favor the model including the parameter, and this chance will remain the same regardless of sample size. Therefore, the AIC is not "consistent"—the probability of choosing the correct model does not approach 1 as the sample size increases. As a result, in a sufficiently large sample the AIC will favor models including too many parameters: the model with the lowest AIC will be sure to include all of the nonzero parameters but will also include some unnecessary ones. This is true of any rule that uses a fixed criterion, such as the conventional .05 significance level, but since the AIC sets a low standard for the inclusion of parameters, it will include a relatively large number of superfluous parameters.

Shibata (1980), however, shows that the AIC has a property that he calls "efficiency." If the true model has an infinite number of parameters, then in a sufficiently large sample the model chosen by the AIC will have smaller expected prediction error than any alternative model. Saying that the true model has an infinite number of parameters amounts to saying that all models that we might actually consider are merely approximations to the true model. This is a popular point of view among data analysts, exemplified by Box's (1979) widely quoted remark that "all models are false, but some are useful." Shibata's result might be described as showing that in a sufficiently large sample the AIC will pick the best approximate model, understood as the model with the greatest predictive power.

The relative appeal of these two principles depends on one's goals. With efficiency, it is to choose the model that gives the better approximation to θ. The parameter estimate that corresponds to a given t-ratio becomes smaller as the sample becomes larger, so in a very large sample the superfluous parameter estimates included as a result of using the AIC will almost certainly be small. Therefore, they will not do much harm to the predictions: the model chosen by the AIC will predict almost as well as the true model. With consistency, the problem is to make a correct choice between $\theta = 0$ and $\theta \neq 0$. From this point of view, there is no distinction among different nonzero values

of θ. Even if the estimate of a superfluous parameter is close to zero, including it is still an incorrect decision.

However, both consistency and efficiency are asymptotic properties. From a practical point of view, what matters is not asymptotic behavior but performance in a given finite sample. The probability that a given criterion will make the "best" choice, whether that is defined in terms of approximation or selection of the correct hypothesis, depends on the actual values of the parameters, which by definition are unknown. In a given sample, even a large one, there is no guarantee that the AIC will pick the model that gives the best predictions.

5.5 CROSS-VALIDATION AND THE AIC

The rationale for the AIC is based on predictive performance in *hypothetical* samples from the same population. "Cross-validation" (Stone, 1977) seeks to obtain an empirical estimate of predictive performance by considering all possible subsamples of the observed sample. The simplest form of cross-validation leaves out samples of size 1, so there are N subsamples, each predicting a single case using the estimates from the rest of the sample. Minimizing the error from "leave-one-out" cross-validation has an intuitive appeal as a principle of model selection, because the parameter estimates are based on almost all of the available data. Stone (1977) showed that choosing the model with the lowest AIC is asymptotically equivalent to choosing the model with the best performance in leave-one-out cross validation. This result holds regardless of the true parameter values. That is, if the sample value of a parameter is more than $\sqrt{2}$ times its standard deviation, then cross-validation in that sample will favor the alternative model, even if the population value of the parameter is zero.

Generalized cross-validation omits subsets of d cases and uses the remaining ones to produce predictions. As the ratio of d/N increases, cross-validation becomes closer to out-of-sample prediction: any given case will appear in the predictive samples more often than it appears in the estimation samples. Shao (1997) shows that, if d/N goes to zero as N goes to infinity, minimizing the prediction errors in cross-validation is equivalent to minimizing the AIC. If d/N approaches 1, then minimizing the prediction errors

is equivalent to using a criterion with a penalty that increases with sample size. Finally, if d/N converges to some value between zero and 1, minimizing the prediction errors is equivalent to using a constant penalty that is greater than 2.0.

Shao's analysis is based on asymptotics and does not show which criterion will yield the best predictions for a given sample and population size, but it shows that the penalty of 2 in the AIC is not arbitrary. Among fixed penalties the value of 2 has a special place: it is the smallest possible value and follows from any fixed choice of d.

5.6   A CLASSICAL PERSPECTIVE ON THE AIC

From a classical perspective, we can consider the probability that the AIC will yield the correct decision, given different values of θ. In terms of the purposes of the AIC, a correct decision means choosing the model that provides the better approximation to θ. For example, if θ is 0.5, then $|\hat{\theta} - \theta| < 0.5$ whenever $\hat{\theta}$ is between zero and 1. That is, the unrestricted model gives the better approximation to the true parameter value if $\hat{\theta}$ is between zero and 1, while the restricted model provides a better approximation if $\hat{\theta}$ is less than zero or greater than 1. The probability that the unrestricted model will give a better approximation can be calculated from a normal distribution with mean θ. Figure 5.1 shows the probability that the $\hat{\theta}$ will be a better approximation to the true value and the probability that the AIC will choose the unrestricted model at various values of θ: for convenience, the standard error of the parameter is assumed to be 1.

When θ is small, the estimate from the unrestricted model will rarely provide a better approximation to the true value of θ, even though the alternative hypothesis $\theta \neq 0$ is true. The AIC will favor the unrestricted model too often; moreover, the cases in which it does so will not be those in which $\hat{\theta}$ is close to the actual value of θ, but those in which it is much larger than that value. For example, if $\theta = 0.1$, then about 8% of the values of $\hat{\theta}$ will be in the range $(0, 0.2)$. For values in this range, the AIC will favor the restricted model: it will favor the alternative model if $\hat{\theta} > 1.41$, in about 9% of the cases, or $\hat{\theta} < -1.41$, about 7%.

When θ is large, however, the AIC will not favor the unrestricted model

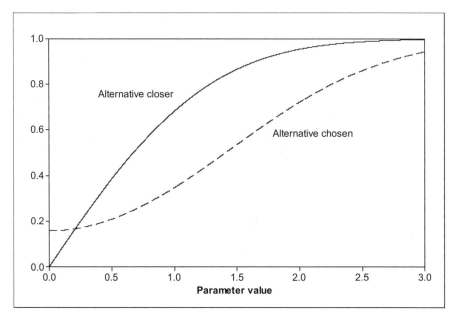

FIGURE 5.1. Example of performance of the AIC.

as often as it should. For example, if $\theta = 3$, $\hat{\theta}$ will almost always be in the range $(0, 6)$, making it a better approximation than the value of zero proposed by the restricted model. Nevertheless, the AIC still has about a 6% chance of favoring the restricted model.

These observations are not meant as a criticism of the AIC: no reasonable model selection criterion would choose the unrestricted model if the estimate of the additional parameter had a t-ratio like 0.2. The point is that from a classical perspective it is not possible to make a general statement about the probability that the AIC will choose the model that provides the better approximation. Conclusions on this point must be based on some assumptions about the possible values of θ. This idea is not easily accommodated within the framework of classical hypothesis testing, but it fits naturally into a Bayesian point of view.

5.7 A BAYESIAN PERSPECTIVE ON THE AIC

As discussed in Chapter 4, differences in the BIC between models are equivalent to one-half the logarithm of a Bayes factor, giving the weight of evidence

in favor of one model over the other. More generally, it is possible to think of any criterion of the form of $D + pf(N)$ in terms of Bayes factors. With reasonably diffuse prior distributions, the resulting Bayes factors will be constant multiples of one another, so their logarithms will differ by a constant. The standard BIC can therefore be thought of as a member of a family of criteria of the form $D + p(\log(N) + c)$. Although these different statistics would yield different conclusions about the choice between particular models, all have a penalty that increases with the log of the sample size.

In order to produce a constant penalty like that used in the AIC, it is necessary to assume that the prior distribution changes with the sample size (Akaike, 1987/1998). More specifically, as the sample increases, the prior distribution must become more favorable to the alternative hypothesis: that is, more concentrated around zero. This may seem like a peculiar assumption, but one can argue that there will generally be a relationship between the extent of prior knowledge and the amount of data collected. When little is known, a small sample will be enough to provide new information about the general contours of the data. It is only when investigators are interested in precise estimates or fine distinctions among models that they will need to collect large amounts of data. If researchers are using data collected by others or given by "nature," the questions they study may adapt to the data: only if a large amount of data are available will researchers be able to move from basic issues to subtle points.

The standard BIC follows from the prior distribution, with the mean equal to the parameter estimate and the standard deviation equal to $\sigma(\theta)\sqrt{N}$, which is equivalent to a single representative observation.[3] If the prior distribution is equivalent to a small fraction b of the sample, then the penalty is $-\log(b)$: the BIC follows from assuming that $b = 1/N$. A prior distribution that is equivalent to a fixed *proportion* of the sample will produce a criterion of the form $D + cp$ (O'Hagan, 1995). A penalty of 2 corresponds to a fraction of about 1/7.4, or about 13.5% of the sample observations.

An advantage of the Bayesian interpretation of the AIC is that it can be used to provide a weight of evidence in favor of different models, which is not possible under the standard predictive rationale. The odds in favor of the

---

[3]If multiple parameters are involved, the covariance matrix for the prior distribution is NI^{-1}, where I is the Fisher information matrix.

model with the smaller AIC are $e^{d/2}$ where d is the difference in the values of the AIC. If more than two models are considered, the odds can be used to produce a complete set of posterior probabilities, or what Burnham and Anderson (2002, p. 75) call "Akaike weights."[4] The relationship between the t-ratio and the odds implied by the AIC is shown in Figure 5.2. Although the odds can favor the null hypothesis, they can never do so very strongly, and t-ratios between about zero and 2 might reasonably be described as inconclusive.

Although the general idea that prior knowledge is usually equivalent to a small but not negligible fraction of the sample is defensible, the precise value is clearly arbitrary. A fraction of 1/20 (.05) implies a penalty of about 3, and a fraction of 1/50 (.02) implies a penalty of a little less than 4. Aitkin (1991) considers the possibility that the prior distribution is equal to the entire sample: that is, the mean is equal to the parameter estimates, and the covariance is equal to the covariance of the parameter estimates. This results in a penalty of log(2), or about .69, setting a lower standard for including new parameters than any other criterion.

A general objection to all of these criteria is that the fraction representing "prior" information is used twice, first to obtain the prior distribution and again for testing. A way to deal with this issue is to set aside a fraction of the data as a "training sample," which is used to obtain a prior distribution but not for hypothesis testing. Because different training samples will yield different distributions, O'Hagan (1995) suggests considering the expected value of all possible divisions of the chosen size. This yields a "fractional Bayes factor" corresponding to the criterion

$$(1 - b)D - p\frac{\log(b)}{1 - b} \qquad (5.2)$$

If the training sample is a single case, the fractional Bayes factor is approximately equal to the standard BIC. The break-even value of the t-statistic is

---

[4]Burnham and Anderson (2004) propose an alternative way to derive the Akaike weights: a combination of the Bayes factor implied by the BIC and the prior odds of the models. If the prior odds favor larger models and do so more strongly as the sample size increases, then it is possible to obtain the same posterior probabilities as those produced by equal prior odds and the fractional prior. However, although Burnham and Anderson offer an argument for the general principle of prior odds' favoring larger models more strongly as the sample increases, they do not make a case for the particular values required to produce the Akaike weights.

2 when the fraction of the training sample (*b*) equals approximately 0.2, and declines toward 1 as *b* approaches 1. The odds implied by the fractional Bayes factor are scaled down to omit the fraction corresponding to the training sample. When *b* = 0.2, the ranking of models will be exactly the same as that obtained from the AIC, but the odds in favor of the preferred model will be only about 0.8 times as large as the odds from the "Akaike weights."

5.8   A GENERAL CLASS OF MODEL SELECTION CRITERIA

The AIC and BIC both have the form $D + p f(N)$, where $f(N)$ is a nondecreasing function of sample size. Although criteria with a fixed penalty are not consistent, $\log(N)$ is not the only function that produces consistency. Hannan and Quinn (1979) showed that the most slowly increasing function that would produce consistency is $c \log(\log(N))$, where c is a positive constant. Although their work was primarily intended as a theoretical contribution, a criterion of

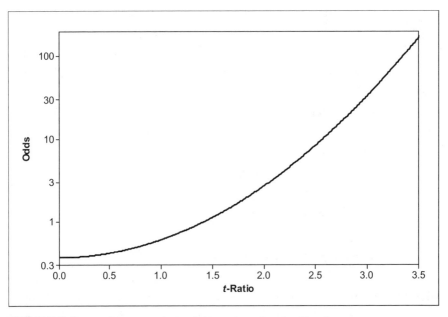

FIGURE 5.2. Odds against the null hypothesis implied by the AIC.

$D + 2p \log(\log(N))$ is sometimes used for model selection.[5] The penalty function $\log(\log(N))$ also increases with sample size, but more slowly than $\log(N)$. In the range of sample sizes typically found in cross-sectional data, the Hannan–Quinn criterion implies only small adjustments for sample size. For example, the values for samples of 50, 500, 5,000, and 50,000 are 2.73, 3.62, 4.28, and 4.76, respectively, which correspond to p-values of .099, .056, .038, and .029.

A criterion in which the penalty increases in proportion to N is not consistent, because the probability of rejecting a false null hypothesis will not increase with sample size. However, any function that increases at a rate betweeen $\log(\log(N))$ and N will produce a consistent criterion. A simple possibility is a penalty of the form $k \log(N)$, where $0 < k \leq 1$. Penalties of this form amount to thinking of the prior distribution as equivalent to N^{1-k} cases. For example, assuming that the prior knowledge is equivalent to the information in $\sqrt{N}$ representative cases produces a penalty of $\log(N)/2$. O'Hagan (1995) suggests that criteria of this form are more robust to misspecification than Bayes factors based on prior distributions representing a constant number of cases.

Kadane and Lazar (2004, p. 283) discuss criteria of the form $D + pf(N)$ and conclude that the choice of penalty "is not a technical matter within the theory, but rather a fundamental issue of the values the statistician-scientist brings to the problem," because there is a "trade-off between parsimony and accuracy (in a specific sense)." The trade-off exists because the inclusion of small effects increases the accuracy of predictions but makes the model less parsimonious. In general terms, the AIC emphasizes the accuracy of predictions, while the BIC emphasizes parsimony. Criteria like those proposed by O'Hagan (1995) and Hannan and Quinn (1979) can be thought of as compromises. There can be no general rule for striking the optimal balance between these goals: the best choice will differ, depending on prior information and the purposes of the investigation.

5.9 SUMMARY AND CONCLUSIONS

After its introduction in the early 1970s, the AIC immediately became popular among scientists and engineers, but it was slow to attract the attention of

---

[5]The choice of $c = 2$ appears to be intended to make the penalty roughly equivalent to the AIC in small samples.

statisticians (Findley and Parzen, 1995/1998). The neglect may have occurred because the AIC did not fit easily into either the frameworks of classical or Bayesian statistics. It did not purport to select the true model, and the sense in which the model chosen by the AIC would provide the "best approxima-tion" was difficult to define. However, the figure of 2 for the penalty can be justified as an estimate of fit in a hypothetical sample or by cross-validation. The AIC can also be regarded as a Bayes factor that results from a prior dis-tribution that is equivalent to a fixed proportion of the sample. There is a case for assuming that the information in the prior generally increases with sample size. Although there is no compelling reason for the particular frac-tion that corresponds to the AIC, the most favorable Bayes factors shown in Table 4.5 suggest that a t-ratio of about $\sqrt{2}$ can be regarded as approximately neutral—providing no evidence either way. As a result, the principle of most favorable Bayes factors justifies a break-even point in the vicinity of the one implied by the AIC.

Compared to classical hypothesis tests, the AIC has the advantage of pro-viding a complete ranking of models. It provides at least a rough sense—and if the "Akaike weights" are used, an exact measure—of the degree of preference. The logic behind the AIC is based on the assumption that the true model may be enormously complex, involving many small parameters, so that rigorously distinguishing between zero and nonzero parameters is of secondary impor-tance: what is needed is just a reasonable approximation. Although there is no guarantee that the AIC will select the model that gives the *best* predictions, the low standard makes it well suited to cases in which we expect many small effects and do not regard Type I errors as very damaging.

Putting these points together, the AIC seems most useful for decisions about control variables. For this purpose, it is generally better to err on the side of including too many variables rather than too few. Mistakenly omit-ting controls creates a risk of bias in estimating the parameters of interest, while including unnecessary ones only reduces the efficiency of estimation. It could be objected that bias is no more important than efficiency—what matters is just the total difference between $\hat{\theta}$ and θ. However, if the sign of θ is of interest, bias is particularly damaging, since it can create a systematic tendency toward "Type S" error. The AIC may also be useful in deciding on primary or secondary structure, but for these purposes there is often a strong preference for simplicity, which would justify a larger penalty.

RECOMMENDED READING

Akaike, H. (1985/1998). Prediction and entropy. In E. Parzen, K. Tanabe, & G. Kitagawa (Eds.), *Selected papers of Hirotugu Akaike* (pp. 387–410). New York: Springer. (First published in Atkinson, A. C., & Fienberg, S. E. (Eds.), *A celebration of statistics* (pp. 1–24). New York: Springer. —A general discussion of the AIC and its connections to other model selection criteria.

Anderson, D. A. (2008). *Model based inference in the life sciences.* New York: Springer. Advocates model selection using the AIC. —Less technical than Burnham and Anderson.

Burnham, K. P., & Anderson, D. R. (2002). *Model selection and multimodel inference* (2nd ed.). New York: Springer. —A comprehensive treatise on model selection using the AIC.

Findley, D. F., & Parzen, E. (1995/1998). A conversation with Hirotugu Akaike. In E. Parzen, K. Tanabe, & G. Kitagawa (Eds.), *Selected papers of Hirotugu Akaike.* New York: Springer. (First published in *Statistical Science, 10,* 104–117.) —Describes the purpose, background, and reception of the AIC.

Kuha, J. (2004). AIC and BIC: Comparisons of assumptions and performance. *Sociological Methods and Research, 33,* 188–229. —A short and relatively accessible account of the rationale of the AIC.

O'Hagan, A. (1995). Fractional Bayes factors for model comparisons. *Journal of the Royal Statistical Society, Series B, 53,* 99–138. —Discusses the idea of taking a fraction of the data to produce a prior distribution, which is important for understanding the Bayesian interpretation of the AIC.

6

Three-Way Decisions

The chapter begins by discussing the difference between substantive and statistical hypotheses. The standard alternative hypothesis, $\theta \neq 0$, does not involve sign. Substantive hypotheses, however, almost always involve sign, suggesting that hypothesis testing should be regarded a three-way choice among $\theta < 0$, $\theta = 0$, and $\theta > 0$. The analysis of three-way choices is difficult in the classical approach but straightforward when using Bayes factors. This chapter examines limits on Bayes factors for three-way choices and shows that Bayes factors give stronger evidence in favor of the appropriately signed alternative than in the choice between $\theta = 0$ and $\theta \neq 0$.

6.1 SUBSTANTIVE AND STATISTICAL HYPOTHESES

Until this point, this book has had little to say about a fundamental question, namely, What hypothesis should be tested? Ideally, the statistical hypothesis should match the substantive hypothesis. As noted in Chapter 2, few theories in the social sciences predict the exact value of a parameter: in most cases, they predict that a parameter will *not* be zero. When testing $\theta = 0$ against the alternative $\theta \neq 0$, the proposition implied by theory is represented by the alternative hypothesis, and the null hypothesis merely represents a skeptic who needs to be convinced—some accounts say a straw man.

However, theories almost always do more than say that a parameter is not zero: they assert that it has a particular sign. Sometimes two different

123

theoretical accounts are presented, one predicting a positive sign, the other a negative sign. However, even if only one theory is offered, an investigator would not normally regard parameter values of zero and the "wrong" sign as equivalent outcomes. A parameter value of zero would simply be regarded as lack of support for the theory, but evidence that it had the wrong sign would be a finding calling out for some explanation. Therefore, with a parameter of theoretical interest, the usual situation is a three-way choice between $\theta < 0$, $\theta = 0$, and $\theta > 0$. This situation raises the question of why hypothesis tests routinely involve the two-way choice between $\theta = 0$ and $\theta \neq 0$, in which *neither* statistical hypothesis represents the hypothesis actually proposed by the investigator. The traditional form is often appropriate for specification tests: for example, testing whether the variance differs in two groups. In such cases, there is no substantive hypothesis being tested; we merely want to know if there is evidence of any difference.

Part of the answer is simply tradition. R. A. Fisher, who popularized the use of significance tests, usually used two-tailed tests, and most early researchers followed him. Once two-tailed tests had come to be the norm, the use of one-tailed tests could be seen as an attempt to get around the accepted standards of evidence (Bross, 1971). Moreover, the critical value for a one-tailed test with significance level of α is the same as the appropriately signed critical value for a two-tailed test with a significance level of 2α. Kaiser (1960) noted the logical problem in drawing conclusions about the sign from a test of the hypothesis that $\theta \neq 0$ and proposed choosing among $\theta < 0$, $\theta = 0$, and $\theta > 0$ by means of two one-tailed tests. However, this would amount to no more than giving a different description of the conclusions: for example, a result would be described as significant at the 2.5% level using a one-tailed test rather than significant at the 5% level using a two-tailed test. The gain from adopting a new description—even a more accurate one—seems small relative to the disruption involved in changing an established tradition.

Another part of the answer is that in the classical approach going from a two-way to a three-way choice makes analysis much more difficult. In terms of the classical approach, a three-way choice can be regarded as a pair of tests:

$$H01: \theta \leq 0 \text{ vs. } HA1: \theta > 0$$

$$H02: \theta \geq 0 \text{ vs. } HA2: \theta < 0$$

with the restriction that H01 and H02 cannot both be false. Given this formulation, an important question is whether or not the zone of rejection should be divided equally between the two tails. The widely accepted principle of minimizing "loss" suggests that the division should depend on judgments about the relative importance of different types of errors (Lehmann, 1957, p. 6). For example, if accepting H01 when HA1 is true is regarded as worse than accepting H01 when HA2 is true, the α level in the second test should be larger. However, Shaffer (2006, p. 19) argues that another widely accepted principle provides "a rationale for using equal-tails tests in asymmetric situations." The details of the argument do not need to be considered here; the point is that, in the classical approach there is room for divergence of opinion on even this very basic issue (see also Wald, 1942, pp. 8–9).

With the Bayesian approach, in contrast, analysis of choices among any number of alternatives is straightforward: one simply specifies a distribution representing each one and then calculates a Bayes factor for every pair of alternatives. The prior probabilities for each alternative can be combined with the Bayes factors to produce posterior probabilities. However, Bayesians have also focused their attention on tests involving $\theta = 0$ and $\theta \neq 0$. Presumably this simply reflects the strength of tradition—these are the hypotheses that are discussed in classical statistical theory and used in empirical research. Although the situation is understandable, it is unfortunate, since it means that a gap remains between substantive and statistical hypotheses. Therefore, this chapter will consider Bayes factors for three-way choices among $\theta < 0$, $\theta = 0$, and $\theta > 0$.

6.2   BAYES FACTORS FOR DIRECTIONAL HYPOTHESES

The three-way decision problem is composed of a point hypothesis, $\theta = 0$, and two "directional hypotheses," $\theta < 0$ and $\theta > 0$. These hypotheses may be called H0, H−, and H+. There will be three different Bayes factors, but given any two, the third is simply their ratio. For example, if $K_{+-} = 10$ and $K_{+0} = 2$, then $K_{0-} = 5$.[1]

---

[1]Positive values indicate support for the first hypothesis indicated in the subscript. In this example, the odds in favor of a positive rather than a negative sign are 10:1, the odds in favor of a positive sign rather than zero are 2:1, and the odds in favor of zero rather than a negative sign are 5:1.

As discussed in Section 2.3.2, many point hypotheses seem unreasonable in principle. Some observers hold that a point hypothesis is *always* false when taken literally: for example, Tukey (1991, p. 100), in the context of testing for differences between groups, asserted that "A and B are always different—in some decimal place—for any A and B. Thus asking 'Are the effects different?' is foolish. What we should be answering first is . . . can we be confident about the direction from A to B? Is it 'up,' 'down,' or 'uncertain'?" Therefore, we will begin by leaving the point hypothesis aside and considering the Bayes factor for the directional hypotheses $\theta < 0$ and $\theta > 0$.

Unless there is some special reason to the contrary, it seems clear that the distributions for $H+$ and $H-$ should be mirror images of each other: $f(\theta|H+) = f(-\theta|H-)$. This can be accomplished by beginning with any symmetrical distribution centered at zero and making the prior distributions for $H+$ and $H-$ proportional to the relevant part of the original range. Previous discussions of Bayes factors have focused on unimodal priors; there is no compelling reason to prefer one distribution over another, so several standard ones will be considered. Once a distribution is selected, the remaining issue is to decide on the dispersion. Figure 6.1 shows the relationship between the dispersion of a normal prior distribution and the Bayes factor for the two directional hypotheses, assuming an estimate of +1.96 and a standard error of 1.0—that is, a positive estimate that is just significant at the 5% level using a two-tailed test.[2] The Bayes factor increases monotonically, approaching a limit of 39 as the dispersion goes to infinity.

The upper limit to the Bayes factor can be understood by recalling the discussion of Bayesian estimation in Section 4.2. Given a diffuse prior distribution, the posterior distribution of θ is proportional to the likelihood function. A t-ratio of 1.96 means that 95% of the posterior probability will be in the range $0 < \theta < 1.96$, 2.5% will be in the range $\theta < 0$, and 2.5% will be in the range $\theta > 1.96$. Therefore, the probability that $\theta > 0$ is .975, and the probability that $\theta < 0$ is .025, resulting in a Bayes factor of $(.975)/(.025) = 39$. More generally, the limit on the Bayes factor for directional hypotheses will be $(1 - p/2)/(p/2)$, where p is the usual p-value (Casella and Berger, 1987).

Thus, with directional hypotheses there is no conflict between classical tests and Bayes factors from diffuse prior distributions. Results that are "sta-

---

[2]The standard deviation refers to the underlying normal distribution. The hypotheses $H-$ and $H+$ are each half-normal distributions.

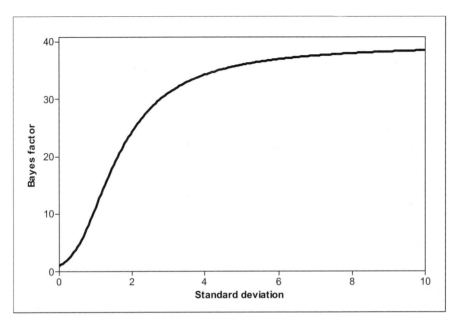

FIGURE 6.1. Influence of the prior distribution on the Bayes factor for sign.

tistically significant" by conventional standards correspond to Bayes factors giving strong evidence about the sign of the parameter. In fact, the conventional standards might be regarded as too conservative, since even a *p*-value of .18 would give a Bayes factor of about 10:1 concerning the sign.

The strength of evidence suggested by the Bayes factor becomes weaker as the dispersion becomes smaller, approaching 1.0 as the dispersion goes to zero. Therefore, it is necessary to decide the best general choice for a prior distribution. A case could be made for a highly dispersed distribution on the grounds that it represents neutrality: within a wide range, all values have approximately the same prior probability. However, as discussed in Section 4.3, no distribution is truly neutral when calculating a Bayes factor. A large dispersion implies that the expected value of θ is large: for example, a standard deviation of 10 implies that the expected value of θ is about 8 under $H+$ (and -8 under $H-$).[3] This does not seem to correspond well to actual research situations: in most cases, a *t*-ratio of 8 for a parameter of theoretical interest would be surprisingly large. Conversely, a small dispersion means a high

---

[3]The mean of a half-normal distribution is $\sigma\sqrt{2}/\sqrt{\pi}$.

degree of confidence that the true value of θ is close to zero. For example, a standard deviation of 0.25 means that under $H+$, the expected value of θ is about 0.2, and if $\theta = 0.2$, then the probability that $\hat{\theta}$ will be greater than or equal to 1.96 is only about .04. That is, it would represent a severely "underpowered" analysis in which a statistically significant result is unlikely under either hypothesis. This is also an unusual situation in research—at least, one would hope so. For normal distributions with standard deviations of 1, 2, and 3, a t-ratio of 1.96 gives Bayes factors of about 11, 24, and 31, respectively. That is, for moderate values of dispersion, a t-ratio of 1.96 provides what could reasonably be called strong evidence about the sign.

The same general pattern is found with any symmetric unimodal distribution. The Bayes factor increases with the dispersion of the prior and approaches a limit of $(1 - [P/2])/(P/2)$. When the expected value of the t-statistic is in the range of about 1.5 to 3, a t-ratio of about 2 gives strong evidence about the sign. For example, if we begin with a logistic distribution with standard deviation 1 (the expected value under $H+$ is 1.39), a t-ratio of 1.96 gives a Bayes factor of 19.3 in favor of $H+$ against $H-$. If $H+$ is represented by a uniform distribution from 0 to 3 (the expected value under $H+$ is 1.5), a t-ratio of 1.96 gives a Bayes factor of 33.5 in favor of $H+$ against $H-$.

6.2.1 Sample Size

For directional hypotheses, the relationship between sample size and the Bayes factor is straightforward. The Bayes factor will obviously favor $H+$ if $\hat{\theta}$ is positive and $H-$ if $\hat{\theta}$ is negative, and the magnitude of the Bayes factor will increase with the absolute value of the t-statistic. In a minimal sample, the Bayes factor in favor of the correct hypothesis will be 1:1—that is, no evidence in either direction. The expected value of the t-ratio will increase with the sample size, so the Bayes factor in favor of the correct hypothesis will go to infinity as the sample goes to infinity. That is, the more evidence, the greater the chance that the Bayes factor will favor the correct hypothesis.[4] This is in contrast to the situation with a point null hypothesis and a two-sided alternative, where, up to a certain point, increases in sample size can increase the chance of favoring a false null hypothesis.

---

[4]If the true parameter is exactly zero—that is, neither directional hypothesis is true—the probabilities of favoring $H+$ and $H-$ will both be .5 at all sample sizes.

6.3 BAYES FACTORS FOR THREE-WAY DECISIONS

The Bayes factor for $H+$ against $H-$ is not affected by the inclusion of a third option. Therefore, this section will focus on the choice between $H0$ and the directional hypotheses. The discussion will assume that the parameter estimate is positive but that it could be applied to a negative estimate simply by reversing the roles of $H+$ and $H-$. Figure 6.2 shows the relationship between the dispersion of the prior distribution and the Bayes factors K_{+0} and K_{-0}, assuming that $\hat{\theta} = 1.96$ with a standard error of 1.0. The hypotheses $H-$ and $H+$ are represented by half-normal distributions; the figures on the horizontal axis represent the standard deviation of the underlying normal distribution. As the standard deviation approaches zero, K_{+0} and K_{-0} both approach 1. As the standard deviation increases, K_{+0} initially increases, reaching a maximum when the standard deviation is about 1.8, and then declines toward zero. In contrast, K_{-0} steadily declines toward zero as the standard deviation increases.

The relationship between the standard deviation and K_{-0} can be under-

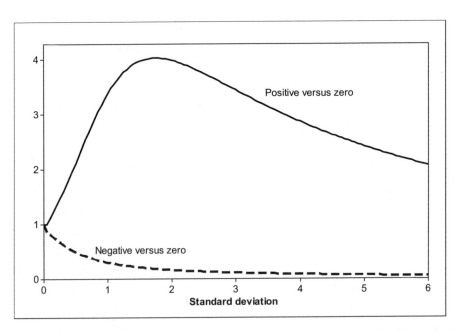

FIGURE 6.2. Influence of the prior distribution on Bayes factors for directional versus null hypotheses.

stood by remembering that $p(x|H-)$ is a weighted average of likelihoods at different values of θ. When the standard deviation of the prior distribution is small, most of the weight is given to values only slightly less than zero, so the likelihood of $H-$ is only slightly smaller than the likelihood of $H0$: in effect, we are choosing between the hypotheses that $\theta = 0$ and θ is slightly smaller than zero. As the standard deviation increases, more of the weight is at parameter values far below zero, where (since the likelihood is small) the likelihood $p(x|H-)$ falls.

The relationship between the standard deviation of the prior distribution and K_{+0} is more complicated because the likelihood $p(x|H1)$ is larger than $p(x|H0)$ at some positive values of $\theta = 0$ and smaller at others. As a result, $p(x|H+)$ may be larger or smaller than $p(x|H0)$, depending on the relative weight given to different values of x in $H+$. When the standard deviation of the prior distribution is near zero, all of the weight is at values of θ for which the likelihood is only slightly greater than the likelihood at $\theta = 0$. As the standard deviation increases, more of the weight will be at values close to the maximum likelihood estimate $\hat{\theta}$, so the Bayes factor will favor $H+$. However, as the standard deviation continues to increase, the weight shifts to values much greater than $\hat{\theta}$, and the Bayes factor becomes more favorable to $H0$. When the standard deviation is very large, almost all of the weight is given to values much greater than $\hat{\theta}$: in effect, we are comparing the hypothesis $\theta = 0$ to the hypothesis that θ is *far greater* than zero. The general pattern is the same as for the Bayes factor of $\theta \neq 0$ against $\theta = 0$, discussed in Chapter 4: there is no upper limit to the possible evidence in favor of $H0$, but there is a limit to the evidence in favor of the alternative hypothesis. Thus, Lindley's paradox—that any test statistic, no matter how large, can count as evidence in favor of the null hypothesis—is still present with a three-way hypothesis test.

Table 6.1 shows the maximum value of K_{+0} at different standard p-values for normal, logistic, and uniform distributions. These figures can be compared to those in Table 4.4, which showed the maximum odds in favor of the alternative hypothesis $\theta \neq 0$ versus $\theta = 0$, given those same distributions. The maximum odds in favor of $H+$ versus $H0$ are always higher than the maximum odds in favor of the hypothesis $\theta \neq 0$ against $\theta = 0$.[5] This occurs because

---

[5]The discussion assumes that the parameter estimate is positive. The Bayes factors involving $H+$ and $H-$ are symmetrical, so the same limits in favor of $H-$ apply if the parameter estimate is negative.

TABLE 6.1. Maximum Odds in Favor of a Directional Hypothesis against $\theta = 0$, Normal, Logistic, and Uniform Prior Distributions

p	t	Normal	Logistic	Uniform
.32	1.00	1.4	1.4	1.5
.15	1.44	2.0	2.0	2.3
.10	1.65	2.6	2.5	3.0
.05	1.96	4.0	3.8	4.7
.01	2.58	13.0	12.3	16.4
.003	2.97	33.5	31.5	43.8
.001	3.29	82.5	77.4	110.8

the hypothesis $\theta \neq 0$ is a combination of two parts: one in which the likelihood is higher than the likelihood of $H0$ and one in which the likelihood is lower. For larger t-ratios, the likelihood of $H-$ is near zero, so the maximum odds in favor of $H+$ are almost exactly twice as large as the maximum odds in favor of $\theta \neq 0$.

6.3.1 Posterior Probabilities in Three-Way Choices

Bayes factors can be used in conjunction with the prior probabilities of the hypotheses to obtain posterior odds. For example, suppose that the alternative hypothesis is represented by a normal distribution with a standard deviation of 3 and we observe a t-ratio of 1.96. The resulting Bayes factor for $\theta = 0$ against the two-sided alternative hypothesis $\theta \neq 0$ is 0.56. If we begin with prior odds of 1:1, the posterior odds in favor of $H0$ are 0.56:1, so the posterior probability of the null hypothesis is $0.56/(0.56+1) = .36$ and the posterior probability of the alternative is $1/(0.56 + 1) = .64$. For the three-way choice, $K + 0$ is 3.45 and $K - 0$ is 0.11. If the prior probabilities of $H+$, $H0$, and $H-$ are equal, the posterior probabilities are $3.45/(3.45+1+.11) = .77$ for $H+$, $1/(3.45 + 1 + .11) = .22$ for $H0$, and $.11/(3.45 + 1 + .11) = .02$ for $H-$.

The difference in the posterior probability of $H0$ could be regarded as a consequence of a difference in the prior probability, rather than the Bayes factors. A two-sided alternative hypothesis is the union of $H+$ and $H-$. If the prior probability of $H0$ is 0.5 and the prior probabilities of $H+$ and $H-$ are each 0.25, the posterior probability of $H0$ is then $0.5 \times 1/(.25 \times 3.45 + .5 \times 1 + .25 \times .11) = 0.36$—the same as that obtained from the Bayes factor for a two-sided alternative hypothesis—while the posterior probabilities of $H+$ and $H-$ are

.62 and .02. In either case, the two-way choice between $\theta = 0$ and $\theta \neq 0$ masks the difference between $H+$ and $H-$. More generally, this example shows that assuming equal prior probabilities implicitly makes the prior probabilities depend on the number of hypotheses considered. As a result, when considering more than two alternatives, it is not possible to ignore or set aside the prior probabilities (Lindley, 1997). This issue will receive more attention when model averaging is discussed in Chapter 7.

6.3.2 Sample Size and Bayes Factors for Three-Way Choices

The effect of sample size on Bayes factors for $\theta = 0$ versus $\theta \neq 0$ was discussed in Section 4.3, and the effect on Bayes factors for the directional hypotheses $\theta < 0$ versus $\theta > 0$ was discussed in Section 6.2. This section will consider the relationship between sample size and the Bayes factors for $\theta = 0$ versus the directional hypotheses $\theta < 0$ and $\theta > 0$. If $\theta = 0$, it is simple: the expected value of the Bayes factors K_{-0} and K_{+0} will go to zero—that is, give increasingly strong evidence in favor of $\theta = 0$—as the sample size increases.

If the true value of θ is greater than zero, all of the values in $\theta < 0$ are farther from the true parameter value than zero is, so the expected value of K_{-0} will always favor $H0$, and as the sample size increases the Bayes factor will favor $H0$ more strongly. The situation is more complicated with K_{+0}. Some of the values in $H+$ are closer to the true value of θ than zero is, while other values are farther. Specifically, all values in the range $0 < \theta < 2\theta$ are closer and therefore will have a higher likelihood than $p(x|H0)$, while values greater than 2θ will have a lower likelihood. Therefore, whether the Bayes factor K_{+0} will favor $H+$ or $H0$ depends on the distribution that represents $H+$. As seen in Figure 6.2, the key issue is the dispersion of the prior distribution: the Bayes factor will favor $H+$ if the dispersion is small relative to θ and will favor $H0$ if the dispersion is large. The relationship between sample size and the Bayes factor K_{+0} differs depending on the dispersion relative to the parameter value. If the dispersion is small, the K_{+0} will favor $H+$ at all sample sizes and will favor $H+$ more strongly as the sample increases. If it is large, the Bayes factor will show increasing odds in favor of the incorrect hypothesis $\theta = 0$ until a certain sample size before turning in favor of $H+$. Conversely, if $\hat{\theta}$ is positive but the Bayes factor favors $\theta = 0$ over $\theta > 0$, that means that the parameter estimate is smaller than expected, given the distribution representing $\theta > 0$.

6.3.3 Prior Distributions for Directional Hypotheses

Work on Bayes factors for two-sided alternatives has focused almost entirely on symmetric unimodal distributions, and this chapter has followed that tradition by defining H+ and H− as halves of a symmetric unimodal distribution. This restriction implies that small values of θ are more probable than large ones, with the most likely values being those that are just slightly greater or less than zero. However, most substantive hypotheses do not just suggest that a parameter will have a particular sign but also that it will have a "substantial" value. That is, some values of θ with the expected sign might be regarded as too small to give much support to the argument that motivated the hypothesis test.

This point suggests that H+ and H− should be represented by distributions with modes at some value other than zero. Many such distributions are possible, but the gamma distribution is a convenient choice because of its flexibility. The gamma distribution has two parameters, known as the "shape" and "scale" parameters. Figure 6.3 shows the density functions for gamma distributions with shape parameters of 2, 4, and 6; the scale param-

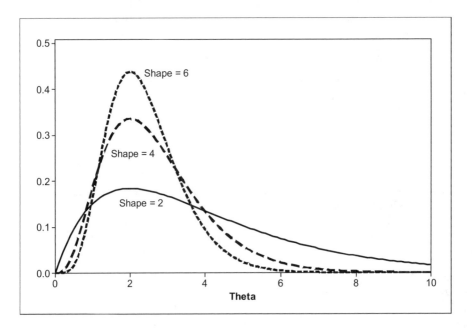

FIGURE 6.3. Examples of gamma distributions with a mode of 2.0.

eters are 2, 0.667, and 0.4, giving each a mode of 2. The distributions all represent $H+$; the hypothesis $\theta < 0$ would be represented by $\Gamma(-x)$, producing a mirror image. The probability density declines to zero at $\theta = 0$, meaning that small values of θ are unlikely. For example, with a shape parameter of 6, the probability that θ is less than 1 is only about 0.05. A larger shape parameter implies more definite expectations about the upper limits to possible values of the parameter. With a shape parameter of 6, the probability that the parameter will be greater than 6 is only about 0.3%; with a shape parameter of 2, it is about 20%.

Table 6.2 shows the maximum possible odds in favor of $H+$ against $H0$, given gamma distributions with shape parameters of 2, 4, and 6 and mode of 2. As in Table 6.1, the standard error of the parameter estimate is assumed to be 1.0, so the prior distributions can be understood in terms of expected t-ratios. The maximums from the gamma distributions are all more favorable to $H+$ than the maximum odds from half-normal and half-logistic distributions shown in Table 6.1. The maximum odds in favor of $H+$ from the gamma distribution with shape parameter 2 are somewhat less favorable than the maximum odds from the uniform distribution, while the maximum odds with shape parameters 4 and 6 are more favorable. Representing directional hypotheses by a gamma distribution rather than halves of a symmetric unimodal distribution means that a given t-ratio provides stronger evidence against the null hypothesis. This effect is not unique to gamma distributions: the general point would apply to any distribution with a nonzero mode—that is, to any distribution under which the most likely parameter values may be "large" rather than almost zero.

The odds in favor of $H+$ are close to the maximums over a wide range

TABLE 6.2. Maximum Odds in Favor of a Directional Hypothesis versus the Null Hypothesis, Gamma Distributions

p	t	2	4	6
.32	1.00	1.4	1.5	1.5
.15	1.44	2.1	2.4	2.5
.10	1.65	2.7	3.1	3.3
.05	1.96	4.3	5.1	5.4
.01	2.58	14.1	17.7	19.7
.003	2.97	36.9	47.5	53.6
.001	3.29	91.2	119.8	136.9

of values of the scale parameter. For example, with a *t*-ratio of 1.96 and a shape parameter of 4, the odds in favor of *H+* are more than 4:1 whenever the scale parameter is between 0.24 and 0.69. These distributions are shown in Figure 6.4. A scale parameter of 0.24 implies fairly exact ideas about the likely values of θ—for example, there is about a 50% chance that it will be between 0.6 and 1.2 and only about a 5% chance that it will be greater than 1.96. That is, in terms of the researcher's expectations, the study is "underpowered." A scale parameter of 0.69 implies much less precise ideas about the values of the parameter—the middle 50% range goes from 1.7 to 3.5, and there is a 5% chance that it will be greater than 5.4. A distribution of this kind seems like a good representation of the expectations that researchers usually bring to an analysis—*t*-ratios of 2 to 3 would be neither surprisingly large nor surprisingly small under the alternative hypothesis. With a shape parameter of 4, a larger scale parameter would mean that the *t*-ratio was expected to be relatively large: for example, with a scale parameter of 1, the middle 50% range goes from 2.5 to 5.1, and the median is 3.7. Given this prior distribution, a *t*-ratio of 1.96 would be somewhat smaller than expected under *H+*, so the evidence would be weaker.

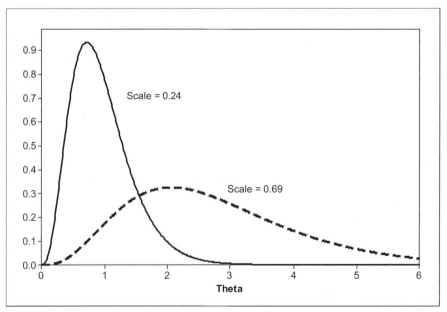

FIGURE 6.4. Two gamma distributions giving odds of 4:1 against null when *t* = 1.96.

A given t-ratio provides strong evidence about the directional hypotheses $\theta < 0$ and $\theta > 0$ when a gamma distribution is used. For example, given a gamma distribution with shape parameter 4 and scale parameter 0.69, a t-ratio of 1.96 gives odds of over 200:1 in favor of $H+$ against $H-$. With a scale parameter of 0.43, which gives the maximum odds in favor of $H+$ against $H0$, the odds in favor of $H+$ against $H-$ are about 90:1. This occurs because $H-$ is understood as a prediction that θ will have a *large* negative value rather than merely a negative one. Thus, compared to a symmetric unimodal distribution, the gamma distribution produces stronger conclusions about both of the comparisons involved in the three-way choice.

6.4   SUMMARY AND CONCLUSIONS

When Jeffreys proposed Bayes factors, he did not think that their conclusions would differ greatly from those of classical hypothesis tests. He recalled that "*I once remarked to Fisher that in nearly all practical applications we should agree, and that when we differed we should both be doubtful*" (Jeffreys, 1977, p. 89).[6] However, since the work of Lindley (1957) and Edwards et al. (1963), most advocates of Bayes factors have argued that the two approaches yield very different conclusions: that Bayes factors are much more favorable to the null hypothesis than are classical tests and that "statistically significant" estimates may even be evidence in favor of the null hypothesis. Hubbard and Lindsay (2008, p. 72) review the literature on Bayes factors and summarize it as showing that "p values exaggerate the evidence against the null hypothesis."

The last two chapters have looked at the reasons that the conclusions from Bayes factors and classical tests may differ. One reason, discussed in Chapter 4, is that Bayes factors depend on the prior distribution regardless of the sample size. A large part of the apparent conflict between Bayes factors and classical hypothesis tests results from the widespread use of the "unit information prior," in the form of the BIC, as the basis for a Bayes factor. The unit information prior is often extremely diffuse, which means that the

---

[6]The remark appears in a letter to Fisher dated May 18, 1937: "It would only be once in a blue moon that we would disagree about the inference to be drawn in any particular case" (Fisher, 1990, p. 162).

resulting Bayes factors tend to be favorable to the null hypothesis. I argued that the unit information prior is not a reasonable standard, and that the only tenable objective choice of a prior distribution is the one that gives the most favorable conclusions about the alternative hypothesis. The most favorable Bayes factors for parameter estimates that are statistically significant at conventional levels give some evidence in favor of the alternative hypothesis $\theta \neq 0$.

A second reason, discussed in this chapter, is that Bayes factors for the three-way choice between $\theta < 0$, $\theta = 0$, $\theta > 0$ are different from those for the conventional choice between $\theta = 0$ and $\theta \neq 0$. The three-way choice is normally a better way to represent the way that researchers usually understand their hypotheses, in which claims that $\theta > 0$ and $\theta < 0$ represent two distinct arguments rather than a single hypothesis. In the three-way choice, the odds against the null hypothesis implied by a given t-ratio are about twice as strong as they are in a two-way choice, so a t-ratio of about 2 implies odds of about 3:1 in favor of the relevant directional hypothesis against the null hypothesis. Conventional levels of significance also translate to strong evidence in the choice between $\theta < 0$ and $\theta > 0$.

A third reason, also discussed in this chapter, is that previous discussions of limits to Bayes factors represent the alternative hypothesis by a symmetric unimodal distribution. Again, this does not seem like the best way to represent most substantive hypotheses, which at least implicitly hold that a parameter will be "large." The idea that a parameter will be large implies that the modes of the distributions representing $\theta < 0$ and $\theta > 0$ should be at values other than zero. With such distributions, the maximum odds in favor of the relevant alternative hypothesis become stronger: a t-ratio of about 2.0 can reasonably be interpreted as producing odds of roughly 4:1. The use of distributions with nonzero modes also increases the odds concerning the sign of the parameter. That is, if a parameter estimate is statistically significant at conventional levels, one of the three hypotheses can (almost) be ruled out.

RECOMMENDED READING

Hurlbert, S. H., & Lombardi, C. M. (2009). Final collapse of the Neyman–Pearson decision theoretic framework and rise of the neo-Fisherian. *Annales Zoologici*

Fennici, 46, 311–349. —Argues that classical tests can and should be interpreted in terms of three outcomes, and includes citations to previous discussions (p. 324).

Kaiser, H. F. (1960). Directional statistical decisions. *Psychological Review, 67,* 160–167. —Raises the problem of reaching conclusions about direction from a test of the hypothesis $\theta = 0$ versus $\theta \neq 0$.

Nickerson, R. (2000). Null hypothesis significance testing: A review of an old and continuing controversy. *Psychological Methods, 5,* 241–301. —Reviews the literature discussing three-way decisions from a clasical perspective (pp. 282–283).

Tukey, J. W. (1991). The philosophy of multiple comparisons. *Statistical Science, 6,* 100–116. —Argues that research should focus on directional hypotheses, not traditional null hypotheses.

7

Model Selection

The chapter begins by discussing the standard procedure of model selection. It then discusses a Bayesian approach based on posterior probabilities and model averaging and illustrates it with examples. In a sense, this approach does not select a model, but it provides estimates for all parameters considered. The main reason for model selection—that is, deciding to treat some parameters as equal to zero—is to make the model more understandable or easier to work with. The chapter then explores some potential risks involved in model selection and the question of whether model selection should proceed from simple to complex or from complex to simple models. Finally, it offers three examples of model selection.

7.1 INTRODUCTION

The standard procedure of model selection is to use a sequence of hypothesis tests with the goal of arriving at a "final" model, or sometimes a small number of contenders. In most cases, the largest model in which all parameter estimates are statistically significant is chosen as the final model. Multiple contenders may be reported if there are several non-nested models in which all parameters are statistically significant or some of the parameter estimates are close to the margin of statistical significance. The basic question in model selection is whether some parameters should be fixed rather than estimated.

This procedure can be, and often is, applied with the AIC or BIC tak-

ing the place of classical hypothesis tests. The AIC and BIC have the advantage of producing a complete ranking of models and not requiring special treatment for non-nested models. As seen in the voting and social mobility examples from Chapter 2, the conclusions from using the AIC, BIC, or classical hypothesis tests can be very different, but the logic of the procedure is the same as when classical hypothesis tests are used. The goal is to select one model, or a few models, and set the others aside.

The standard procedure of model selection can be regarded as an extension of the Neyman–Pearson approach to testing hypotheses: the goal is to make the best decision among alternatives. However, the Neyman–Pearson theory involves a choice between two alternatives: as discussed in Section 6.1, even going from two to three alternatives makes analysis much more difficult. As a result, statistical theory provides little guidance about selection among a large number of alternatives, and there is no assurance that the standard procedure is optimal in any sense. In fact, it seems clear that confidence intervals from the final model will understate the degree of uncertainty, no matter how carefully that model is chosen. The statement that the $1 - \alpha$ confidence interval has a $1 - \alpha$ chance of including the true parameter value is based on the assumption that the model is correctly specified, but in reality there is always some uncertainty about whether that is the case. The standard confidence intervals do not take uncertainty about the model into account.

7.2 BAYESIAN MODEL SELECTION

The central principle of the Bayesian approach is to calculate the probabilities of different models rather than making a decision to accept or reject. The prior distributions for the parameters can be combined with the evidence of the data to give Bayes factors for each pair of models, which can be combined with the prior probabilities to give the relative posterior probabilities of all models. Because all possible models are considered, the sequence in which they are estimated is irrelevant, and non-nested models do not need special treatment.

If the number of models is large, it is impractical to specify prior distributions and probabilities for each one. Therefore, Bayesian model selection is usually based on a standard prior distribution and prior probabilities. The

usual approach is to use the BIC, which implicitly amounts to choosing the unit information prior, and equal prior probabilities for each model.[1] In Chapter 4, I argued that unit information prior does not provide a reasonable general standard—the prior distribution, and therefore the Bayes factor and the posterior probabilities, varies in ways that depend on irrelevant features of the data. However, the AIC is defensible as a general standard. The results in Table 4.4 show that, when choosing between $\theta = 0$ and $\theta \neq 0$, given a t-ratio of about 1.4 the maximum odds in favor of the alternative hypothesis are about 1.2 or 1.3 to 1. The "Akaike weights" give odds of 1:1 when the absolute value of the t-ratio is equal to the square root of 2, so they can be justified by the principle of using a prior distribution that is close to the most favorable one. This argument does not give a reason to use a penalty of *exactly* 2.0, but using a slightly different one would produce similar conclusions.

Table 7.1 shows an example in which the AIC is used to produce posterior probabilities. In order to keep the number of models manageable, the

TABLE 7.1. Posterior Probabilities of Models Predicting Democracy

Model	Predictors	SSE	p	AIC	Posterior probability
1	None	581.7	0	986.7	.000
2	GDP	426.3	1	940.5	.086
3	Education	454.9	1	950.6	.001
4	Urbanization	506.2	1	967.2	.000
5	Fractionalization	508.1	1	967.8	.000
6	GDP, education	419.0	2	939.9	.120
7	GDP, urbanization	424.0	2	941.7	.048
8	GDP, fractionalization	415.5	2	944.7	.231
9	Education, urbanization	451.2	2	951.3	.000
10	Education, fractionalization	438.0	2	946.7	.004
11	Urbanization, fractionalization	462.3	2	955.1	.000
12	GDP, education, urbanization	415.6	3	940.6	.083
13	GDP, education, fractionalization	410.6	3	938.7	.215
14	GDP, urbanization, fractionalization	414.7	3	940.3	.099
15	Education, urbanization, fractionalization	433.6	3	947.1	.003
16	All	408.9	4	940.1	.108

[1]A set of nested models can be understood as a combination of a number of hypotheses. If prior probabilities of 0.5 are assumed for every hypothesis, then every model will have the same prior probability.

example is a simple one: a linear regression in which the dependent variable is a rating of the degree of democracy in 155 nations. There are four independent variables: the logarithm of per-capita GDP, the rate of enrollment in educational institutions, the percent living in urban areas, and an index of ethnolinguistic fractionalization (Norris, 2009). There are $2^4 = 16$ possible subsets of the independent variables, and it is assumed that each of the 16 regression models has the same prior probability.

The lowest AIC, and therefore the highest posterior probability, occurs for Model 8, which includes per-capita GDP and ethnolinguistic fractionalization as predictors. However, it would be misleading to focus on that model, since its posterior probability is only about .23, and there are three other models with posterior probabilities over .10 and one with a posterior probability of .099.

In a general way, the posterior probabilities based on the AIC lead to the same conclusions in this case as conventional model selection using classical tests in this case. Among the models including two or more predictors, Model 8 is the only one in which all are statistically significant at the 5% level, so it would normally be chosen as the final mode. However, fractionalization does not remain statistically significant when education is added to the model, so a careful investigator would realize that there was a good deal of uncertainty about the relative impact of education and ethnolinguistic fractionalization. This conclusion, however, depends on the exercise of judgment: an investigator who simply followed a .05 level of significance would conclude that Model 8 was the only acceptable model. With posterior probabilities, no judgment is necessary: the figures directly show that there is a good deal of uncertainty about which model is best.

The sums of posterior probabilities of the models can be combined to obtain the probability that a particular parameter is not zero: the probabilities are .99, .53, .34, and .66 for GDP, education, urbanization, and fractionalization, respectively. These results illustrate a subtle but important difference from the conventional practice. In Model 16, urbanization has a t-ratio of about -0.8, and the absolute value of its t-ratio is below 1.0 in all of the models that include GDP, so an investigator following the usual procedure of model selection would simply exclude it from further consideration. However, there is only weak evidence against the proposition that urbanization has an effect, and the posterior probability is not very different from those

for education and fractionalization. This uncertainty is a necessary effect of using the AIC: with a t-ratio of 0.8, the odds in favor of the null hypothesis are about 2:1 (compare Models 16 and 13), and even with a t-ratio of exactly zero, the odds would be only e:1. The AIC can produce strong evidence *against* a null hypothesis, but only weak evidence in favor of one. Therefore, use of the AIC will often lead to situations like this one, in which several models have a substantial posterior probability.

7.2.1 Model Averaging

The posterior probabilities of the models can be used to compute posterior distributions for the parameters. That is, rather than saying that a parameter is or is not zero, we can say that there is some probability that it is zero, or any given value. Table 7.2 shows the average parameter estimates and standard errors using the weights from Table 7.1, along with the estimates and standard errors from Models 8, the "final" model, and 16, the model including all independent variables.[2]

Compared to the estimates from Model 8, the weighted average estimate for log GDP is about the same, but the weighted standard error is considerably larger. The weighted average for ethnolinguistic fractionalization is considerably smaller than the estimate from Model 8, while the standard error is about the same size. Compared to the estimates from Model 16, the weighted average for log GDP is about the same, as is its standard error; the weighted average for fractionalization is somewhat smaller, and its standard error is slightly smaller. Finally, the weighted averages for education and urbanization have the same sign but are closer to zero than the estimates from Model 16.

A practical difficulty with this approach is that it may require estimating a very large number of models. For example, in the economic growth example there are 67 potential control variables, resulting in about 10^{20} possible

---

[2]This is an example of what Sala-i-Martin et al. (2004) call "Bayesian averaging of classical estimates." A pure Bayesian approach would use the same prior distribution to produce both the weights and the estimates. With a diffuse prior distribution like the unit information prior, the Bayesian estimates are almost the same as the classical ones. With a less diffuse distribution, they are somewhat different but require more effort to compute, so there is a practical advantage to using the classical estimates.

TABLE 7.2. Parameter Estimates and Standard Errors from Regressions Predicting Economic Growth

	Average	Model 16	Model 8
Log GDP	.506	.480	.529
	(.161)	(.159)	(.091)
Education	0.008	0.015	
	(.047)	(.010)	
Urban	−.002	−.007	
	(.017)	(.007)	
Fractionalization	−.718	−.950	−1.166
	(.584)	(.604)	(.585)

combinations, too many to estimate even given modern computing power. However, usually many of the potential models fit poorly and therefore have posterior probabilities close to zero. Therefore, one way to deal with this difficulty is to devise methods to identify the smaller group of models that need to be estimated. Another is to select and estimate a random sample of models—the size of the random sample can be chosen to give whatever degree of precision is desired (Sala-i-Martin et al., 2004, p. 819).

7.2.2 Bayesian Model Selection and Bayesian Estimation

Model averaging based on posterior probabilities results in a probability distribution for each parameter; thus, in a sense it always "selects" the full model. This point raises the question of how Bayesian model selection differs from Bayesian estimation, which also combines a prior distribution for the parameters with the evidence of the data to produce a posterior distribution.

The posterior distribution from model averaging corresponds to the distribution that would be obtained from estimation using a prior distribution with a "spike" of probability at or near the value of zero for each parameter. Two objections might be raised against a prior distribution of this kind, one theoretical and one practical. The theoretical objection is that the idea of a spike of probability at or very near zero may not be credible. In the economic growth example, one could argue that all of the variables considered almost certainly have *some* influence. From this point of view, a reasonable prior distribution might have a mode of zero, representing an inclination to think that smaller parameter values are more likely, but without a definite

spike: a multivariate normal distribution would be an obvious possibility. The practical objection is that the marginal posterior distribution that results from Bayesian averaging will be a combination of a continuous distribution and a spike at zero. As a result, it will not be possible to reconstruct the distribution, even approximately, from the weighted mean and standard error. To give an accurate sense of the posterior distribution, it will be necessary to show figures or a table with multiple columns (see Sala-i-Martin et al., 2004, for examples). When there are many parameters, it may be difficult for readers, or the investigators themselves, to understand the marginal distributions. The joint distribution will be even more difficult to grasp. When Bayesian estimation is applied using a multivariate normal prior distribution for the regression parameters, the posterior distribution will also be approximately multivariate normal, so the marginal distributions will be given by the parameter estimates and standard errors.

Thus, the choice between Bayesian model averaging and Bayesian estimation is partly a matter of the choice of prior distributions and partly a matter of convenience in estimation and interpretation. Bayesian estimation of multiple parameters involves multiple integrals, so it is computationally demanding. Although computing the posterior probabilities requires the estimation of a large number of models, the calculations are straightforward. Therefore, model averaging based on posterior probabilities could be seen as a more practical way to reach the same goal. However, advances in software and computational power have made Bayesian estimation more feasible, so the advantage of model averaging has diminished, if not disappeared.

7.3   THE VALUE OF MODEL SELECTION

The implication of the discussion in the preceding section is that, if the goal is prediction, model selection is usually not called for. As Kadane and Dickey (1980, p. 265) observe, "One should not deliberately exclude a cost-free variable from influence on one's predictor, provided that one maintains the freedom to use it in the optimal way." Model averaging and Bayesian estimation are alternative ways of using variables in an optimal way.

However, in many cases, the primary goal of research is not prediction but rather some kind of understanding. For this purpose, a model with a large number of parameters, even optimally estimated ones, can produce what Dempster (1971, p. 62) calls "confusion," in which "too many dimen-

sions . . . are insufficiently determined by available facts, so that . . . insights from the model are muffled." The risk of confusion means that including a variable is not "free," so there is a benefit to selecting a simpler model. For example, in the social mobility example discussed in Section 2.6.3, a model in which there is more or less mobility is easier to grasp than a model in which there are different patterns of mobility.

There also may be practical advantages to selecting a simpler model. Sometimes an investigator wants to use a model as a starting point to investigate other issues in more depth: for example, to consider functional form, interactions, or the possibility of correlation among the errors for different cases. Having a reasonably large number of degrees of freedom to work with makes it easier to investigate these issues, so there is a benefit to model selection in small samples like the economic growth data. Even when the number of cases is large, it is useful to have a model that can be estimated quickly and easily, and maximum likelihood estimation is usually easier than Bayesian estimation or model averaging.[3] Therefore, when choosing a model for further investigation, it may be desirable to make a definite decision to include or exclude a parameter.

Model selection is not the only way of reducing "confusion." An alternative is to treat parameters as random variables: this idea is the basis of hierarchical or multilevel modeling (Gelman and Hill, 2007). Which approach is better depends on the nature of the problem. For example, it would normally be more reasonable to treat the parameters for dummy variables representing the American states as random variables rather than to set some to zero. That is, it is more reasonable to say that "state" makes a difference than it is to say that some states make a difference and others do not. However, if prior knowledge suggested a regional classification, it might be useful to combine the states into regional groups.

7.4 THE RISKS OF MODEL SELECTION

In the standard practice of model selection, a sequence of models is considered; at each step, a variable (or group of related variables) is added to or

---

[3]Sala-i-Martin et al. (2004) carried out about 80 million regressions to produce their averages.

removed from the previous model. One risk of model selection is that the final model may depend on the sequence in which variables are considered. The results for the economic growth example illustrate this point. The final models produced by beginning with a simple model and adding variables differed from those produced by beginning with the full model and removing variables. For example, Models 2 and 5 in Table 2.2 both used a *p*-value of .05 as the standard for inclusion. Starting with a simple model and adding variables resulted in a final model with nine predictors other than ethnolinguistic fractionalization, while starting with the full model and removing variables resulted in a final model with 12. Moreover, only four of those variables were the same. Although this example involves an automatic method of model selection, the issue is equally relevant when the search is guided by the investigator's judgment: different investigators who considered parameters in a different order might arrive at different models. The problem is not just that the investigator's preferences or beliefs might affect the outcome of the analysis, but that they would affect it in an unknown way.

A second risk is that the final model may include some variables that have no real relationship to the outcome. To some extent, this is an obvious consequence of using any model selection criterion. For example, if we consider 50 variables that have no real relationship to a dependent variable, we can expect about 2.5 of them to be statistically significant at the 5% level. However, Freedman (1983) shows that the risk can be much greater when the analysis proceeds in stages, as it usually does. He considered an example in which all variables were independent draws from a standard normal distribution: that is, the dependent variable had no relation to any of the predictors. With 100 cases, 50 independent variables, and a two-step screening process, he found that the final model contained an average of five variables that were statistically significant at the 5% level—about twice the number that would be expected from the simple calculation. Although Freedman did not consider stepwise regression, Lukacs, Burnham, and Anderson (2010) found that it produced poor results in a similar situation. Freedman and Pee (1989) suggest that a large number of predictors relative to the number of observations increases the chance of spurious significant results.

One approach to this problem is to fit all possible models, or as large a subset as can reasonably be calculated, and to calculate averages as described

in Section 7.2. An alternative is to apply standard methods of model selection beginning from a number of starting points. If different models are obtained from different starting points, they can be combined into a single comprehensive model, and the search can proceed from that point. Hoover and Perez (1999) offer a simulation study of model selection using a modified version of stepwise regression that applies a variety of specification tests to each model. They find that the procedure does a good job of identifying the true model if a variety of starting points are used. Although more research is needed on these issues, one conclusion seems clear: results based on a single sequence of tests are problematic, particularly when the number of variables is large relative to the number of observations.

7.4.1   Simple to Complex or Complex to Simple?

The usual practice of model selection is to begin with a simple model and consider adding parameters. However, a number of econometricians, notably Hendry (1995) and Mizon (1977), have argued for a "general-to-specific" approach in which one begins with a complex model and considers imposing restrictions (Hansen, 1996).[4] Starting with a complex model can be shown to be optimal under some conditions (Anderson, 1962). The reason can be understood by considering a regression in which the true model is:

$$y = \alpha + \beta_1 x_1 + \beta_2 x_2 + e; \ e \sim N(0, \sigma^2) \tag{7.1}$$

If β_1 is positive, β_2 is negative, and x_1 and x_2 have a positive correlation, then the correlation between each predictor and the dependent variable may be near zero. A search strategy that began with the null model, then considered a model including only x_1, then considered a model including only x_2, and then terminated the search would miss the true model. A strategy that began with the model including both variables and then considered models including only x_1 and x_2 would find it. However, it is not possible to make definitive judgments about more complicated situations, and arguments have been

---

[4]This is sometimes known as the "LSE approach," since much of its early development took place at the London School of Economics. Although proponents have focused on time series, the issue applies more broadly.

made on behalf of both approaches (see Hoover and Perez, 1999, pp. 168–170, for a summary).

In most cases, it is not possible to begin with a *completely* general model (Hansen, 1996). For example, in the economic growth example, the number of parameters required to estimate a model involving all two-way interactions among the 67 predictors would far exceed the number of cases. An investigator who wanted to consider interactions would have no alternative to starting from a relatively simple model: for example, one that included only the main effects. Moreover, the theoretical argument for the general-to-specific approach is based on asymptotic considerations. The results of Freedman and Pee (1989) show that fitting a large number of parameters relative to the number of observations can increase the risk of spurious significant results. Again, the conclusion that can be drawn with the most confidence is that when searching for models a number of different sequences should be used.

7.5   EXAMPLES OF MODEL SELECTION

This section will consider three examples of model selection. The first involves social mobility in 16 nations; these data were analyzed by Raftery (1986; 1995a) in articles advocating the BIC and by Weakliem (1999) in a critique. The second and third examples were discussed in Chapter 2: social mobility in the United States and Britain and interactions between race and other factors in race and voting choices.

7.5.1   Social Mobility in 16 Nations

Grusky and Hauser (1984) analyzed data consisting of 16 three-by-three tables for intergenerational mobility in different nations. The data for one of the nations (Australia) are shown in Table 7.3.[5] Grusky and Hauser estimated the model

$$\log(n_{ijk}) = \alpha_{ik} + \beta_{jk} + \phi_{1k}\,P1 + \phi_{2k}\,P2 + \phi_{3k}\,P3$$

---

[5] See Raftery (1995a) or Weakliem (1999) for the complete data.

TABLE 7.3. Example of a 3 × 3 Mobility Table and Model of Association

Nonmanual	291	170	29
Manual	290	608	37
Farm	81	171	175
Nonmanual	P1	0	P4
Manual	0	P2	0
Farm	0	0	P3

where i indexes father's occupation, j indexes son's occupation, and k indexes nation. The ϕ parameters can be interpreted as representing the strength of "inheritance" in each occupation in that nation. This is sometimes called the "quasi-independence" model, since it implies that the father's and son's occupations are independent except for the inheritance effect. The quasi-independence model leaves 1 degree of freedom for each nation. Although it could be rejected using classical tests (a deviance of 150 with 16 degrees of freedom, giving a p-value of less than 10^{-16}), Grusky and Hauser (1984) accepted it on the grounds that it accounted for the great majority of the association. Raftery (1986) pointed out that the BIC supported this decision. With 113,556 cases in the whole sample, the BIC for the quasi-independence model is 895.0. The BIC for the "saturated" model fitting each cell exactly is 931.2, implying odds of about 70 million to one in favor of the quasi-independence model.

This example is well known in the literature on Bayesian model selection: Raftery (1995a) featured it in an article on Bayesian model selection, Weakliem (1999) discussed it in detail in a critique of the BIC, and Efron and Gous (2001) returned to it in a comparison of Bayesian and classical approaches to model selection. However, none of these authors gave any serious attention to the saturated model. Efron and Gous (2001, p. 231) said that "standard hypothesis tests and confidence intervals would show that the sociometric [i.e., quasi-independence] model does not fit the data perfectly but that deviations from the model are quite small," but did not examine those deviations. One reason for this neglect is that the interpretation of the relevant parameters is not straightforward: there are many possible ways to define a "deviation" parameter, all of which produce a perfect fit to the data. In order to evaluate the size of the parameter estimates, it is necessary to

define them in a way that can be easily understood, and this requires attention to the substantive question.

A possibility is indicated in the second part of Table 7.3: P4 is a dummy variable for the association between fathers in nonmanual occupations and sons in farming. The rationale for representing it in this fashion is that, because nonmanual occupations generally provide more income, prestige, and other resources, the sons of white-collar fathers are more likely to be able to realize their preferences among occupations. The extra parameter can therefore be interpreted as representing preference between farm and blue-collar occupations: a positive sign would indicate that sons of white-collar fathers favored farming over blue-collar occupations, and a negative sign would indicate the opposite.

In the saturated model, the median values are 1.5, 0.16, and 2.9 for the white-collar, blue-collar, and farm "inheritance" parameters, respectively, and 0.33 for the "preference" parameter.[6] The additional parameter cannot reasonably be regarded as unimportant: it is considerably smaller than the white-collar and farm inheritance parameters but larger than the blue-collar inheritance parameter. Ironically, model selection was not really necessary in this example, since the parameters from the saturated model could be interpreted in their own right.[7]

This issue is connected to the cost of "confusion" discussed in Section 7.3. The obvious way to avoid confusion is to use a simpler model—this was the major reason that Grusky and Hauser (1984) chose the quasi-independence model even though they were not aware of the BIC. However, parameters can be defined in different ways, some of which are more informative than others. One way to think of the saturated model is as including a specific parameter for each combination of father's and son's occupation in each nation, in effect, saying that every possibility is unique. From this perspective, the saturated model does not contribute to our understanding of social mobility. However, if the model is understood in the way proposed in Table 7.3, then it can be

---

[6]The parameter estimates are not independent, so different ways of representing the off-diagonal association lead to different estimates of the inheritance parameters. However, the general conclusions are robust under alternative specifications.

[7]Gelman and Rubin (1999, p. 408) noted the neglect of the saturated model.

informative. The general point illustrated by this example is that, if possible, parameters should be defined so that their estimates can be interpreted as "large" or "small."

7.5.2   Social Mobility in Britain and the United States

The second example involves the social mobility data for the 19th and 20th centuries discussed in Section 2.6.3. In the "uniform difference" model, the association between the father's and son's occupation is a product of parameters representing the pattern (γ) and a parameter (ϕ) representing the strength of association:

$$\log(\hat{n}_{ijk}) = \beta_{ik} + \beta_{jk} + \phi_k\gamma_{ij} \qquad (7.2)$$

The parameters representing the association between father's and son's occupation are 1.44 in 19th-century Britain, 1.26 in 20th-century Britain, 0.59 in 19th-century America, and 0.90 in 20th-century America. The gap between the nations was only about half as large in the 20th century, mostly because the association increased (that is, mobility declined) in the United States.

The uniform difference model is attractive because it is easy to interpret and provides straightforward answers to an important question about mobility. However, classical tests show that it does not fit the data (a deviance of 108.1 with 45 degrees of freedom, for a p-value of about .0000004). The question is whether the classical tests are merely registering small and unsystematic discrepancies, or whether they are revealing some important features of the data. According to classical tests, Model 4, which holds that there were different patterns of mobility in the 19th and 20th centuries, fits significantly better than the uniform difference model (reducing the deviance by 60 while using 15 degrees of freedom). A comparison of the residuals from the models indicated that the greatest improvement in fit involved skilled and unskilled manual workers.[8] There was more "inheritance" in each category and less mobility between them in the 19th century: that is, the barriers between the two kinds of manual occupations appear to have declined between the 19th and 20th centuries. A change of this kind seems plausible, since the rise of

---

[8]Semiskilled workers are included in the skilled category.

industry created semiskilled jobs and new kinds of skilled work that lacked a traditional system of apprenticeship.

Even Model 4 could be rejected at the conventional 5% level. Examination of the residuals from this model indicates that it fits well for Britain and the 20th-century United States but much less well in the 19th-century United States. The total Pearson chi-square is 47.2; of this, 28.6 occurs in the 19th-century United States. Again, the largest residuals involved manual workers—the model underestimated inheritance and overestimated mobility between the manual groups.

Putting these results together, the most important change in the pattern of mobility seems to have been that the barriers between skilled and unskilled manual workers were larger in the 19th century, particularly in the United States. A model that adds a variable for the contrast between types of manual occupation to Model 3 (shown as Model 3a in Table 7.4) gives a deviance of 67.3 with 42 degrees of freedom. The estimates for the new parameter are .28, .35, .02, and zero for 19th-century Britain, 19th-century America, 20th-century Britain, and 20th-century America, respectively.[9]

The discrepancies from Model 3 were not trivial or erratic: it was possible to give at least some of them a reasonable substantive interpretation and to obtain a substantially better fit while using only a few additional param-

TABLE 7.4. Fit Statistics for Models of Social Mobility in the United States and Britain

Model	Association	Deviance	df	AIC
1	No association	1,747.3	64	1,819.3
2	No differences in association	268.9	48	372.9
3	Different amounts	108.1	45	218.1
3a	Different amounts and manual	67.3	42	**171.3**
4	Amount by nation, pattern by time	48.1	30	188.1
5	Amount by time, pattern by nation	69.0	30	209.0
6	Different patterns	0	0	200.0

Note. Bold type indicates the best fitting model according to that criterion.

---

[9]The variable is coded +1 for skilled manual sons of skilled manual fathers and unskilled manual sons of unskilled manual fathers, and −1 for unskilled manual sons of skilled manual fathers and skilled manual sons of unskilled manual fathers. The 20th-century United States is the reference category.

eters. Of course, that will not always be the case—sometimes discrepancies will be too small to be of interest or will show no discernible pattern. However, the fact that a model can be rejected against a more complex model is evidence that it is useful to continue searching. This point follows from the difference in the way that the alternative hypothesis is understood in Bayesian and classical tests involving multiple parameters. With a Bayes factor, the alternative is that all of the parameters are not zero; with a classical significance test, the alternative is that *some* of the parameters are not zero. Thus, if a simpler model is rejected against a more complex one by a classical test, the appropriate response is not necessarily to accept the more complex model; rather, it may be to continue searching.

Although the uniform difference model can be rejected against several more complex models, it is still useful in providing a summary of differences in mobility. A parallel is the use of linear regression to represent a nonlinear relationship. In a nonlinear relationship, there is no single value for $\partial y/\partial x$: it differs, depending on the value of x. However, the coefficient in a linear regression provides an average value for the slope, which is useful as a first approximation. If the relationship is very far from being linear, the average will be of less value and may even be misleading for some purposes. The closeness of the approximation provided by the simple model can be assessed in light of the more complex model. In the present case, the conclusion that American social mobility declined between the 19th and 20th centuries stands and is even strengthened by the inclusion of the new parameters. When the manual parameters are included, the parameters representing the magnitude of the primary pattern of association are 0.58 and 1.07 in 19th- and 20th-century America, and 1.46 and 1.51 in 19th- and 20th-century Britain.

Even the model including the extra parameters for manual groups could be rejected at conventional significance levels against the saturated model ($p = .008$), so there is a good chance that there are other systematic discrepancies. However, at this point we can be fairly confident that further refinements would not alter the conclusions about general changes in mobility. Thus, it would be reasonable to stop the investigation at this point and accept Model 3a as a useful approximation. However, it would also be reasonable to attempt to model and interpret the remaining discrepancies. Which of these courses should be chosen would depend on the goals of the investigator.

7.5.3   Interactions between State and Race in Voting Choices

The existence of state differences in support for the different parties is obvious to even casual observers of American politics. However, the figures in Table 2.7 suggested that the pattern of state differences was not the same among blacks and whites. Table 7.5 shows fit statistics from a number of models: the first includes the main effects of state and race, while the second adds interactions between them (these were Models 1 and 5 in Table 2.7). Including the interaction reduces the deviance by 151 while using 39 degrees of freedom, a highly significant difference. The next step is to consider ways of representing the pattern of state differences among blacks and whites. The third model holds that there are state differences among whites but not among blacks—this was Model 6 in Table 2.7. This model fits better than the model of no interaction while using the same number of degrees of freedom, but it can still be rejected against the model of interaction between race and state. Therefore, it is necessary to search for intermediate models.

One possible intermediate model holds that the same pattern of state differences is found in both races but that it is stronger among whites: this is the "uniform difference" model discussed in the example of social mobility in Britain and the United States. Models 1 and 3 are both special cases of this model: in Model 1, the ϕ parameter representing the relative strength of the pattern among blacks is 1.0 and in Model 3 it is zero. The estimated value in Model 4 is $-.39$: that is, black voters tend to be more Democratic in states where white voters are more Republican. However, although Model 4 gives a statistically significant improvement over Models 1 and 3, it can still be rejected against Model 2. In Model 5, state has the same effects on voters of

TABLE 7.5. Fit Statistics for Models of Democratic versus Republican Vote, Interactions of Race and State

Model	Interactions	Deviance	p	AIC
1	None	13,903	56	14,015
2	Interactions	13,753	95	13,945
3	Nonblack only	13,843	56	13,955
4	Uniform difference	13,837	57	13,951
5	Southern blacks	13,830	57	13,944
6	Blacks by region	13,822	63	13,948

both races outside the South, but southern blacks are distinct.[10] This model fits better than Model 4 while using the same number of degrees of freedom, but it can still be rejected against Model 2. Finally, Model 6 extends the idea of Model 5 by classifying the states into seven regions and including dummy variables for blacks in each one. This model does not result in a significant improvement over Model 5, and among black voters there are no statistically significant differences among any of the regions outside the South.

A straightforward application of classical hypothesis tests implies that Model 2 should be accepted: all of the alternatives can be rejected against it at any standard level of significance. If there were a substantial number of voters from each race in all states, it would be possible to examine the estimates from each state and compare the patterns for blacks and whites. However, because the number of black voters is very small in many states, it is difficult to interpret the parameters from this model: in Dempster's (1971) terms, it leads to confusion rather than insight. Therefore, it would be reasonable to adopt Model 5, in which southern blacks are distinctive, on the grounds that it captures an important part of the interaction between state and race while using only one extra parameter. The AIC is slightly lower for Model 5 than for Model 2, but this is a secondary consideration: the main reason for preferring Model 5 is that it is easier to interpret. At the same time, the significance test suggests that there may be other systematic patterns that remain to be detected.[11]

7.6   SUMMARY AND CONCLUSIONS

Model selection should be based on a combination of classical tests and the AIC. Classical tests are useful in assessing goodness of fit: they tell us whether it is necessary to go beyond the set of existing models and develop new ones. It is sometimes objected that, given enough data, classical tests will "reject" a model because of trivial discrepancies. For example, Jeffreys (1961, p. 391) said that "there has not been a single date in the history of the

---

[10]In effect, this model adds a new "state" composed of southern black voters.

[11]Since the exit poll sample includes a fairly small number of precincts in each state, the sampling variation is larger than it would be in a random sample of voters. A more detailed analysis of interactions involving state would need to take account of this point.

law of gravitation when a modern significance test would not have rejected all laws and left us with no law." With a goodness-of-fit, however, "rejecting" a model is merely an indication that there is something to be explained. As Cox (comment on Rubin, 1971, p. 375) observed, significance tests "would have indicated unexplained discrepancies between experiment and theory, and that is their usefulness; on any approach to the analysis of data, whether the theory should be *used* involves other considerations." The AIC is useful as an approximation to the most favorable Bayes factor. It provides a ranking of all models considered and can be used to calculate posterior probabilities of each model, which classical tests cannot do. For the purposes of prediction, one should consider the probabilities of all models rather than "accepting" one and rejecting the others, but when trying to develop new models it may be useful to focus on one possibility. However, in either case the posterior probabilities provide important information.

RECOMMENDED READING

Dempster, A. P. (1971). Model searching and estimation in the logic of inference. In V. P. Godambe & D. A. Sprott (Eds.), *Foundations of statistical inference* (pp. 56–76). Toronto and Montreal: Holt, Rinehart & Winston. —Argues for model selection as a means of avoiding "confusion."

Freedman, D. A. (1983). A note on screening regression equations. *American statistician, 37,* 152–155. —A simple example showing the risk of spurious "significant" results in model selection.

Gelman, A., & Rubin, D. B. (1995). Avoiding model selection in Bayesian social research. *Sociological Methodology, 25,* 165–173. —Argues that model selection is usually not necessary and that analysis should be based on Bayesian estimation of a general model.

Hoover, K. D., & Perez, S. J. (1999). Data mining reconsidered: Encompassing and the general-to-specific approach to specification search. *Econometrics Journal, 2,* 167–191. —Offers a set of rules designed to represent the "LSE" approach and carries out a simulation study to evaluate its effectiveness.

Raftery, A. E. (1995). Bayesian model selection in social research. *Sociological Methodology, 25,* 111–163. —Discusses model selection and model averaging, with a focus on the BIC.

Sala-i-Martin, X., Doppelhofer, G., & Miller, R. I. (2004). Determinants of long-term economic growth: A Bayesian averaging of classical estimates (BACE) approach. *American Economic Review, 94,* 813–835. —A detailed illustration of model averaging (using the BIC) applied to economic growth data.

Hypothesis Tests

This chapter begins with a discussion of the strength of evidence provided by a test. Many accounts hold that Bayes factors are considerably more favorable to the null hypothesis than are classical tests, but I argue that both approaches lead to the conclusion that a p-value of about .05 provides moderate evidence against the null hypothesis. The chapter then discusses the situations in which hypothesis tests are or are not appropriate. Finally, I argue that it is important to distinguish tests of particular propositions from tests of a theory. Hypothesis tests are useful in establishing specific facts, but, given the nature of most theories in the social sciences, no single test can provide strong favorable evidence. To evaluate theories, it is necessary to focus on multiple implications. The chapter concludes with some recommendations.

8.1 HYPOTHESIS TESTS AND THE STRENGTH OF EVIDENCE

As discussed in Chapters 3 and 4, both classical and Bayesian approaches imply that a t-ratio of about 2 can normally be interpreted as evidence against the null hypothesis. Comparing the strength of evidence implied by the two approaches, however, is difficult. Berger and Sellke (1987) assert that "most non-specialists interpret p precisely as $Pr(H0|x)$." Similarly, Raftery (1995a, pp. 138–139), when offering guidelines for interpreting Bayes factors, says, "I prefer to define 'strong evidence' as corresponding to posterior odds of 20:1 . . . (by analogy with the intention behind the standard .05 significance

level)." Johnson (2014) proposes that .005 should be the default standard of "statistical significance" on the grounds that this is the level required to obtain a most favorable Bayes factor of 20:1 or more.[1]

It is not clear that Berger and Sellke (1987) are correct in saying that researchers generally interpret a *p*-value as the posterior probability of the null hypothesis: for example, a *p*-value between .1 and .5 is usually dismissed as "nonsignificant" rather than taken to mean that the null hypothesis is probably false. However, they identify an important problem, namely, that it is difficult to say how a *p*-value *should* be interpreted from a classical perspective. When hypothesis tests were introduced, the .05 level was usually treated as suggestive but not strong evidence. R. A. Fisher (1958, p. 139), discussing a *p*-value of .03, said that it meant "we cannot ignore the possibility" of a real difference but that "the data do not . . . demonstrate this point beyond possibility of doubt." Jeffreys (1961, p. 435) wrote that "users of these [classical] tests speak of the 5 per cent. point in much the same way as I should speak of the $K = 10^{-1/2}$ [about 3:1 odds against the null hypothesis] point, and of the 1 per cent. point as I should speak of the $K = 10^{-1}$." As time went on, there seems to have been a gradual shift toward treating the .05 level as *strong* evidence.

Lindley's (1953) proposal to choose a significance level in order to minimize "cost" provides a way to judge the strength of evidence provided by a *p*-value. As discussed in Section 3.4, if Type I and Type II errors are counted equally, the optimal α level can be as high as .3, but a moderate preference for the null hypothesis makes the optimal rule considerably more conservative. If a Type I error is five times as important as a Type II error, the optimal α level is never greater than .032 (a *t*-ratio of 2.14) in a two-tailed test. That is, if we begin with odds of 5:1 in favor of the null hypothesis, it will always take a *p*-value of .032 or less to make us choose the alternative hypothesis. The pattern of optimal α levels therefore implies that a *t*-ratio of about 2.0 can be interpreted as giving odds of somewhat less than 5:1 against the hypothesis that the parameter equals zero.

Another relevant calculation is provided by Sellke, Bayarri, and Berger

---

[1]His definition of the most favorable Bayes factor applies the classical principle of "uniformly most powerful" tests to Bayes factors. See Johnson (2013, 2014) for details on his approach.

(2001, p. 63). Suppose that a number of null hypotheses are tested, half of which are true. The chance of getting a p-value of .05 when the null hypothesis is true will be $f(1.96) + f(-1.96)$, where $f(x)$ is the normal density function. The chance of getting a p-value of .05 when the null hypothesis is false will be $f(1.96 - \theta) + f(-1.96 - \theta)$, where θ is the actual parameter value (assuming a standard error of 1.0). The minimum ratio of "false positives" to correct rejections of the null hypothesis, which will occur when $\theta = 1.96$, will be a little less than 1:3. The corresponding calculation for $p = .01$ shows that at least 7% will represent "false positives."

Both of these calculations support the interpretation of Fisher and Jeffreys: the .05 level represents evidence that is strong enough to be of interest but far from definitive. To obtain odds of 20:1, a p-value of substantially less than .01 is required. These standards are quite similar to those suggested by Bayes factors (see Chapter 6). That is, Bayesian and classical tests, when properly interpreted, lead to similar conclusions. Jeffreys (1937, p. 259) once said that "Fisher's practice does not follow from his postulates, but it, or something very like it, follows from mine." Although most later work has emphasized the possible difference between Bayesian and classical tests, the analysis in this book suggests that his judgment was fairly accurate.

To summarize, under normal circumstances a test statistic that is "statistically significant" at the 5% level provides some evidence that the parameter is not zero and fairly strong evidence that it does not have the opposite sign to $\hat{\theta}$. A "nonsignificant" test statistic shows that the null hypothesis is consistent with the data but provides little or no evidence in favor of that hypothesis. "Normal circumstances" means that the observed parameter estimate is in the range that could reasonably be expected under the alternative hypothesis. If the observed parameter estimate is much larger or much smaller than would be expected under the alternative hypothesis, then a given t-ratio implies weaker evidence. Even if researchers do not have definite prior distributions for the parameters, they should consider the plausibility of the observed estimate: if it is "remarkably large," that should be regarded as weakening, not strengthening, the evidence against the null hypothesis. Researchers might reexamine their previous views and decide that the observed estimate is in the range that would have been expected, but in that case they should make that argument explicitly.

These interpretations are based on the most favorable Bayes factor, which

depends only on the test statistic, not on the sample size. With a Bayes factor based on a fixed prior distribution, the value of the test statistic required to produce evidence against the null hypothesis increases as the sample increases. This feature is often claimed as an advantage, since it means that any Bayes factor will approach 100% success in making the correct decision as the sample size goes to infinity. However, in most research, the sample size is fixed, and the goal is to make the best decision possible given the data. Even if it is possible to obtain more information, there is no general standard for the size beyond which the Bayes factor based on a particular distribution would outperform a classical test: that is, there is no way to know if the sample is "large enough" in terms of the problem at hand. Therefore, there is no practical value in adjusting the α level for sample size.

The Bayesian approach does more than provide an alternative justification of the conventional interpretation of tests: it clarifies several points that are obscure in the classical approach. First, it provides a way to express the meaning of significance levels. It is hard to judge the strength of evidence provided by a given p-value—for example, whether .05 amounts to "some evidence" or "strong evidence." The relative odds given by Bayes factors provide a straightforward and understandable way of judging the strength of evidence. This point suggests that it would be useful to routinely report the implied odds from most favorable distributions. This would require some kind of convention about which distributions to consider, but limits like those shown in Table 6.2 provide a starting point (see also Sellke et al., 2001).

Second, from the perspective of classical theory it is not clear whether conventional standards of significance should be treated in a flexible or a rigid fashion (see Section 2.3.4). In a Bayesian approach, there is no doubt on this point: the evidence provided by a Bayes factor is a matter of degree. General recognition of this point would help to reduce the distortion of evidence resulting from current publication practices, in which results that are just above the critical value for conventional levels of significance are more likely to be published than those that are just below that value. An obvious consequence of this practice is that evidence that falls just short of statistical significance often remains unknown. A less obvious but equally important one is that results that are just significant by conventional standards tend to be given too much credence: when reported in the press or in textbooks, they are likely to be summarized as "a peer-reviewed study finds." Treating

a test statistic as a scale of evidence would mean that results on both sides of the conventional dividing line would be recognized as suggestive but not conclusive.

8.2   WHEN SHOULD HYPOTHESES BE TESTED?

As discussed in Chapter 3, there is a close connection between confidence intervals and classical hypothesis tests: to say that the null hypothesis $\theta = 0$ is not rejected at the α level is equivalent to saying that the $1 - \alpha$ confidence interval includes zero. However, tests and confidence intervals suggest somewhat different conclusions, which can be illustrated by the example of social mobility in Britain and the United States. In the model of a common pattern of mobility (Equation 7.2) the association parameters in 19th- and 20th-century Britain are 1.44 and 1.26, respectively, for a difference of 0.18 with a standard error of 0.116. A test of the hypothesis that the association is the same at both times gives a t-ratio of 1.55, for a p-value of .12. Depending on how one interprets results that are "almost" significant, the conclusion would be either that there is no evidence of change or that there is very weak evidence. The most favorable Bayes factor is close to 1, meaning virtually no evidence one way or the other.[2]

Alternatively, the comparison between 19th- and 20th-century Britain could be made by considering the confidence interval for the difference. In the Bayesian approach, if we begin with a diffuse prior distribution—in effect, saying we have no idea about how large any difference is likely to be— the posterior distribution is approximately normal, with a mean of 0.18 and standard deviation of 0.116. This distribution implies that there is about a 94% chance that the association was smaller in the 20th century. Essentially the same conclusion could be drawn from classical confidence intervals. The posterior probability of a decline in the association is somewhat lower if the prior distribution is less dispersed, but still substantial given reasonable choices. For example, if the prior distribution is normal with a mean of zero

---

[2]As discussed in Section 7.5.2, it is possible to improve on the model of a common pattern of mobility, but the parameters from this model provide a useful example for illustrating the difference between hypothesis tests and confidence intervals.

and a standard deviation of 0.25, the posterior distribution gives a 91% probability of a decline.

To summarize, if the difference in parameter estimates is evaluated by a hypothesis test, there is little or no evidence of any change in the association, but if it is evaluated by a confidence interval, we can be fairly sure that the association declined between the 19th and 20th centuries. Therefore, it is necessary to decide which approach should be employed. Many observers have claimed that tests of point null hypotheses are overused. Edwards et al. (1963, p. 235) state that "Bayesians are unlikely to consider a sharp null hypothesis nearly so often as do the consumers of classical statistics." Wolfowitz (1967/1980, p. 441), a distinguished classical statistician, notes that "many statistical problems which are treated as problems in testing hypotheses are not really such problems at all." However, there have been few systematic discussions of when hypothesis tests are or are not appropriate.

The clearest case for testing a point hypothesis occurs when there is an appreciable chance that it is exactly true: in Bayesian terms, when there is a mass of probability at a specific value. Jeffreys (1937, pp. 35–41) held that this assumption is generally justified on the ground that simpler "laws" have higher initial probability. He illustrated his claim by the example of "the inverse square law of force in electrostatics, in which the index has been shown experimentally to be –2 within $\frac{1}{21,600}$. . . . The only law within the admissible range that has an appreciable prior probability is the exact inverse square one, and it is unnecessary to consider any other" (Jeffreys, 1937, p. 51). In the physical sciences, sometimes a theory implies that a parameter will have a specific value; moreover, experience has shown that physical constants are often small integers. With rare exceptions, neither of these considerations applies in the social sciences. For example, the proposition that the association between fathers' and sons' occupations was *exactly* the same in the two centuries does not seem intrinsically more likely than the proposition that it differed by some small amount, say 1%. Moreover, in terms of theory, the distinction between these two possibilities is uninteresting: in both cases, we would conclude that mobility stayed about the same. In contrast, a small difference in a physical constant could have important theoretical or practical implications.

Alternatively, a point null hypothesis can be used as an approximation to the interval hypothesis that $-\delta < \theta < \delta$, where δ is a small value relative to the

standard error of the parameter estimate. The null hypothesis then amounts to the claim that the parameter value is much smaller than the observed estimate. Testing a hypothesis of this kind amounts to assuming that there is a strongly "spiked" prior distribution in which a substantial amount of probability is concentrated in a small range near θ_0. This interpretation is plausible for many problems in the social sciences. Experience shows that any two arbitrarily chosen variables are likely to have some small association with each other, even after including reasonable control variables, while substantive hypotheses generally propose some specific mechanism that is expected to produce a "large" association. We can therefore think of a spike in probability near zero as representing what Lykken (1968/1970, p. 270) calls the "ambient noise level" of correlation that would still be found if the substantive hypothesis were false. However, in the social mobility example, the possibility of change does not depend on any single mechanism: there were many social and economic changes between the 19th and 20th centuries that might have affected the association between the father's and son's occupation. It would be surprising if none of these made any difference, or if they happened to exactly offset each other. The question is not a matter of testing a proposition about a specific factor that is thought to affect mobility but rather one of estimating the amount of change, so a confidence interval using a fairly diffuse prior distribution seems more suitable than a hypothesis test.

Another reason for hypothesis testing is that including an additional parameter may have some "cost": as Lindley (1953) pointed out, a cost is formally equivalent to a difference in the prior probability. For example, including more control variables usually reduces the precision of the estimates of parameters of interest, and additional parameters representing nonlinearity may make a model more difficult to estimate or interpret. The idea of a "cost" of including additional parameters, however, is less relevant to parameters of theoretical interest. For example, a model in which the association between father's and son's occupation is the same in 19th- and 20th-century Britain and a model in which it differs are about equally easy to estimate and understand.

Finally, it is sometimes said that simple models are inherently preferable to more complex models. R. A. Fisher, in commenting on Jeffreys's views of statistical inference, said that "simpler specifications are preferred to more complicated ones, not, I think, necessarily because they are more probable or

more likely, but because they are simpler" (Fisher, 1934, p. 8). Many observers have appealed to "Occam's razor" or the "principle of parsimony" as a basic principle of scientific investigation. Kemeny (1953) argues that even if nature is not simple, the principle of parsimony is useful in constructing models. If we begin with the assumption that the world is infinitely complex, we will immediately exhaust the degrees of freedom in the sample; if we begin with a simple model, we can modify and improve it to fit the observed facts.

However, if the principle of parsimony is accepted, it raises the question of how to define simplicity. There are usually many ways to reduce the number of parameters that would not be regarded as making the model simpler: for example, combining two categories that did not have any substantive qualities in common. Keuzenkamp and McAleer (1995) offer other examples in which the number of parameters does not seem like a good index of complexity. In this case, the statement that "the association changed between the 19th and 20th centuries in the United States but stayed the same in Britain" might be regarded as more complex than "the association changed between the 19th and 20th centuries" even though it requires fewer parameters to fit the corresponding model.

To summarize, there is no reason to routinely test null hypotheses involving parameters of interest. We should ask if it is reasonable to think of a "spike" of probability at or very close to zero. This seems reasonable if a specific mechanism suggesting a "substantial" parameter value has been proposed, but if there are many factors that might plausibly affect the value of a parameter, we can usually assume that there is *some* difference: the question is whether we can be confident about its direction. Most comparisons of nations or widely separated times, like those in the social mobility example, should be thought of in terms of judging direction rather than testing a null hypothesis.

8.3 THE ROLE OF HYPOTHESIS TESTS

Some critics of hypothesis tests have challenged defenders to point to cases in which their use has led to new discoveries or the refutation of prominent theories. Mason (1991, pp. 343–344) asks a rhetorical question: "Has major progress in the social sciences been aided by the notion of statistical signifi-

cance, or confidence intervals, or standard errors? Show me." Summers (1991, p. 130) asserted that there are no cases in which "a meaningful hypothesis about economic behavior . . . has fallen into disrepute because of a formal statistical test." Keuzenkamp and Magnus (1995, p. 21), after quoting Summers and other skeptics, appealed, "We invite readers to name a paper that contains significance tests which significantly changed the way economists think about some economic proposition."

Such challenges miss the point: the main value of hypothesis tests is a more mundane one—what Merton (1987) calls "establishing the phenomenon," or determining if there is something to be explained. Assessing the fit of models can be regarded as a form of "establishing the phenomenon," since it gives an answer to the question of whether there is a systematic discrepancy. When outcomes can be affected by a large number of factors, it is often difficult to be sure about the facts: for example, are two variables correlated? Hypothesis tests are useful for this purpose. There are cases in which a relationship is strong enough to be obvious without any test. Summers (1991, p. 143), for example, says that for most important "stylized facts," the "regularity . . . was sufficiently clear cut that formal techniques were not necessary to perceive it." However, in light of the human tendency to see patterns where none exist, we should be suspicious even of the regularities that appear to be clear. Other regularities are too small to be apparent without a test, but paying attention to small differences may be important for the assessment of theories.

Criticisms like those of Mason or Summers reflect an association of hypothesis testing with the idea of a crucial test confirming or refuting a theory. However, as Giere (1975, p. 220) points out, "Testing of statistical hypotheses [is] epistemologically prior to the testing of general theories." By establishing, with a greater or lesser degree of certainty, the facts to be explained, hypothesis tests provide a system of "roots" for the growth of scientific theories (Giere, 1975, p. 258). Even if Summers is correct, the answer to Mason's question is "yes"—not because hypothesis tests or confidence intervals have produced major breakthroughs, but because they have led to slightly better judgments about many individual facts. A significance test or confidence interval gives more and better information than a statement like "it is obvious that there is a relationship between these variables."

8.3.1   Specification and Goodness-of-Fit Tests

In most cases, not all models can be specified in advance, so the task of research might better be called model discovery or model development rather than model selection. Goodness-of-fit and specification tests play an important role in this process. Often the alternative model considered in a goodness-of-fit test is undesirable because it is difficult to estimate or interpret. In this case, the response to the rejection of a model should be a search for intermediate models, and specification tests can help to suggest the kinds of modifications that will lead to improvement.

A study by Jung, Shavit, Vishwanathan, and Hilbe (2014) provides an example of the value of specification tests. The study reported a strong effect of the gender of hurricane names (in interaction with the severity of the hurricane) on deaths, which was interpreted as evidence of the effect of gender stereotypes on behavior. The relevant estimates were highly significant using classical tests, and the BIC also favored their inclusion. However, the estimates were based on a specification in which the logarithm of deaths was proportional to the value of the damage caused by the hurricane. A specification test for nonlinearity would have shown that the model they used was inaccurate: examples of such tests include polynomial regression including powers of damage or a test for autocorrelation in the residuals if the data are ordered by the amount of damage. A model in which the logarithm of deaths was proportional to the logarithm of damage provides a much better fit, and in this model the parameters involving gender are not statistically significant. Although using the logarithm of damage is a fairly obvious alternative, it was not necessary to think of it in advance—a specification test would show the general direction of change that was required, and a process of trial and error would lead to an adequate model.

8.3.2   Testing and Replication

In principle, a hypothesis test could establish a fact with complete certainty or arbitrarily close to certainty: for example, a t-ratio of 10 would leave virtually no doubt. However, in addition to the uncertainty implied by the test statistic, there is usually room for questions about model specification and often about data quality. Also, in a strict sense any conclusions apply only to the

specific conditions that produced the observed data. There is consequently a limit to the degree of certainty that can be provided by a hypothesis test based on a single set of data. Even if we are sure that something more than chance is going on in that dataset, we cannot rule out the possibility that it is merely some peculiarity of those data rather than a more general rule. Consequently, establishing the phenomenon requires replication as well as hypothesis tests. As R. A. Fisher (1926/1992, p. 83) observed, "A scientific fact should be regarded as experimentally established only if a properly designed experiment *rarely fails* to give this [.05] level of significance" [emphasis in original]. With observational data, one could say that a fact is established only if we can state the conditions under which a statistically significant estimate can regularly be found. For this purpose, replication is not limited to exact reproduction of a study: in order to know the conditions under which a phenomenon regularly occurs, we need to vary those conditions.

8.4 OVERFITTING

Section 7.4 discussed the risk of overfitting, which can be a result of the process of model selection. In classical statistics, some protection against overfitting is provided by goodness-of-fit tests. For example, a researcher who is considering a number of independent variables can begin by including all and carrying out an *F*-test of the null hypothesis that all of the coefficients are zero versus the alternative that at least one is not zero. If the null hypothesis is not rejected, then the investigator should refrain from any further searching. However, although this procedure would be effective in an extreme case in which none of the proposed predictors has any relation with the dependent variable, it would not be effective if the predictors include a few with nonzero coefficients. In that case, the null hypothesis would probably be rejected. The investigator would then search for combinations of predictors that provide a better fit to the data, resulting in a final model that includes a number of superfluous ones. A goodness-of-fit test could also be used at the end of the search process, by an *F*-test of the group of "discarded" variables. An unusually high *p*-value would suggest that the fit of the proposed model is "too good to be true." However, this is also fairly weak protection.

The next line of defense against overfitting is to adjust significance levels

for multiple testing. The general idea is that a given test statistic should be evaluated differently depending on how many other hypotheses are tested: for example, a t-ratio of 2.5 becomes less impressive if we learn that it is the largest one obtained in testing 20 potential independent variables. However, although the general idea is clear, deciding on the optimal correction is difficult. There is a large literature on this subject, which is reviewed by Shaffer (1995).

In the Bayesian approach, the protection against overfitting comes from prior probabilities. For example, suppose that we have 50 predictor variables and find that the p-value of the overall F-statistic is 0.5, but that one of the t-ratios is about 2.5. In the classical approach, we would disregard the single "significant" estimate on the grounds that it is only one of a large number of variables tested. However, in the Bayesian approach, the only relevant evidence is the likelihood of the models including and excluding this variable. According to the most favorable Bayes factor, a t-ratio of 2.5 gives odds of about 5:1 or 6:1 in favor of the hypothesis that the coefficient is not zero: whether other hypotheses have been tested is irrelevant.[3] The posterior odds in favor of the hypothesis are a product of the prior odds and the Bayes factor, so if the prior odds that this coefficient is not zero are 1:1, then the conclusion is that the coefficient is probably not zero. However, if the prior odds that *at least one of the coefficients* is not zero are 1:1, and the individual hypotheses $\beta_i \neq 0$ are independent, then the prior odds in favor of the proposition that any particular coefficient is zero are about 70:1 (Jeffreys, 1938). As a result, the posterior odds in favor of the proposition that the coefficient is zero are still substantial, about 10 or 15 to 1. If the group of variables had been regarded as potential controls and the one with the t-ratio of 2.5 had not been singled out for special attention beforehand, then prior odds of 70:1 would seem more appropriate than prior odds of 1:1.

Even if a model was not thought of before observing the data, it is possible to make an approximate judgment about its prior probability. For example, in the case of social mobility in the United States and Britain, one of the models included parameters for the manual groups (Model 3a in Table 7.4). Adding these parameters produced a substantial improvement in fit, reduc-

---

[3]To keep the calculations simple, I assume a test of $\beta = 0$ against $\beta \neq 0$ rather than the three-way test discussed in Chapter 6.

ing the deviance by 42 while using 3 degrees of freedom, and the Akaike weights give odds of about 25,000,000:1 in favor of their inclusion. However, this model was developed after examining the data rather than specified in advance, so the evidence should clearly be discounted to some extent. A rough calculation can be made by supposing that the prior odds of the model of a common pattern of mobility versus different patterns are 1:1 and then asking how many "reasonable" models of different patterns might exist. A "reasonable" model in this sense is one that could be given a plausible substantive interpretation: possibilities include models that treat a single occupational category as distinctive, models involving mobility between two related categories, and models that distinguish between the "diagonal" (father and son in the same category) and other cells. Although there are quite a few possibilities, it seems that it would be difficult to think of as many as 100. If we suppose that there are 100 mutually exclusive alternatives, and that each one is equally likely, the prior odds of each one against the model of a common pattern is 1:100, and the posterior probability of the model adding parameters for the manual groups against the model of a common pattern is about 250,000:1. That is, even after discounting for a lower probability, we can be confident in the finding about changes in mobility between skilled and unskilled manual occupations.

8.5 HYPOTHESIS TESTS AND THE DEVELOPMENT OF THEORY

As discussed in Section 2.4, many observers argue that the use of hypothesis tests has impeded the development of theory. One popular line of criticism is that the usual practice of research in conjunction with conventional hypothesis tests gives researchers many opportunities to obtain statistically significant results, and that a large proportion of these results are in fact spurious. The possibility of spurious "findings" is enhanced because in the social sciences theoretical predictions usually involve the *signs* of the parameters rather than exact values. An estimate that is statistically significant, has the expected sign, and is judged to be "substantively important" is counted as support for the theory, but it is usually possible to think of a number of plausible arguments that a parameter will have a particular sign. Stinch-

combe (1968, p. 13) noted that "a student who cannot think of at least three sensible explanations for any correlation that he is interested in should probably choose another profession." He was referring to sociology, but the point applies to the social sciences more generally: Meehl (1978) made a similar observation about psychology. The alternative explanations include not only substantive ones but also accounts involving some kind of mistake in measurement or analysis, such as the omission of an important control variable.

One response to this analysis is that there should be more focus on prediction: a hypothesis developed after looking at the data might not be acceptable until it had survived a test using new data. This approach would move the practice of research closer to the model proposed by Popper (1959), in which science progresses by making falsifiable predictions. Strict adherence would require a major change in publication practices, since predictions would have to be offered in advance in order to establish that they had not been developed after looking at the data. For example, Young and Kerr (2011) propose that research publications should have two parts, one in which a fraction of the sample is used for modeling and another in which the model is tested on the remaining data, ideally by a separate team of researchers.

Popper's approach rests on the principle that prediction is the only test of a theory, and that "accommodation," or explaining an observed regularity, has no value as evidence. Although Popper goes further than most, prediction is generally accepted as superior to accommodation. However, it is surprisingly difficult to give a logically compelling argument in favor of this preference. The likelihood principle, which is a foundation of the Bayesian approach, implies that accommodation and prediction are of equal value (Leamer, 1978, p. 292). Given the same potential explanation and the same evidence, why should the date at which the explanation was proposed matter? After reviewing the arguments, Lipton (2004; see also Simon, 1955/1977) concludes that the only valid reason is that accommodation raises the possibility of "fudging"—introducing an extraneous element in order to fit the data. This amounts to saying that the link between theory and hypothesis is not perfect—that there are a number of more or less plausible interpretations of a theory that yield different hypotheses. If the hypothesis follows unambiguously from the theory, then it does not matter whether it was offered before or after observing the data, but if there is any ambiguity researchers who observe the data first will tend to choose an interpretation that is more

consistent with what they observe. In reality, there is a good deal of ambiguity in any theory, so it is reasonable to question hypotheses offered after examining the data. The fact that a hypothesis is developed "post hoc" is not a weakness in itself, but it suggests that we should examine the reasoning more closely than if the hypothesis had been offered in advance.

The implication is that accommodation is less compelling than prediction but that it does have value as evidence; that is, it is not just a source of hypotheses. If some phenomenon occurs in the observed data, and the theory as understood before observing the data does not account for that phenomenon but a modifed version does, then the modified version of the theory should be regarded as more likely or accurate than the original form. Simon (1968/1977) offered a model of science in which a researcher begins with a theory but is willing to modify it to account for striking features of the data. The modified version of the theory may suggest additional implications that can be tested by using the same data or new data. In this approach, although new data are valuable, it is also important to get as much information as possible out of the available data. Simon's model seems to provide a better fit to the way that scientific research—including research that is generally regarded as successful—actually proceeds than Popper's does.

Moreover, even if prediction generally provides stronger evidence than accommodation, there is variation within both categories: that is, both prediction and accommodation can be made more informative. The most direct way is to tighten the logical connections between theory and hypotheses (Diekmann, 2011). This reduces the chance of "fudging" in accommodation and also increases the value of prediction. If the link between theory and hypothesis is uncertain, then even a successful prediction does not provide strong support for the theory that is supposed to have generated the hypothesis.

A second way is to offer more precise hypotheses. If a prediction involves only the sign of a parameter, then even a successful prediction cannot provide much support for the underlying theory. It merely implies that at least one of the arguments predicting that sign is correct, and usually it is possible to think of a number of alternatives. The more precise a prediction, the more difficult it is to think of alternative arguments that lead to the same prediction, so confirmation provides stronger evidence for the theory (Meehl, 1978; Cohen, 1994).

A third way is to consider multiple implications of a theory. Cochran (1965, p. 252) recalled that "when asked in a meeting what could be done to clarify the step from association to causation, Sir Ronald Fisher replied: 'Make your theories elaborate.' The reply puzzled me, since by Occam's razor the advice usually given is to make theories as simple as is consistent with the known data. What Sir Ronald meant, as the subsequent discussion showed, is that when constructing a causal hypothesis one should envisage as many *different* consequences of its truth as possible." The more predictions that a theory offers, the more difficult to think of an alternative that duplicates *all* of them. Therefore, by considering a variety of different hypotheses implied by a theory, it is potentially possible to find strong evidence for or against that theory.

8.5.1   Making a Theory Elaborate

There are several different ways in which additional consequences might be derived from a theory. One is to consider the effects of a variable on other outcomes. For example, the prediction that ethnolingustic fragmentation might affect economic growth is based on the propositions that it makes cooperation across ethnic lines more difficult and that cooperation across ethnic lines enhances economic growth. Therefore, one might investigate the relationship between fragmentation and various forms of cooperation, or between cooperation across ethnic lines and economic growth.

A second way is to offer hypotheses about the effects of several different variables on a single outcome. This is relevant to the work of Kanazawa (2007) on parental appearance and the sex ratio of their children. The hypothesis was derived from the generalized Trivers–Willard hypothesis, which holds that parents with heritable traits that have more impact on the reproductive success of one sex are more likely to have children of that sex. A convincing test of the generalized Trivers–Willard hypothesis would consider a wide range of implications rather than focusing on a single one. Researchers sometimes produce a series of papers examining a single prediction from a theory. However, this practice makes it likely that the unsuccessful predictions will not be published or will be relegated to the status of "controls" in a paper that highlights the successful one.

A third way of deriving consequences from a theory is to consider other

units of analysis. For example, the study on the relationship between socio-economic development and fertility used the nation as the unit of analysis, because data on both variables are readily available at the national level. However, the substantive argument does not seem to be tied to the nation: it seems applicable to any unit that develops distinctive norms of fertility. Estimating the relationship using subnational units would be valuable, not just in providing more observations but also in extending the upper limits of the observed range of socioeconomic development. This point raises the question of which other units might be theoretically appropriate. It would seem fairly safe to consider large territorial units like the American states, but it is not clear whether the hypothesis could reasonably be applied to smaller units such as cities or to nongeographical units such as ethnic groups. This point, however, illustrates another benefit of the effort to "make theories elaborate": it forces one to specify the original argument more precisely.

A fourth way is to consider interaction effects. An ordinary regression coefficient can be interpreted as the effect of a one-unit change in the independent variable on the expected value of the dependent variable. However, in the social sciences, the idea that one variable has a uniform effect on another is often implausible: rather than one effect, there should be many different effects (Gelman, 2015; Schwartz, Gatto, and Campbell, 2012). For example, although higher income is generally associated with a greater chance of voting Republican, it is likely that an increase in income would not affect all people in the same way. Consequently, interactions are likely to be very common in the social sciences, and a successful theory will predict not only the main effects but also the pattern of interactions.

Consideration of multiple implications can increase the value of prediction, but it is particularly important for accommodation. Researchers often encounter unexpected patterns when analyzing data. If the theory under consideration can plausibly explain these patterns, that is additional evidence in its favor; if not, that could be regarded either as negative evidence or as a problem suggesting that the theory needs further development.

8.5.2 Evaluation of Multiple Implications

The focus on multiple implications of theories echoes the concerns of some early critics of hypothesis tests. Kendall (1957/1970, p. 87) noted that "tradi-

tional tests of significance have been developed to study the probable correct-ness or incorrectness of *single, isolated* statements" but that in much empiri-cal research "there is a series of loosely interrelated hypotheses which must be looked at in combination." Lipset, Trow, and Coleman (1956/1970, p. 86) proposed that causality could be tested "by establishing further hypotheses which would be true if the relation is a causal one, false if it is not." The implication of these points, however, is not that hypothesis tests are useless or misleading: a parameter that has the expected sign and a *p*-value of .30 is less impressive evidence than one that has the expected sign and a *p*-value of .03. The correct implication is that the most important consideration is the pattern of results, not a single test (Coleman, 1958). Ironically, this seems to have been Fisher's own position: Yates (1951, p. 33), one of his closest asso-ciates, said that "emphasis on tests of significance, and the consideration of the results of each experiment in isolation, have had the unfortunate con-sequence that scientific workers have often regarded the execution of a test of significance . . . as the ultimate objective. Results are significant or not significant and that is the end of it."

Fisher's remark about making one's theory elaborate has frequently been quoted but does not seem to have had much impact on practice. One of the factors that has prevented it from being more widely followed is the absence of a standard method for evaluating several directional hypotheses at once. Meehl (1978) observes that when multiple implications are consid-ered, researchers often take a "scorecard" approach of counting the successes and failures. For example, if four parameters were statistically significant with the predicted sign and one was statistically significant with the oppo-site sign, that would be taken as generally favorable evidence for the theory that generated the predictions. However, this would not be the correct con-clusion: although the result would be strong evidence that something more than chance was at work, it would have a low probability under the proposed theory. If θ is positive, the chance that $\hat{\theta}$ will be negative and statistically significant at the .05 level is .025 or less, so even a single significant estimate with the "wrong" sign will count heavily against a theory that predicts a posi-tive value. The result would suggest that one should attempt to think of a new theory that was consistent with the pattern, either by modifying the existing theory or starting from scratch.

On the other hand, correctly predicting a pattern of signs can provide strong evidence even if none of the estimates is statistically significant. In this case, a "scorecard" approach is appropriate. For example, predicting 9 out of 10 signs correctly would give substantial evidence in favor of a theory. Although such calculations could be made more precise, the evaluation of multiple implications generally depends on judgment rather than on any one test. For example, some hypotheses might be regarded as central and therefore given more weight in the assessment. When considering multiple implications, it is important to include all results that are theoretically relevant: as Gelman and Loken (2014, p. 465) point out, the analysis should report "all relevant comparisons, not just . . . whatever happens to be statistically significant."

8.6 SUMMARY AND CONCLUSIONS

The major claim of this book is that classical hypothesis tests, Bayesian hypothesis tests, and the AIC are not in conflict and that all have value in model selection. Significance tests of the kind proposed by Fisher are useful in showing when a model needs further development, while the Bayesian and Neyman–Pearson approaches are useful when evaluating specific parameters. Bayes factors and classical tests imply the same general conclusions, but in most cases the Bayesian interpretation is more straightforward. If the observed parameter estimate is "reasonable" under the alternative hypothesis—not surprisingly large or disappointingly small—a t-ratio of about 2 provides moderate evidence in favor of that hypothesis. Saying that the parameter estimate is reasonable amounts to taking the Bayes factor that is most favorable to the alternative hypothesis as a standard. If the parameter estimate does *not* seem reasonable under the alternative hypothesis, the Bayesian approach can be applied using a prior distribution appropriate to the specific case. The AIC is a convenient general criterion for model selection that can be justified as an approximation to the evidence provided by the most favorable Bayes factor and can be used to calculate the corresponding posterior probabilities.

In the most general sense, this book is a defense of conventional hypothesis tests. Some standard is necessary in order to distinguish between results

that can reasonably be ascribed to chance and those that cannot. Although any standard is to some extent arbitrary, the .05 and .01 conventions are not bad choices. Moreover, there is no need to adjust those standards based on sample size. However, there are a number of ways in which conventional practice could be improved:

- Researchers should realize that a *p*-value of .05, although it provides some evidence against the null hypothesis, does not provide *strong* evidence against it.

- Confidence intervals or standard errors should always be shown for parameters of interest. The practice of showing only an indication of significance level (usually with *, **, and *** for significance at the .05, .01, and .001 levels) discards a substantial amount of information in order to save a small amount of space.

- Significance levels should be interpreted flexibly. There is nothing wrong with noting that a *t*-ratio of 1.90 is close to the .05 level of significance. Of course, this should be done consistently, not just when it helps to support the researcher's preferred interpretation.

- A closely related point is that inference should not be based solely on the "best" model if there are other models that have a substantial posterior probability. The other contenders should be considered too, whether they are examined individually or combined to produce averages.

- There are cases in which a relationship between variables, or a difference between groups, seems almost certain in principle. In such cases, there is no reason to give the proposition $\theta = 0$ the "benefit of the doubt," so there is no need for a hypothesis test. Instead, the issue is to judge the likely direction of the relationship, which can be done using confidence intervals.

- Systematic and routine use of hypothesis tests is appropriate in the process of model specification. A standard set of specification tests like that proposed by Hoover and Perez (1999) is a good starting point, although it might be modified or augmented to suit the particular situation.

- Finally, the evaluation of theories should be distinguished from the evaluation of hypotheses. By considering multiple consequences, it is possible

to obtain strong evidence in favor of one theory over another, even if the theories only make predictions about the signs of parameters. Much of the criticism of hypothesis tests is a response to a real problem—the focus on isolated results. But hypothesis tests are not the cause of the problem— rather, when properly used, they are an important part of the solution.

RECOMMENDED READING

Fisher, R. A. (1926/1992). The arrangement of field experiments. *Journal of the Ministry of Agriculture of Great Britain, 33,* 503–513. —A statement of Fisher's views about the roles of hypothesis testing and replication in establishing knowledge.

Gelman, A. (2015). The connection between varying treatment effects and the crisis of unreplicable research: A Bayesian perspective. *Journal of Management, 41,* 632–643. —Argues that interaction effects are pervasive and should be modeled explicitly.

Giere, R. N. (1975). The epistemological roots of scientific knowledge. *Minnesota Studies in the Philosophy of Science, 6,* 212–261. —Maintains that hypothesis tests help to provide the "roots" for scientific theories.

Jeffreys, H. (1937). *Scientific inference* (2nd ed., Chap. 4). Cambridge, UK: Cambridge University Press. —Argues that simpler theories have a higher prior probability.

Meehl, P. E. (1978). Theoretical risks and tabular asterisks: Sir Karl, Sir Ronald, and the slow progress of soft psychology. *Journal of Consulting and Clinical Psychology, 46,* 806–834. —Criticizes the standard use of hypothesis tests. Argues for a Popperian approach in which theories make precise predictions that can be taken as null hypotheses.

Rosenberg, M. (1968). *The logic of survey analysis.* New York: Basic Books. —Offers examples of using hypotheses about interactions to develop and test theories.

Simon, H. A. (1968/1977). On judging the plausibility of theories. In *Models of discovery* (pp. 25–46). Dordrecht, The Netherlands: D. Reidel. (First published in *Studies in Logic and the Foundations of Mathematics, 52,* 439–459.) —Proposes that the development of scientific theories involves both accommodation and prediction.

Summers, L. H. (1991). The scientific illusion in empirical macroeconomics. *Scandinavian Journal of Economics, 93,* 129–148. —Criticizes hypothesis tests as part of the "scientific illusion."

References

Aitkin, M. (1991). Posterior Bayes factors. *Journal of the Royal Statistical Society, Series B, 53,* 111–142.

Akaike, H. (1974/1998). A new look at the statistical model identification. In E. Parzen, K. Tanabe, & G. Kitagawa (Eds.), *Selected papers of Hirotugu Akaike* (pp. 215–222). New York: Springer. (First published in *IEEE Transactions on Automatic Control, 19,* 716–723.)

Akaike, H. (1987/1998). Factor analysis and the AIC. In E. Parzen, K. Tanabe, & G. Kitagawa (Eds.), *Selected papers of Hirotugu Akaike* (pp. 371–386). New York: Springer. (First published in *Psychometrika, 52,* 317–332.)

Alesina, A., Devleeschauwer, A., Easterly, W., Kurlat, S., & Wacziarg, R. (2003). Fractionalization. *Journal of Economic Growth, 8,* 155–194.

Amemiya, T. (1980). Selection of regressors. *International Economic Review, 21,* 331–354.

Anderson, D. A. (2008). *Model based inference in the life sciences.* New York: Springer.

Anderson, T. W. (1962). The choice of the degree of a polynomial regression as a multiple decision problem. *Annals of Mathematical Statistics, 33,* 255–265.

Anscombe, F. J. (1961). Examination of residuals. In *Proceedings of the fourth Berkeley symposium on mathematical statistics and probability* (Vol. 1, pp. 1–37). Berkeley: University of California Press.

Anscombe, F. J. (1963). Tests of goodness of fit. *Journal of the Royal Statistical Society, Series B, 25,* 81–94.

Anscombe, F. J. (1967). Topics in the investigation of linear relations fitted by the method of least squares. *Journal of the Royal Statistical Society, Series B, 90,* 1–52.

Arrow, K. J. (1960/1984). Decision theory and the choice of a level of significance for the t-test. In *Collected papers of Kenneth J. Arrow* (Vol. 4, pp. 66–76). Cambridge, MA: Harvard University Press. (First published in I. Olkin (Ed.), *Contributions to probability and statistics* (pp. 70–78). Stanford, CA: Stanford University Press.)

Atkinson, A. C. (1978). Posterior probabilities for choosing a regression model. *Biometrika, 65,* 39–48.

Barnard, G. A. (1947). [Review of the book *Sequential analysis,* by A. Wald]. *Journal of the American Statistical Association, 42,* 658–665.

Barnard, G. A. (1967). The use of the likelihood function in statistical practice. In *Proceedings of the fifth Berkeley symposium on mathematical statistics and probability* (Vol. 1, pp. 27–40). Berkeley: University of California Press.

Barnard, G. A. (1972). [Review of *The logic of statistical inference*, by I. Hacking]. *British Journal for the Philosophy of Science, 23*, 123–132.

Barnard, G. A., Jenkins, G. M., & Winsten, C. B. (1962). Likelihood inference and time series. *Journal of the Royal Statistical Society, Series A, 125*, 321–372.

Bartlett, M. S. (1940). The present position of mathematical statistics. *Journal of the Royal Statistical Society, 103*, 1–29.

Berger, J. O., & Delampady, M. (1987). Testing precise hypotheses. *Statistical Science, 2*, 317–352.

Berger, J. O., & Pericchi, L. R. (1996). The intrinsic Bayes factor for model selection and prediction. *Journal of the American Statistical Association, 91*, 109–122.

Berger, J. O., & Sellke, T. (1987). Testing a point null hypothesis: The irreconcilability of *p*-values and evidence. *Journal of the American Statistical Association, 82*, 112–122.

Berk, R. A., & Brewer, M. (1978). Feet of clay in hobnail boots: An assessment of statistical inference in applied research. *Evaluation Studies Review Annual, 3*, 190–214.

Berk, R. A., Western, B., & Weiss, R. E. (1995). Statistical inference for apparent populations. *Sociological Methodology, 25*, 421–458.

Berkson, J. (1938). Some difficulties of interpretation encountered in the application of the chi-square test. *Journal of the American Statistical Association, 33*, 526–536.

Berkson, J. (1942/1970). Tests of significance considered as evidence. In D. E. Morrison & R. Henkel (Eds.), *The significance test controversy* (pp. 285–294). Chicago: Aldine. (First published in *Journal of the American Statistical Association, 37*, 325–335.)

Box, G. E. P. (1979). Robustness in the strategy of scientific model-building. In R. L. Lauer & G. N. Wilkinson (Eds.), *Robustness in statistics* (pp. 201–236). New York: Academic Press.

Box, G. E. P., & Tiao, G. C. (1973). *Bayesian inference in statistical analysis*. New York: Wiley.

Bross, I. D. J. (1971). Critical levels, statistical language, and scientific inference. In V. P. Godambe & D. A. Sprott (Eds.), *Foundations of statistical inference* (pp. 501–513). Toronto and Montreal: Holt, Rinehart & Winston.

Burnham, K. P., & Anderson, D. R. (2002). *Model selection and multimodel inference* (2nd ed.). New York: Springer.

Burnham, K. P., & Anderson, D. R. (2004). Multimodel inference: Understanding AIC and BIC in model selection. *Sociological Methods and Research, 33*, 261–304.

Casella, G., & Berger, R. L. (1987). Reconciling Bayesian and frequentist evidence in the one-sided testing problem. *Journal of the American Statistical Association, 82*, 106–111.

Chamberlin, T. C. (1890/1965). The method of multiple working hypotheses. *Science, 148*, 754–759. (First published in *Science, 15*, 92–96.)

Christensen, R. (2005). Testing Fisher, Neyman, Pearson, and Bayes. *American Statistician, 59*, 121–126.

Cochran, W. G. (1952). The χ^2 test of goodness of fit. *Annals of Mathematical Statistics, 23*, 315–345.

Cochran, W. G. (1965). The planning of observational studies of human populations. *Journal of the Royal Statistical Society, Series A, 128*, 234–266.

Cohen, J. (1988). *Statistical power analysis for the behavioral sciences* (2nd ed.). Hillsdale, NJ: L. Erlbaum.

Cohen, J. (1994). The earth is round ($p < .05$). *American Psychologist, 49*, 997–1000.

Coleman, J. S. (1958). Letter to the editor. *American Journal of Sociology, 64*, 59–60.

Cowles, M., & Davis, C. (1982). On the origins of the .05 level of statistical significance. *American Psychologist, 37*, 553–558.

Cox, D. R. (1977). The role of significance tests. *Scandinavian Journal of Statistics, 4*, 49–70.

Cox, D. R. (1982). Statistical significance tests. *British Journal of Clinical Pharmacology, 14*, 325–331.

Cox, D. R. (2006). *Principles of statistical inference.* Cambridge, UK: Cambridge University Press.

Cramér, H. (1955). *The elements of probability theory and some of its applications.* New York: Wiley.

Das, C. (1994). Decision making by classical procedures using an optimal level of significance. *European Journal of Operational Research, 73*, 76–84.

Davidson, R., Godfrey, L., & MacKinnon, J. G. (1985). A simplified version of the differencing test. *International Economic Review, 26*, 639–647.

Davis, J. A. (1958/1970). Some pitfalls of data analysis without a formal criterion. In D. E. Morrison & R. Henkel (Eds.), *The significance test controversy* (pp. 91–93). Chicago: Aldine. (First published in *American Journal of Sociology, 63*, 445–446.)

Dempster, A. P. (1971). Model searching and estimation in the logic of inference. In V. P. Godambe & D. A. Sprott (Eds.), *Foundations of statistical inference* (pp. 56–76). Toronto and Montreal: Holt, Rinehart & Winston.

Dickey, J. M., & Lientz, B. P. (1970). The weighted likelihood ratio, sharp hypotheses about chances, the order of a Markov chain. *Annals of mathematical statistics, 41*, 214–226.

Diekmann, A. (2011). Are most published research findings false?. *Jahrbücher für nationalökonomie und statistik, 231*, 628–635.

Edwards, W., Lindman, H., & Savage, L. J. (1963). Bayesian statistical inference for psychological research. *Psychological Review, 70*, 193–242.

Efron, B., & Gous, A. (2001). Scales of evidence for model selection: Fisher versus Jeffreys. In P. Lahiri (Ed.), *Model selection* (pp. 208–256). Beachwood, OH: Institute of Mathematical Statistics.

Erikson, R., & Goldthorpe, J. H. (1992). *The constant flux: A study of class mobility in industrial societies.* Oxford, UK: Oxford University Press.

Findley, D. F., & Parzen, E. (1995/1998). A conversation with Hirotugu Akaike. In E. Parzen, K. Tanabe, & G. Kitagawa (Eds.), *Selected papers of Hirotugu Akaike.* New York: Springer. (First published in *Statistical Science, 10*, 104–117.)

Fisher, R. A. (1926/1992). The arrangement of field experiments. In S. Kotz & N. L. Johnson (Eds.), *Breakthroughs in statistics* (Vol. 2, pp. 82–91). New York: Springer. (First published in *Journal of the Ministry of Agriculture of Great Britain, 33,* 503–513.)

Fisher, R. A. (1929). The statistical method in psychical research. *Proceedings of the Society for Psychical Research, 39,* 189–192.

Fisher, R. A. (1934). Probability, likelihood and quantity of information in the logic of uncertain inference. *Proceedings of the Royal Society of London, Section A, 146,* 1–8.

Fisher, R. A. (1937). *The design of experiments* (2nd ed.) [first edition 1935]. Edinburgh: Oliver and Boyd.

Fisher, R. A. (1958). *Statistical methods for research workers* (13th ed.) [first edition 1925]. New York: Hafner.

Fisher, R. A. (1990). *Statistical inference and analysis: Selected correspondence of R. A. Fisher* (J. A. Bennett, Ed.). Oxford, UK: Oxford University Press.

Freedman, D. A. (1983). A note on screening regression equations. *American Statistician, 37,* 152–155.

Freedman, L. S., & Pee, D. (1989). Return to a note on screening regression equations. *American Statistician, 43,* 279–282.

Gelman, A. (2015). The connection between varying treatment effects and the crisis of unreplicable research: A Bayesian perspective. *Journal of Management, 41,* 632–643.

Gelman, A., & Hill, J. (2007). *Data analysis using regression and multilevel/hierarchical models.* New York: Cambridge University Press.

Gelman, A., & Loken, E. (2014). The statistical crisis in science. *American Scientist, 102,* 460–465.

Gelman, A., & Rubin, D. B. (1995). Avoiding model selection in Bayesian social research. *Sociological Methodology, 25,* 165–173.

Gelman, A., & Rubin, D. B. (1999). Evaluating and using statistical methods in the social sciences. *Sociological Methods and Research, 27,* 403–410.

Gelman, A., & Tuerlinckx, F. (2000). Type S error rates for classical and Bayesian single and multiple comparison procedures. *Computational Statistics, 15,* 373–390.

Gelman, A., & Weakliem, D. (2009). Of beauty, sex, and power. *American Scientist, 97,* 310–316.

Gerber, A. S., & Malhotra, N. (2008). Publication bias in empirical social research: Do arbitrary significance levels distort published results? *Sociological Methods and Research, 37,* 3–30.

Giere, R. N. (1972). The significance test controversy. *British Journal for the Philosophy of Science, 23,* 170–181.

Giere, R. N. (1975). The epistemological roots of scientific knowledge. *Minnesota Studies in the Philosophy of Science, 6,* 212–261.

Gill, J. (1999). The insignificance of null hypothesis significance testing. *American Journal of Political Science, 52,* 647–674.

Good, I. J. (1950). *Probability and the weighting of evidence.* London: C. Griffin.

Good, I. J. (1983). *Good thinking*. Minneapolis: University of Minnesota Press.

Greenhouse, J., & Wasserman, L. (1996). A practical, robust method for Bayesian model selection: A case study in the analysis of clinical trials. *IMS Lecture Notes—Monograph Series, 29*, 41–62.

Grusky, D. B., & Hauser, R. M. (1984). Comparative social mobility revisited: Models of convergence and divergence in sixteen countries. *American Sociological Review, 49*, 19–38.

Haavelmo, T. (1944). The pobability approach in econometrics. *Econometrica, 12*(Suppl.), 1–115.

Hagood, M. J., & Price, D. O. (1952). *Statistics for sociologists* (2nd ed.). New York: Henry Holt.

Hannan, E. J., & Quinn, B. G. (1979). The determination of the order of an autoregression. *Journal of the Royal Statistical Society, Series B, 41*, 190–195.

Hansen, B. (1996). Methodology: Alchemy or science? *Economic Journal, 106*, 1398–1413.

Hauser, R. M. (1995). Better rules for better decisions. *Sociological methodology, 25*, 175–183.

Heckman, J. J. (1979). Sample selection bias as a specification error. *Econometrica, 47*, 153–161.

Hendry, D. (1995). *Dynamic econometrics*. Oxford, UK: Oxford University Press.

Hendry, D. F., & Krolzig, H.-M. (2004). We ran one regression. *Oxford Bulletin of Economics and Statistics, 66*, 799–810.

Hocking, R. R. (1976). The analysis and selection of variables in linear regression. *Biometrics, 32*, 1–49.

Hoffman, R. K., Minkin, V. I., & Carpenter, B. K. (1997). Ockham's razor and chemistry. *HYLE–International Journal for Philosophy of Chemistry, 3*, 3–28.

Hoover, K. D., & Perez, S. J. (1999). Data mining reconsidered: Encompassing and the general-to-specific approach to specification search. *Econometrics Journal, 2*, 167–191.

Howson, C., & Urbach, P. (1994). Probability, uncertainty and the practice of statistics. In G. Wright & P. Ayton (Eds.), *Subjective probability* (pp. 39–51). Chichester, UK: Wiley.

Hubbard, R., & Lindsay, R. M. (2008). Why P values are not a useful measure of evidence in significance testing. *Theory and Psychology, 18*(1), 69–88.

Hurvich, C. M. (1997). Mean square over degrees of freedom: New perspectives on a model selection treasure. In D. R. Brillinger, L. T. Fernholz, & S. Morgenthaler (Eds.), *The practice of data analysis* (pp. 203–216). Princeton, NJ: Princeton University Press.

Hurvich, C. M., & Tsai, C.-L. (1989). Regression and time series model selection in small samples. *Biometrika, 76*, 297–307.

Ioannidis, J. P. A. (2005). Why most published research findings are false. *PLoS Medicine, 2*, 696–701.

Jackson, E. F., & Curtis, R. F. (1972). Effects of vertical mobility and status inconsistency: A body of negative evidence. *American Sociological Review, 37*, 701–713.

Jaynes, E. T. (1976). Confidence intervals vs. Bayesian intervals. In W. L. Harper &

C. A. Hooker (Eds.), *Foundations of probability theory, statistical inference, and statistical theories of science* (Vol. 2; pp. 175–257). Dordrecht, The Netherlands: D. Reidel.

Jeffreys, H. (1937). *Scientific inference* (2nd ed.) [first edition 1931]. Cambridge, UK: Cambridge University Press.

Jeffreys, H. (1938). Significance tests when several degrees of freedom arise simultaneously. *Proceedings of the Royal Society of London, Series A, 165,* 161–198.

Jeffreys, H. (1961). *Theory of probability* (3rd ed.) [first edition 1938]. Oxford, UK: Oxford University Press.

Jeffreys, H. (1977). Probability theory in geophysics. *IMA Journal of Applied Mathematics, 19,* 87–96.

Jeffreys, H. (1980). Some general points in probability theory. In A. Zellner (Ed.), *Bayesian analysis in economics and statistics* (pp. 451–453). Amsterdam: North-Holland.

Johnson, V. E. (2013). Uniformly most powerful Bayesian tests. *Annals of Statistics, 41,* 1716–1741.

Johnson, V. E. (2014). Revised standards for statistical evidence. *Proceedings of the National Academy of Sciences, 110,* 19313–19317.

Johnstone, D. J. (1986). Tests of significance in theory and practice. *The Statistician, 35,* 491–504.

Johnstone, D. J. (1989). On the necessity for random sampling. *British Journal for the Philosophy of Science, 40,* 443–457.

Jung, K., Shavit, S., Vishwanathan, M., & Hilbe, J. (2014). Female hurricanes are deadlier than male hurricanes. *Proceedings of the National Academy of Sciences, 111,* 8782–8787.

Kadane, J. B., & Dickey, J. M. (1980). Bayesian decision theory and the simplification of models. In J. Kmenta & J. B. Ramsey (Eds.), *Evaluation of econometric models* (pp. 245–268). New York: Academic Press.

Kadane, J. B., & Lazar, N. A. (2004). Methods and criteria for model selection. *Journal of the American Statistical Association, 99,* 279–290.

Kaiser, H. F. (1960). Directional statistical decisions. *Psychological Review, 67,* 160–167.

Kanazawa, S. (2007). Beautiful parents have more daughters: A further implication of the generalized Trivers–Willard hypothesis. *Journal of Theoretical Biology, 244,* 133–140.

Kass, R. E., & Raftery, A. E. (1995). Bayes factors. *Journal of the American Statistical Association, 90,* 773–795.

Kass, R. E., & Wasserman, L. (1995). A reference Bayesian test for nested hypotheses and its relationship to the Schwartz criterion. *Journal of the American Statistical Association, 90,* 928–934.

Kemeny, J. (1953). The use of simplicity in induction. *Philosophical Review, 62,* 391–408.

Kempthorne, O. (1976). Of what use are tests of significance and tests of hypotheses? *Communications in Statistics—Theory and Methods, 5,* 763–777.

Kendall, P. (1957/1970). Note on significance tests. In D. E. Morrison & R. Henkel

(Eds.), *The significance test controversy* (pp. 87–90). Chicago: Aldine. (First published in R. K. Merton, G. G. Reader, & P. Kendall, *The student physician* (pp. 301–305). Cambridge, MA: Harvard University Press.)

Keuzenkamp, H. A., & Magnus, J. R. (1995). On tests and significance in econometrics. *Journal of Econometrics, 67,* 5–24.

Keuzenkamp, H. A., & McAleer, M. (1995). Simplicity, scientific inference, and econometric modelling. *Economic Journal, 105,* 1–21.

Krantz, D. H. (1999). The null hypothesis testing controversy in psychology. *Journal of the American Statistical Association, 44,* 1372–1381.

Kullback, S. (1959). *Information theory and statistics.* New York: Wiley.

Kullback, S., & Leibler, R. A. (1951). On information and sufficiency. *Annals of Mathematical Statistics, 22,* 79–86.

Leahey, E. (2005). Alphas and asterisks: The development of statistical significance testing standards in sociology. *Social Forces, 84,* 1–24.

Leamer, E. E. (1978). *Specification searches.* New York: Wiley.

Ledley, R. S., & Lusted, L. B. (1959). Reasoning foundations of medical diagnosis. *Science,* 130 (3366), 9–21.

Lehmann, E. L. (1957). A theory of some multiple decision problems, I. *Annals of Mathematical Statistics, 28,* 1–25.

Lehmann, E. L. (1958). Significance level and power. *Annals of Mathematical Statistics, 29,* 1167–1176.

Lehmann, E. L. (1959). *Testing statistical hypotheses.* New York: Wiley.

Lindley, D. V. (1953). Statistical inference. *Journal of the Royal Statistical Society, Series B, 15,* 30–76.

Lindley, D. V. (1957). A statistical paradox. *Biometrika, 44,* 187–192.

Lindley, D. V. (1965). *An introduction to probability and statistics from a Bayesian viewpoint.* Cambridge, UK: Cambridge University Press.

Lindley, D. V. (1997). Some comments on Bayes factors. *Journal of Statistical Planning and Inference, 61,* 181–189.

Lindley, D. V. (2000). The philosophy of statistics. *Journal of the Royal Statistical Society, Series D, 49,* 293–337.

Lindsey, J. K. (1997). *Applying generalized linear models.* New York: Springer.

Lipset, S. M., Trow, M., & Coleman, J. S. (1956/1970). Statistical problems. In D. E. Morrison & R. Henkel (Eds.), *The significance test controversy* (pp. 81–86). Chicago: Aldine. (First published in *Union democracy.* Glencoe, IL: Free Press.)

Lipton, P. (2004). *Inference to the best explanation* (2nd ed.). London: Routledge.

Long, J., & Ferrie, J. (2008). *Intergenerational occupational mobility in Britain and the U.S. since 1850.* Unpublished manuscript.

Long, J., & Ferrie, J. (2013). Intergenerational occupational mobility in Britain and the U.S. since 1850. *American Economic Review, 103,* 1109–1137.

Lukacs, P. M., Burnham, K. P., & Anderson, D. A. (2010). Model selection bias and Freedman's paradox. *Annals of the Institute of Statistical Mathematics, 62,* 117–125.

Lykken, D. (1968/1970). Statistical significance in psychological research. In D. E. Morrison & R. Henkel (Eds.), *The significance test controversy* (pp. 267–279). Chicago: Aldine. (First published in *Psychological Bulletin, 70,* 151–159.)

Mallows, C. L. (1973). Some comments on C_p. *Technometrics, 15,* 661–675.

Mason, W. M. (1991). Freedman is right as far as he goes, but there is more, and it's worse: Statisticians could help. *Sociological Methodology, 21,* 337–351.

McCloskey, D. (1998). Quarreling with Ken. *Eastern Economic Journal, 24,* 111–115.

McCloskey, D. N. (1985). The loss function has been mislaid: The rhetoric of significance tests. *American Economic Review, 75,* 201–205.

McCloskey, D. N. (1996). *The vices of economists: The virtues of the bourgeoisie.* Amsterdam: Amsterdam University Press.

McCullagh, P., & Nelder, J. A. (1989). *Generalized linear models* (2nd ed.). London: Chapman & Hall.

Meehl, P. E. (1978). Theoretical risks and tabular asterisks: Sir Karl, Sir Ronald, and the slow progress of soft psychology. *Journal of Consulting and Clinical Psychology, 46,* 806–834.

Merton, R. K. (1945). Sociological theory. *American Journal of Sociology, 50,* 462–473.

Merton, R. K. (1987). Three fragments from a sociologist's notebooks. *Annual Review of Sociology, 13*(1), 1–29.

Mizon, G. E. (1977). Model selection procedures. In M. J. Artis & A. R. Nobay (Eds.), *Studies in modern economic analysis* (pp. 97–120). Oxford, UK: Basil Blackwell.

Morgan, S. L., & Winship, C. (2015). *Counterfactuals and causal inference* (2nd ed.). New York: Cambridge University Press.

Morrison, D. E., & Henkel, R. (1969/1970). Significance tests reconsidered. In D. E. Morrison & R. Henkel (Eds.), *The significance test controversy* (pp. 182–198). Chicago: Aldine. (First published in *The American Sociologist, 4,* 131–140.)

Morrison, D. E., & Henkel, R. (Eds.). (1970). *The significance test controversy.* Chicago: Aldine.

Mosteller, F., & Bush, R. B. (1954). Selected quantitative techniques. In G. Lindzey (Ed.), *Handbook of social psychology* (pp. 289–334). Cambridge, MA: Addison-Wesley.

Mulligan, C. B., Sala-i-Martin, X., & Gil, R. (2003). *Do democracies have different public policies than nondemocracies?* NBER Working Paper No. 10040.

Myrskylä, M., Kohler, H.-P., & Billari, F. C. (2009). Advances in development reverse fertility declines. *Nature, 460,* 741–743.

Neyman, J. (1952). *Lectures and conferences on mathematical statistics and probability* (2nd ed.). Washington, DC: U.S. Department of Agriculture.

Neyman, J. (1977). Frequentist probability and frequentist statistics. *Synthese, 36,* 97–131.

Neyman, J., & Pearson, E. S. (1933/1967). The testing of statistical hypotheses in relation to probabilities a priori. In J. Neyman & E. S. Pearson, *Joint Statistical Papers* (pp. 186–202). Berkeley and Los Angeles: University of California Press. (First published in *Proceedings of the Cambridge Philosophical Society, 24,* 492–510.)

Norris, P. (2009). *Democracy crossnational data, release 3.0.* Available at *www.hks.harvard.edu/fs/pnorris/Data/Data.htm.*

O'Hagan, A. (1995). Fractional Bayes factors for model comparisons. *Journal of the Royal Statistical Society, Series B, 53,* 99–138.

Pearson, E. S. (1939). "Student" as statistician. *Biometrika, 30,* 210–250.

Peters, C. C. (1933). Note on a misconception of statistical significance. *American Journal of Sociology, 39,* 231–236.

Popper, K. R. (1959). *The logic of scientific discovery.* New York: Basic Books.

Quandt, R. E. (1980). Classical and Bayesian hypothesis testing: A compromise. *Metroeconomica, 32,* 173–180.

Raftery, A. E. (1986). Choosing models for cross-classifications. *American Sociological Review, 51,* 145–146.

Raftery, A. E. (1995a). Bayesian model selection in social research. *Sociological Methodology, 25,* 111–163.

Raftery, A. E. (1995b). Rejoinder: Model selection is unavoidable in social research. *Sociological Methodology, 25,* 185–195.

Rosnow, R. L., & Rosenthal, R. (1989). Statistical procedures and the justification of knowledge in psychological science. *American Psychologist, 44,* 1276–1284.

Ross, F. A. (1933). Ecology and the statistical method. *American Journal of Sociology, 38,* 507–522.

Rubin, H. (1971). Occam's razor needs new blades. In V. P. Godambe & D. A. Sprott (Eds.), *Foundations of statistical inference* (pp. 374–377). Montreal and Toronto: Holt, Rinehart & Winston.

Sala-i-Martin, X., Doppelhofer, G., & Miller, R. I. (2004). Determinants of long-term economic growth: A Bayesian averaging of classical estimates (BACE) approach. *American Economic Review, 94,* 813–835.

Savage, L. J. (1962). Bayesian statistics. In R. E. Machol & P. Gray (Eds.), *Recent developments in information and decision processes* (pp. 161–194). New York: Macmillan.

Savage, L. J., Bartlett, M. S., Barnard, G. A., Cox, D. R., Pearson, E. S., & Smith, C. A. B. (1962). *The foundations of statistical inference: A discussion.* London: Methuen.

Schrodt, P. A. (2014). Seven deadly sins of contemporary quantitative political analysis. *Journal of Peace Research, 51,* 287–300.

Schwartz, G. (1978). Estimating the dimension of a model. *Annals of Statistics, 6,* 461–464.

Schwartz, S., Gatto, N. M., & Campbell, U. B. (2012). Extending the sufficient component cause model to describe the stable unit treatment value assumption (SUTVA). *Epidemiologic Perspectives and Innovations, 9,* 1–11.

Sellke, T., Bayarri, M. J., & Berger, J. O. (2001). Calibration of p values for testing precise null hypotheses. *American Statistician, 55,* 62–71.

Shaffer, J. P. (1995). Multiple hypothesis testing. *Annual Review of Psychology, 46,* 561–584.

Shaffer, J. P. (2006). Recent developments towards optimality in multiple hypothesis testing. *IMS lecture notes—monograph series. Second Lehmann symposium—optimality, 49,* 16–32.

Shao, J. (1997). An asymptotic theory for model selection. *Statistica Sinica, 7,* 221–264.

Shibata, R. (1980). Asymptotically efficient selection of the order of the model for estimating parameters of a linear process. *Annals of Statistics, 8,* 147–164.

Simon, H. A. (1955/1977). Prediction and hindsight as confirmatory evidence. In *Models of Discovery* (pp. 20–24). Dordrecht, The Netherlands: D. Reidel. (First published in *Philosophy of Science, 22,* 227–230.)

Simon, H. A. (1968/1977). On judging the plausibility of theories. In *Models of discovery* (pp. 25–46). Dordrecht, The Netherlands: D. Reidel. (First published in *Studies in Logic and the Foundations of Mathematics, 52,* 439–459.)

Startz, R. (2014a). Choosing the more likely hypothesis. *Foundations and Trends in Econometrics, 7,* 1–70.

Startz, R. (2014b). On the implicit BIC prior. *Economics Bulletin, 34,* 766–771.

Sterling, T. D. (1959/1970). Publication decisions and their possible effects on inferences drawn from tests of significance—and vice versa. In D. E. Morrison & R. Henkel (Eds.), *The significance test controversy* (pp. 295–300). Chicago: Aldine. (First published in *Journal of the American Statistical Association, 54,* 30–34.)

Sterne, J. A. C., & Davey-Smith, G. (2001). Sifting the evidence: What's wrong with significance tests? *British Medical Journal, 322,* 226–231.

Stinchcombe, A. L. (1968). *Constructing social theories.* New York: Harcourt, Brace & World.

Stone, M. (1977). Asymptotics for and against cross-validation. *Biometrika, 64,* 29–35.

Stuart, A. (1954). Too good to be true? *Journal of the Royal Statistical Society, Series C, 3,* 29–32.

Summers, L. H. (1991). The scientific illusion in empirical macroeconomics. *Scandinavian Journal of Economics, 93,* 129–148.

Teräsvirta, T., & Mellin, I. (1986). Model selection criteria and model selection tests in regression models. *Scandinavian Journal of Statistics, 13,* 159–171.

Tukey, J. W. (1960). Conclusions vs. decisions. *Technometrics, 2,* 423–433.

Tukey, J. W. (1969/1986). Analyzing data: Sanctification or detective work? In L. V. Jones (Ed.), *The collected works of John W. Tukey* (Vol. 4, pp. 721–737). Monterey, CA: Wadsworth & Brooks/Cole. (First published in *American Psychologist, 24,* 83–91.)

Tukey, J. W. (1991). The philosophy of multiple comparisons. *Statistical Science, 6,* 100–116.

Wagenmakers, E.-J. (2007). A practical solution to the pervasive problem of *p*-values. *Psychonomic Bulletin, 14,* 779–804.

Wald, A. (1942). *On the principles of statistical inference.* Notre Dame, IN: University of Notre Dame Press.

Wald, A. (1950). *Statistical decision functions.* New York: Wiley.

Wallis, A. W., & Roberts, H. V. (1956). *Statistics: A new approach.* Glencoe, IL: Free Press.

Waugh, A. E. (1943). *Elements of statistical method* (2nd ed.). New York: McGraw-Hill.

Weakliem, D. L. (1992). Comparing non-nested models for contingency tables. *Sociological Methodology, 22,* 147–178.

Weakliem, D. L. (1999). A critique of the Bayesian information criterion for model selection. *Sociological Methods and Research, 27,* 359–397.

Weakliem, D. L. (2004). Introduction to the special issue on model selection. *Sociological Methods and Research, 33,* 167–187.

Wilkinson, L. (1999). Statistical methods in psychology journals: Guidelines and explanations. *American Psychologist, 54*(8), 594–604.

Wilson, E. B. (1952). *An introduction to scientific research.* New York: McGraw-Hill.

Wolfowitz, J. (1967/1980). Remarks on the theory of testing hypotheses. In *Selected papers.* New York: Springer-Verlag. (First published in *New York Statistician, 18,* 1–3.)

Xie, Y. (1992). The log-multiplicative layer effect model for comparing mobility tables. *American Sociological Review, 57,* 380–395.

Xie, Y. (1999). The tension between generality and accuracy. *Sociological Methods and Research, 27,* 428–435.

Yates, F. (1951). The influence of *Statistical Methods for Research Workers* on the development of the science of statistics. *Journal of the American Statistical Association, 46,* 19–34.

Young, S. S., & Kerr, A. (2011). Deming, data, and observational studies. *Significance, 8*(3), 116–120.

Yule, G. U., & Kendall, M. G. (1950). *Introduction to the theory of statistics* (14th ed.). London: Charles Griffin.

Ziliak, S. T., & McCloskey, D. N. (2008). *The cult of statistical significance.* Ann Arbor: University of Michigan Press.

Author Index

191

Subject Index

Probability function, models and, 7
p-value
  defined, 47
  hypothesis tests and strength of evidence, 158–162
  likelihood principle and, 25–26, 71–72
  meaning of, 25
  multiple-parameter hypothesis testing, 6
  one-parameter hypothesis testing, 5
  recommendations for using, 177
  significance levels and, 20–21, 70
  significance tests, 47–50

R

Random sampling
  classical hypothesis testing and, 43–46
  conventional hypothesis testing and, 17–18
Regression models, Akaike information criterion for, 112
Replications, 167–168

S

Sample size
  Akaike information criterion and, 111
  Bayes factors for directional hypotheses and, 128
  Bayes factors for three-way decisions and, 132
  choosing a significance level in small samples, 62–63
  effects of, 22–23, 70–71
  influence on Bayes factors, 85–88
Sampling. See also Random sampling
  classical hypothesis testing and, 17–18, 68
Secondary structure, 15–16
Significance levels
  ad hoc adjustments in conventional practice, 61–62
  adjusting to defend against overfitting, 168–169
  arbitrary nature of, 21–22, 70
  choosing
    implications of, 63–65
    one-tailed tests, 57–60
    overview and description of, 53–57

  in small samples, 62–63
  tests with multiple degrees of freedom, 60–61
  flexible versus inflexible interpretation of, 20–21, 70
  hypothesis tests and strength of evidence, 158–162
  recommendations for using, 177
Significance tests
  description of, 46–48
  model comparison and, 48–50
Simple models, principle of parsimony, 164–165
Small samples
  the Akaike information criterion in, 111
  choosing a significance level, 62–63
Social mobility example. See Comparative social mobility example
Specification tests, 167
Specific-to-general model selection, 148–149
Spurious findings, 170
Standard errors, recommendations for using, 177
Statistical hypotheses, 123–125
Statistical significance
  alternative to the conventional standards of, 2–3
  conventional standard of, 2
  criticisms of, 26–27
  critics and defenders, 12–13
  introduction to, 1–2
  sample size and, 22, 23
  spurious findings, 170
  substantive significance and, 22
Subjectivist approach, to Bayesian hypothesis testing, 91, 101
Substantive hypotheses, 123–125
Substantive significance
  conventional approach, 61
  in one-parameter hypothesis testing, 5
  statistical significance and, 22
Symmetry, lack of in conventional hypothesis testing, 24–25, 71

T

Theory
  deriving consequences from and making elaborate, 173–174

About the Author

David L. Weakliem, PhD, is Professor of Sociology at the University of Connecticut. He has been a fellow at the Center for Advanced Study in the Behavioral Sciences at Stanford University and at the Australian National University. Dr. Weakliem is Editor-in-Chief of *Comparative Sociology* and a past Deputy Editor of the *American Sociological Review.*